Land Use, Open Space, and the Government Process

edited by
**Edward Ellis Smith
Durward S. Riggs**

A study performed by Jones & Stokes Associates,
Sacramento, California, commissioned by the
Commonwealth Club of California,
founded in 1903.

The Praeger Special Studies program—
utilizing the most modern and efficient book
production techniques and a selective
worldwide distribution network—makes
available to the academic, government, and
business communities significant, timely
research in U.S. and international economic, social, and political development.

Land Use, Open Space, and the Government Process

The San Francisco Bay Area Experience

PRAEGER SPECIAL STUDIES IN U.S. ECONOMIC, SOCIAL, AND POLITICAL ISSUES

Praeger Publishers   New York   Washington   London

Library of Congress Cataloging in Publication Data

Jones & Stokes Associates.
    Land use, open space, and the government process.

    (Praeger special studies in U.S. economic, social,
and political issues)
    "Commissioned by the Commonwealth Club of California."
    Bibliography: p.
    Includes index.
    1. Regional planning—San Francisco Bay region.
2. Land—California—San Francisco Bay region.
3. Open spaces—San Francisco Bay region.   I. Smith,
Edward Ellis, ed.   II. Riggs, Durward S., ed.
III. Commonwealth Club of California, San Francisco.
IV. Title.
HT394.S25J66   1975   309.2'5'097946   74-14048
ISBN 0-275-05700-3

PRAEGER PUBLISHERS
111 Fourth Avenue, New York, N.Y. 10003, U.S.A.
5, Cromwell Place, London SW7 2JL, England

Published in the United States of America in 1974
by Praeger Publishers, Inc.

Spanish galleons passed San Francisco Bay for almost 200 years without recognizing it. However, Richard Henry Dana, Jr., in his *Two Years Before the Mast* and *Twenty-Four Years After** described the magnificent Bay Area in all its pristine beauty before its ravishment by successive waves of California immigrants.

It was in the winter of 1835-6 [Dana wrote much later] that the ship *Alert*, in . . . her voyage for hides on the remote and almost unknown coast of California, floated into the vast solitude of the Bay of San Francisco. All around was the stillness of nature. One vessel, a Russian, lay at anchor there, but during our whole stay not a sail came or went. . . . Our anchorage was between a small island, called Yerba Buena, a gravel beach in a little bight or cove of the same name, formed by two small projecting points. Beyond, to the westward of the landing place, were dreary sand-hills, with little grass to be seen, and few trees, and beyond them higher hills, steep and barren, their sides gullied by rains. Some five or six miles beyond the landing place, to the right, was a ruinous Presidio and some three or four miles to the left was the Mission of Dolores, as ruinous as the Presidio. . . . Over a region far beyond our sight there were no other human habitations except that an enterprising Yankee, years in advance of his time, had put up, on the rising ground above the landing, a shanty of rough boards, where he carried on a very small retail trade between the hide ships and the Indians. Vast banks of fog . . . drove in through the entrance, and covered the whole bay; and when they disappeared, we saw a few wellwooded islands, the sand-hills on the west, the grassy and wooded slopes on the east, and the vast stretch of the bay to the southward . . . still longer stretches to the northward and northeastward, where we understood smaller bays spread out and large rivers poured in their tributes of waters. There were no settlements on those bays or rivers. . . . Not only in the neighborhood of our anchorage, but the entire region was a solitude. . . .

The "vast solitude" of the San Francisco Bay that Dana found 140 years ago has now become a clamorous, bustling, megalopolis. In fact, Dana saw a markedly changed Bay Area when he returned, 25 years later, in 1859.

---

*Richard Henry Dana, Jr., *Two Years Before the Mast* and *Twenty-Four Years After* (Boston: Houghton Mifflin Company, 1969), pp. 375, 377.

When I . . . looked . . . over the City of San Francisco [he claimed] with its storehouses, towers, and steeples; its courthouses, theatres, and hospitals;. . . its fortresses and light-houses; its wharves and harbor, with their thousand-ton clipper ships, more in number than London or Liverpool sheltered that day . . . and the sole emporium of a new world, the awakened Pacific; when I looked across the bay to the eastward, and beheld a beautiful town on the fertile, wooded shores of the Contra Costa, and steamers, large and small, the ferryboats . . . and capacious freighters and passenger-carriers . . . with lines of their smoke in the horizon, when I saw all these things, and reflected on what I once . . . saw here, and what now surrounded me, I could scarcely keep my hold on reality at all, or the genuineness of anything, and seemed to myself like one who had moved in "worlds not realized."*

The process of transforming the San Francisco Bay Area from pastoral quietude into a workplace, residence, and playground had already commenced.

In 1970, more than 4.6 million people claimed the Bay Area, its 9 counties and 45 cities, as home. The population now probably exceeds 5 million, having increased by more than 2,000 times compared with 1859 when Dana considered he had been in "worlds not realized." Viewed in that context the San Francisco Bay Area represents one of the most significant urban areas in the United States and, indeed, the world. Administrative boundaries, of course, arbitrarily delineate it; but without them, the Bay Area could realistically be categorized as a major city of the planet.

For example, it accommodates the western terminals of three transcontinental railways, two principal international airports, and seven seaports. The Bay Area employed almost 2 million persons during 1970. As an indication of construction activity, more than 50,000 family dwelling units go up in the Area each year. San Francisco's skyline reflects constant innovation. Three major universities of international fame and a number of notable institutions of higher learning make the Bay Area a mecca for students and scholars.

Since Dana's time phenomenal growth in immigration and the expansion of tourism (San Francisco's tourist industry in dollar volume and numbers per annum exceeds that of the Republic of China, Israel, or Indonesia) makes it apparent that the Bay Area beckons the traveller as well as the permanent settler. More than 2 million tourists visit San Francisco each year.

Quite obviously, industry, institutions, and people find the Bay Area desirable, many of them preferring it to other great metropolitan areas. Its mild climate and striking topographical contrasts combine with open space, more than half of its 7.5 million acres, scattered throughout the nine counties to make the area noteworthy, if not unique. Only in recent years has open space planning assumed significance; and, just as its climate has been fortuitous, so has its existing open space seemingly come from good fortune.

---

*Ibid.

An attempt to analyze comparatively open space, to say nothing of planning, in the Bay Area with other regions in the United States is difficult because of the Bay's distinctive topography factor. Perhaps Washington's Puget Sound represents an exception.

More appropriate precedents exist abroad. Stockholm, with more than 300 years of city planning, stands as a classic example for a consideration of open space policy. From 1640 to 1850, virtually no private ownership of land existed in that city. The municipality or the crown, owners of most of the land, simply issued "ground-fee" permits to users. By 1866, however, private ownership had generally replaced this system. Then the government began to allow individuals full title to land at many times exceeding the ground fee. Stockholm today must purchase land needed in its development plans, although in 1953 Parliament enabled the city to buy land before the disclosure of a specific development plan.

The British "new town" experiment, initiated in 1946 to relieve growth pressures on London, caused the first town, designed as "totally independent," to be built approximately thirty miles away from London. The authorities made housing available, persuaded industry to develop in the area, and established a cultural center, subsequently unsuccessful in attracting major cultural events. Unfortunately, after some years, theatres and restaurants closed. A dreary, uniform architectural style had already contributed to an apathetic attitude among the town's residents. However, as planners learned from their mistakes and made changes, the "new towns" continued to increase and they now number 17. A major concept of this experiment centered on the creation of attractive cities to move people *into*, in contradistinction to most American urban renewal plans which concentrate more on moving people *out* of, existing high density areas into other areas that unfortunately soon become high density.

From these examples, it might be concluded that a lack of planning has stood the Bay Area in good stead vis-a-vis open space. But other factors have brought the Bay Area to its present, relatively auspicious, open space situation. And planning has indeed become necessary.

Fortunate as the Bay Area has been, it does not lack open space problems. Thus, we note that open space requirements cannot be isolated from general land use and city planning considerations and that it must be viewed within the context of complex, interlocking governmental processes.

Many agencies in the Bay Area presently have various advisory or regulatory powers; however, no regional agency concerned primarily with open space needs, and with the requisite implementation capacity, exists. That the population in the nine-county area now approximates 5 million, and will reach an estimated 5.5 million by 1980, alone indicates the need for planning.

The economics of open space preservation, of course, must be kept in mind. A lack of funds often precludes the purchase of land. But land acquisition by the state represents only one means of obtaining open space. A serious question exists, furthermore, regarding the real meaning of "open space." The City of San Francisco has aggregated open space around buildings by zoning. In addition, we note the numerous laws and regulatory agencies that have suddenly appeared on the California scene, mandated to preserve open space and protect the environment. Government now has substantial powers in the use and development of private property. Even the smallest property owners in the Bay Area must presently cope with Environmental Impact Reports, the Bay Area Conservation and Development Commission, the California Coastal Zone Conservation Commission, the Environmental Protection Agency, the Bay Area Air Pollution Control Board, and possible litigation instituted by almost any interested group or person.

Farmers in counties that have accepted the Williamson Act* continue to contract with the counties, agreeing not to subdivide their lands in consideration for taxation on the value of their lands for agricultural purposes. Thus the lands still return property tax revenues to the state and the farms remain open space. Although public parks provide open space they remove lands from the tax rolls and require constant surveillance in attempting to eliminate crime and litter.

Logic requires an essential balance of open space with the peoples' needs, and with aesthetics. Nor may individual rights, always preeminent, be ignored. And, as one specialist has pointed out, "San Francisco, Paris, Rome, and Venice might not exist, if overzealous environmentalists had prevailed." Clearly, serious conflicts exist regarding the use of our lands and the enhancement of our environment.

* * *

Having in mind the multiplicity of problems associated with open space in the San Francisco Bay Area, the Commonwealth Club of California, in line with its tradition., decided some time ago to examine this phenomenon. Accordingly, the Club commissioned Jones & Stokes Associates, a distinguished consulting firm in Sacramento, to gather the necessary data and enlist the required expertise for an in-depth study. Jones & Stokes thus provided the basic research, but it drew on the knowledge and assistance of many others. Paul Watt, Director, Robert Olson, Assistant Director, and William J. Francken, Chief Graphic Designer of the Metropolitan Transportation Commission in Berkeley assisted in preparing the essential maps. Pacific Gas and Electric Company and the Redwood Empire Association graciously provided representative photographs from their collections. The directors and staff members of Bay Area public and private agencies kindly provided their time and competence in responding to questions, and scores of individuals, too numerous to mention, made valuable comments.

Finally, the foresight of Justice Wakefield Taylor, who chairs the Research Committee of the Commonwealth Club of California, provided the impetus for this study.

Edward Ellis Smith
Durward S. Riggs
editors

---

*Passed in 1965 by the California legislature, the Williamson Act authorized cities and counties to make contracts with landowners to maintain land in agricultural or compatible uses, providing a tax concession with government agencies. (See p. 80 for a more detailed discussion of the act.)

CONTENTS

PART II: OPEN SPACE PRESERVATION

Chapter   Page

LIST OF TABLES, FIGURES, AND PHOTOGRAPHS

TOP OF MT. TAMALPAIS, LOOKING TOWARD S.F. ON A FOGGY DAY.

Worden Collection, Wells Fargo Bank History Room, San Francisco, California

I

OPEN SPACE
AND THE BAY AREA

No consensus exists among the general public, its elected representatives, or professional planners concerning the open space that should be preserved in the Bay Area. An identification of the region's open space requirements remains important, however, not only to establish goals, but also as a first step to develop an open space program.

INVENTORY OF EXISTING OPEN SPACE

Although most of the Bay Area's 7.5 million acres of land may be classified as open space, no guarantee exists that it will so remain, because 21 square miles of land annually converts to urban use.[1] The commitment of land to open space use may be categorized as follows:

1. *Permanent* open space comprises public and private park and open space land held expressly for park or open space purposes, including local, regional, state, and federal parks, wildlife refuges, and the holdings of private conservation organizations.

2. *Semipermanent* open space includes public and privately owned land for which a strong commitment to continued open use exists. Watershed lands, academic institutional lands, military reservations, and Bureau of Land Management holdings belong to this category of public lands. Privately held lands qualifying as semipermanent open space include private golf courses, cemeteries, and quasi-public recreation areas (YMCA and Boy Scout Camps, for example).

3. *Temporary* open space includes private lands under Williamson Act contracts that provide for the commitment of land to open space uses for a minimum of ten years.

Table 1 recapitulates existing publicly owned urban and regional open space lands and private lands under Williamson Act contract, but it does not include some 10,000 acres of private golf courses, 4,700 acres of cemetery lands, 4,300 acres held by conservation organizations, more than 7,000 acres belonging to Stanford University and other private colleges, and quasi-public and private recreational acreage.

REGIONAL OPEN SPACE REQUIREMENTS

The planning program of the Association of Bay Area Governments (ABAG) has experienced difficulty in defining the regional open space system. The Regional Plan, prepared in 1970, calls for the permanent commitment of

TABLE 1

The Status of Open Space Preservation: The Regional Open Space (all areas in acres) System

County	Target Size of System	Permanently Preserved Land in Public Ownership[a]	Deficit in Permanently Preserved Land	Percent of Target Permanently Preserved	Semipermanently Preserved land in Public Ownership	Temporarily Preserved Land under Williamson Act Contract[b]	Total
Alameda	423,465	78,422	345,043	18.5	32,677	143,996	255,095
Contra Costa	307,585	53,930	253,655	17.5	24,108	50,309	128,347
Marin	277,494	87,706	189,788	31.6	21,409	85,009	194,124
Napa	399,850	49,620	350,230	12.4	38,722	60,691	149,033
San Francisco	34,773	33,718	1,055	97.0	1,064	0	34,782
San Mateo	219,404	60,198	159,206	27.5	24,164	40,039	124,401
Santa Clara	634,899	34,245	600,654	5.4	32,113	285,362	351,720
Solano	358,500	59,684	298,816	16.6	8,816	158,934	227,434
Sonoma	781,268	30,431	750,837	3.9	11,295	221,399	263,125
Total	3,437,243	487,954	2,949,289	14.2	194,368	1,045,740	1,728,061

4

County	Deficit in Open Space Commitment	Percent of Target Preserved	Publicly Owned Lands in Areas for Controlled Development	Local Open Space Now in Public Ownership
Alameda	168,370	60.2	100	5,227
Contra Costa	179,238	41.7	0	3,078
Marin	83,370	70.0	415	1,000
Napa	250,817	37.2	0	36
San Francisco	0		0	1,700
San Mateo	95,003	56.5	1,500	837
Santa Clara	283,179	55.3	1,140	1,605
Solano	131,066	63.4	81	376
Sonoma	518,143	33.6	0	437
Total	1,709,182	50.2	2,236	14,296

aIncludes acreage figures for San Francisco Bay.
bIncludes Williamson Act lands in areas designated for controlled urban development.

Source: Association of Bay Area Governments, *Regional Plan* (Berkeley: ABAG, 1970).

5

FIGURE 1

Bay Area Open Space—ABAG Regional Plan, 1970-90

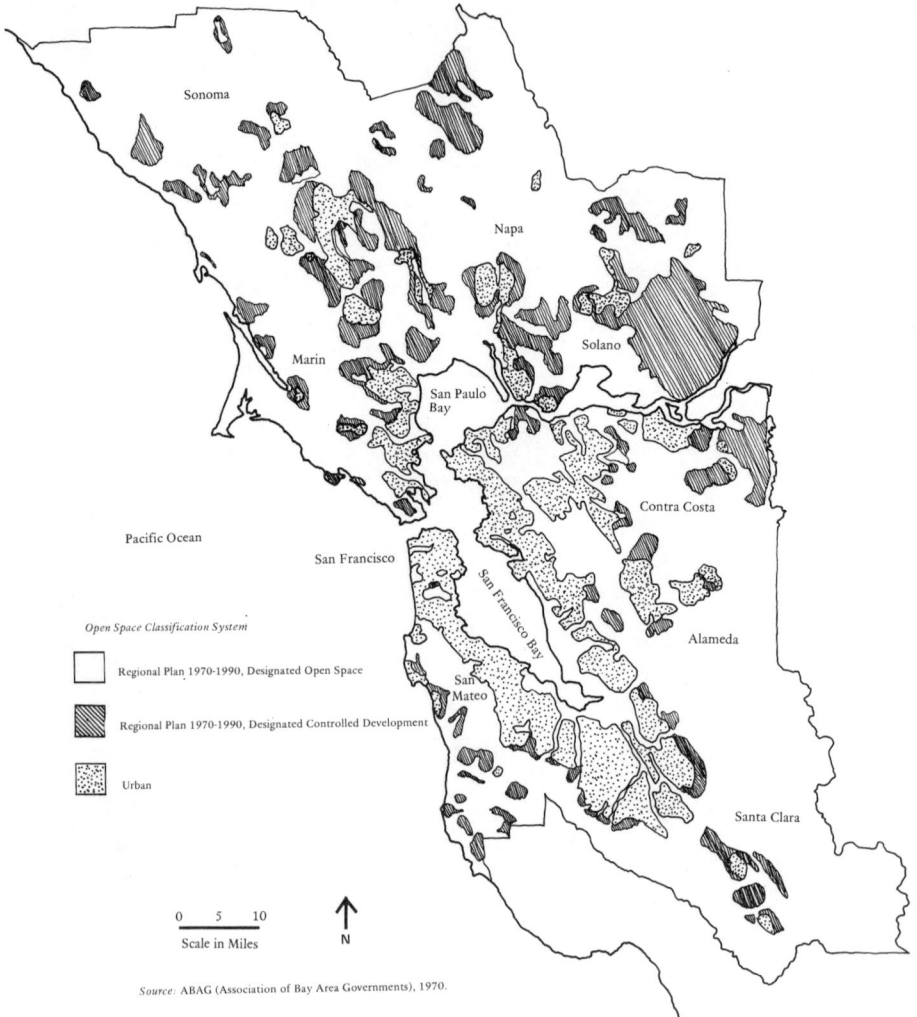

Source: ABAG (Association of Bay Area Governments), 1970.

6

TABLE 2

Location and Size of the Bay Area Regional Open Space System
(Land Area in Acres)

County	The Regional Open Space System			Classification of the Permanent Regional Open Space System by Purpose					
	Permanent Open Space	Controlled Development Areas	Total Area	I Preservation of Natural and Human Resources	II Managed Resource Production	III Outdoor Recreation	IV Shaping Urban Growth	V Health, Welfare and Well-being	VI Public Safety
Alameda	423,500	10,700	434,200	200,000	279,600	159,500	329,900	228,400	33,700
Contra Costa	307,600	75,000	382,600	139,500	238,300	123,500	225,000	93,000	9,600
Marin	277,500	45,700	323,200	197,000	213,000	159,600	137,700	94,900	6,500
Napa	399,900	77,100	477,000	177,900	294,900	188,400	161,800	270,500	31,600
San Francisco	34,800	0	34,800	34,800	30,400	34,800	34,300	31,700	0
San Mateo	219,400	32,000	251,400	184,400	132,000	159,500	188,300	76,200	17,300
Santa Clara	634,900	48,400	683,300	144,100	435,200	126,100	599,300	392,900	53,700
Solano	358,500	188,300	546,800	134,100	318,700	107,400	118,200	186,900	132,000
Sonoma	781,300	150,800	932,100	367,400	297,800	304,900	526,200	110,000	341,000
Total	3,437,400	628,000	4,065,400	1,579,200	2,239,900	1,363,700	2,320,700	1,484,500	625,400

Source: Association of Bay Area Governments, Regional Open Space Plan, Phase II, San Francisco Bay Region (Summary) (1972).

3.4 million acres as regional open space[2] (see Figure 1), based on "the region's natural features, location policies for urban development, comprehensive open space goals, and criteria determining regional open space significance, location, space and development character."[3] The plan also includes 628,000 acres of controlled development areas between the outer limits of areas designated for development by 1990, and permanent open space. These areas would be reserved for urban expansion, if needed, after 1990.[4] Table 2 shows the open space targets for each county and six resource classifications.

URBAN SPACE REQUIREMENTS

The regional open space system, including only areas of 100 acres or more, does not address the equally critical provision for open space within existing and proposed urban areas. Standards for open space acreages per 1,000 persons, although of questionable practical value for planning purposes, represent one method of expressing urban open space requirements for the region. ABAG has suggested the following standards for the Bay Area:[5]

Parks and recreation areas	15 acres/1,000
Private open space	5 acres/1,000
Other green space for health, welfare, and well-being	10 acres/1,000
Total urban open space	30 acres/1,000

A projected population of 7,496,000, in the year 2000 would require approximately 225,000 acres of urban open space. If the standards were applied only to the projected population increase of 2,865,000, roughly 86,000 acres would be needed to serve new development. Currently preserved public and private open space clearly falls far short of these suggested requirements, although precise figures are unavailable.

STATUS OF OPEN SPACE PRESERVATION

Table 1 shows currently preserved regional open space, the target size of the open space system, and the deficit in both permanently preserved land and land committed to open space use by acres and percentage for each county.

Excepting San Francisco County, substantial deficits exist in permanently preserved land for each county. However, they represent, for the most part, a deficit in the amount of publicly owned undeveloped land. In 1968 experts estimated the sum of $1.9 billion to acquire the needed open space land in the area.[6] That such an amount could be made available during the next 30 years remains highly unlikely. Consequently, the institution and enforcement of rigorous land use controls for the protection of presently existing open space becomes even more important. Judiciously utilizing available funds to purchase the most vital open space areas under threat of urban development remains essential.

NOTES

1. Eckbo, Dean, Austin, & Williams, *Open Space: The Choices Before California* (San Francisco: Diablo Press, 1965), p. 15.

2. Association of Bay Area Governments, *Regional Open Space Plan Phase II, San Francisco Bay Region* (Summary) (1972), p. 2.

3. Association of Bay Area Governments, *Regional Plan 1970: 1990 San Francisco Bay Region* (1970), p. 20.

4. Association of Bay Area Governments, *Regional Open Space Plan, Phase II*, op. cit.

5. Association of Bay Area Governments, *Regional Open Space Element, Supplemental Report RP-3* (1969), p. 47.

6. Development Research Associates, "Economic Analysis of a Regional Open Space Program" (San Francisco: People for Open Space, 1969), p. 33.

REGIONAL POPULATION
AND LAND USE

Its mild climate, beautiful and variegated natural landscape, diverse and relatively stable economy, rich cultural heritage, and progressive problem-solving attitudes distinguish the San Francisco Bay region. In approximately 30 years the population has more than doubled. The rapid pace of urbanization, however, has created serious environmental problems, including the relentless conversion of the natural landscape to intensive urban use.[1]

THE HISTORICAL URBANIZATION PATTERN

Prior to the Gold Rush of 1849, cattle grazing and agricultural activities centered around the three small towns of Yerba Buena, San Jose, and Sonoma, and upon some 100 large ranchos granted by Spanish and Mexican authorities, which became the major enterprises in the Bay region. With the discovery of gold in the Sierras, fortune seekers crowded San Francisco (nee Yerba Buena), swelling its population from 1,000 to 30,000 in only three years.

This hectic period generated a host of new towns platted in the prevalent rectangular grid fashion popular in the East. Situated along the Bay and river routes that provided convenient transportation to Sacramento and the gold diggings, many towns—Oakland, Alameda, Pittsburg, Alviso, Benicia, and Napa—were speculative ventures, launched by men primarily interested in selling real estate. Some towns—Antioch, Union City, Petaluma, and Suisun—became shipping points for agricultural products destined for San Francisco. Belmont, San Bruno, and San Leandro developed originally as way-stations along the main land routes. Later, Livermore, Pleasanton, Brentwood, Gilroy, and others established along the new railroad lines.

Despite the 1855 depression that abruptly ended the Gold Rush, San Francisco maintained its new-found status as the commercial, financial, and shipping center of California and the West. The expansion of agricultural enterprises throughout the region and the phenomenal railroad building led by the Big Four (Charles Crocker, Mark Hopkins, Collis P. Huntington, and Leland Stanford) of the Central Pacific, later the Southern Pacific, prevailed in the period 1855-1900. More than any other single enterprise, railroad building paced the Bay region's continued growth and economic expansion. In the 1860s, railways were completed between San Jose and San Francisco, Sacramento and Vallejo, and in the Napa and lower Santa Clara valleys. When the Transcontinental Railroad reached its Oakland terminus in 1869, it created a direct link to eastern markets.

As gold fever abated and disillusioned miners turned toward the soil, communities in the fertile valleys developed into a second ring of settlements around the Bay, including San Jose, Santa Clara, Napa, St. Helena, Sebastopol, Bloomfield, Healdsburg, Rio Vista, Fairfield, and Walnut Creek. San Jose, the first Bay Area town, founded in 1777, soon became the most important agricultural center in the abundantly fertile Santa Clara Valley. Early in this period, farmers introduced prunes, wine grapes, and dairy farming, but diversification did not become the hallmark of Bay Area agriculture until the 1880s.

A rivalry for economic leadership developed among San Francisco, Oakland, and Vallejo during this period. San Francisco continued its rapid growth, boosted by the great silver strike of the Comstock mining area during the 1860s and 1870s. The East Bay became the regional railhead and, consequently, the significant locus of manufacturing activity, while San Francisco consolidated its position as the regional financial, shipping, and cultural center.

Other significant developments during the period included the founding of the University of California in the "country" north of Oakland, around which Berkeley thrived. San Francisco's Golden Gate Park, the first of a legacy of great parks, was established in the early 1870s. The creation of resorts and recreation areas—notably Pacific Congress Springs (Saratoga), Calistoga, San Rafael, and Half Moon Bay—indicated the increasing sophistication and affluence of the Bay Area's population.

By 1880 the San Francisco Bay Area had become a regional entity with a population of 422,000, of which 234,000 resided in San Francisco itself. Oakland and Alameda accounted for 40,000 and Vallejo, 6,000 people. Excepting San Jose, Bay Area communities remained largely rural, with populations of 3,000 or less.

An increasing regional economic stability characterized Bay Area development during the last two decades of the nineteenth century. A significant shift toward fruit production strikingly transformed the value and appearance of rural valleys. Subsequent increases in the fruit-processing industry contributed significantly to the growth of San Jose, which boasted a population of 21,500 by 1900. Industrial expansion began in the 1880s with the establishment of smelting and explosives plants along the coast of Contra Costa County. Standard Oil's Richmond refinery was the first of six that eventually located in the area.

In the last decade of the century, residential dispersion began in the East Bay, made possible by the successful introduction and rapid expansion of electric railway systems, enabling people to live further from their offices and shops. The railways sparked a flurry of land promotion activity that encouraged residential development north and south of downtown Oakland. By 1900 "Greater Oakland" exceeded 16 square miles of incorporated territory with a population of 67,000.

The Peninsula, on the contrary, displayed very slow growth. Many financial leaders of the period—Ralston, Spreckles, Crocker, Roth, Parrott, Pullman,

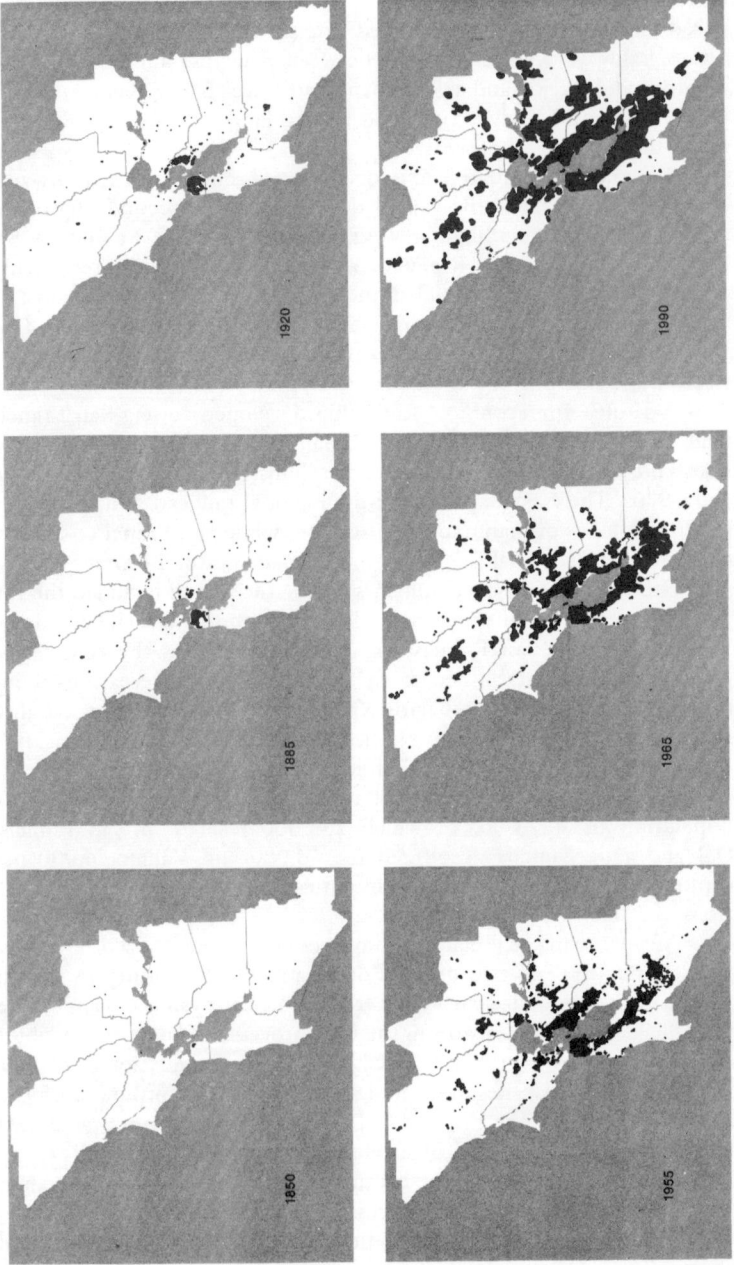

FIGURE 2

Form of the Region, 1850-1990

1850

1885

1920

1955

1965

1990

Source: ABAG, 1970.

12

Mills, and Stanford—then owned spacious country estates on the Peninsula, and thus much of it has remained primarily residential in nature. In 1891, Leland Stanford donated his extensive holdings to Leland Stanford, Jr. College, endowing a university to the memory of his son. A major portion of that Stanford property, in the hills toward the Pacific, remains undeveloped.

Trends established toward the end of the nineteenth century continued until 1920. The East Bay became distinctly urban because of an aggressive industrial expansion campaign that capitalized on the turmoil resulting from the 1906 San Francisco earthquake and fire and the improvement of shipping and rail facilities. Richmond emerged as an urban community by 1920, with a population of almost 17,000.

Almost 75 percent of the Bay Area's 1920 population of 1,183,000 resided in two dense urban agglomerations on both sides of the Bay with approximate population densities of 5,900 persons per square mile.[2] Although the automobile became a common sight by 1920—increasingly supported by numerous gas stations, car lots, and repair shops, as well as a rapid rate of state and county road construction—its use was primarily recreational. Automobile commuting, still costly, had not come into its own. Furthermore, outlying communities, particularly on the Peninsula, offered little employment opportunity.

Due to centripetal factors in the 1920s and 1930s, the Bay region became inclined toward low-density suburban growth. By 1960, urban population density had decreased to 2,500 persons per square mile. After several relatively stable decades, San Mateo County began to grow, as numerous subdivisions were gradually built along the Bay shore. Between 1920 and 1930 the county's population had more than doubled to 77,000 people. In the ensuing decade an additional 44,000 people settled on the Peninsula. The 1927 decision to locate San Francisco's municipal airport on part of the former Mills property in San Bruno encouraged Peninsula development. Despite the growth of agriculture in the Santa Clara Valley, increases in the food processing industry, and the establishment of Moffett Field in 1931, San Jose experienced uncrowded development.

Alameda County similarly experienced low-density development that absorbed most of an increase of 170,000 persons between 1920 and 1940. Albany, San Leandro, and Hayward, on the periphery of the built-up area, registered greater relative gains than Oakland and Berkeley. The fact that 25 percent of the 50,000 daily San Francisco ferry commuters from Alameda drove their automobiles in 1930, whereas five years earlier virtually all had used connecting rail services, indicated the increasing role of the automobile in urban growth patterns. The completion of the Bay Bridge in 1937 and the Golden Gate Bridge a year later accentuated this trend.

During the late 1920s, Richmond, still the main urban area of Contra Costa County, developed port facilities that spurred industrial growth. The Berkeley Hills then formed a significant barrier between the eastern county and the employment centers west of the "Hills." Marin County, to the north, typified the search for more space, as the small cities within commuting range of San Francisco registered significant population gains, doubling the county's population between 1920 and 1940. Only the cities within Solano, Napa, and Sonoma counties failed to register appreciable gains.

World War II marked the major turning point in the Bay Area's growth and development. More than 500,000 persons moved into the region between

1940 and 1945, joining the massive war materiel production effort for the Pacific Theatre of operations. Military establishments in the region employed thousands: shipbuilding facilities at Hunters Point, South San Francisco, Sausalito, Richmond, and Mare Island; explosives manufacturing plants at Port Chicago and along the north Contra Costa bayshore. Richmond, a noteworthy example of the impact of the war industry on the Bay Area, in addition to the huge Kaiser-operated shipyards, had 55 major war industries. In less than three years its population expanded from 23,000 to more than 100,000. Relatively little land on the urban peripheries accommodated the population increase during the war years. However, the massive postwar influx of newcomers and the baby boom generated an enormous demand for new homes, industries, shopping facilities, schools, community centers, and industrial plants. Suburban expansion has continued, with the region averaging nearly 1 million new residents per decade since 1940, increasing from 1,734,000 in 1940 to 4,631,000 in 1970 (see Table 3).

Since 1955, Santa Clara County has consistently shown the greatest growth in the area. Its population has increased six times, from 175,000 in 1940 to more than 1 million in 1970. The rapid development of the aerospace and electronics industries, in 1970 accounting for 27 percent or more than

TABLE 3

Population of the Bay Area, 1940-70
(in thousands of persons)

County	1940	1950	1955[a]	1960	1965[b]	1970
Alameda	513	740	825	903	1,023	1,073
Contra Costa	101	299	338	409	495	556
Marin	53	86	111	147	186	207
Napa	29	47	56	66	73	79
San Francisco	635	775	740	740	742	716
San Mateo	112	236	345	444	517	557
Santa Clara	175	291	428	642	901	1,066
Solano	49	105	116	135	160	172
Sonoma	69	103	125	147	182	205
Nine-county total	1,736	2,682	—	3,633	—	4,631
Percent change in growth rate by decade:						
Bay Area region	10.0	55.0	—	31.0	—	25.0
State	21.7	55.3	—	48.5	—	27.0
Nation	7.2	14.5	—	18.4	—	11.6

[a] Integral estimates of total population in California counties for July 1, 1955.
[b] Integral estimates of total population in California counties for July 1, 1965.
Source: California Department of Finance, U.S. Department of Commerce, Bureau of the Census.

114,000 workers of the county's total employment, provided the primary stimulus.[3] Alameda and Contra Costa counties have registered population increases approximating 550,000 during the last 30 years and accounted for 32 percent of the region's population growth during the last decade. Contra Costa County's population is four times greater than in 1940, undergoing increased urbanization. San Mateo County's greatest growth occurred during the 1950s when the population almost doubled, from 236,000 to 444,000. In 1970 it encompassed 557,000 persons, although growth has since declined because most of the easily developed land along the Bay shore has been exploited.

Population growth in Napa, Marin, Sonoma, and Solano counties has lagged, compared to the four southern Bay Area counties. They accounted for only 17 percent of the region's increase between 1960 and 1970. Of these counties, Marin has recorded the greatest increase, more than doubling in population between 1950 and 1970. San Francisco's 47 square miles, urbanized since the 1940s, have registered a gradual population decrease resulting from accelerated suburban migration in the postwar period.

URBAN LAND USE PATTERNS

Natural geographic features have determined the Bay Area's growth patterns (see Figure 3). The Santa Cruz Mountains and the Diablo Range, and its northwestern extension the Berkeley Hills, form the major branches of the Coast Ranges in the south. A parallel series of ridges extend north of the Bay, merging into the Mendocino Highlands. Between the mountain ridges lie several fertile valleys, including Santa Clara, Napa, Sonoma, Cotati, Diablo, San Ramon, and Livermore. The Santa Clara Valley, by far the largest, is 50 miles long and 15 miles wide.

Development has tended to concentrate in areas adjacent to the Bay and in the valleys. A virtually continuous metropolis composed of 5 counties, 45 cities, and 75 percent of the Bay Area's population surrounds the Bay from the Golden Gate on the west to the Carquinez Straits in the northeast. In addition to San Francisco, at the tip of the Peninsula, this metropolitan area encompasses the Peninsula's bayside, the northern Santa Clara Valley, the East Bay lands, and the San Pablo Bayshore from the cities of Richmond to Crockett, bounded by the Santa Cruz Mountains on the west and the Diablo and Berkeley ranges on the east. Extensive marshes and salt ponds, covering more than 40,000 acres, surround the southern portion of the Bay below the San Mateo-Hayward Bridge. Few major areas remain undeveloped except for the tidelands, the San Bruno Mountains immediately south of San Francisco, the Stanford University land holdings in Palo Alto and Menlo Park, the Alviso-Agnew and Berryessa areas north of San Jose, and extensive agricultural lands north and south of the city of Fremont.

Manufacturing and industrial plants are concentrated along narrow bands paralleling the Bayshore Highway, the Nimitz Freeway, and Interstate 80. Industry now has heavily centered in the South-of-Market area in San Francisco, in South San Francisco, at the Ford and General Motors plants in Milpitas and Fremont, along a continuous belt from Oakland to Emeryville, and at Point Richmond. Only in Santa Clara County does industrial activity

FIGURE 3

Population Growth Associated with Economic Growth Alternatives, San Francisco Bay Region, 1970-2000

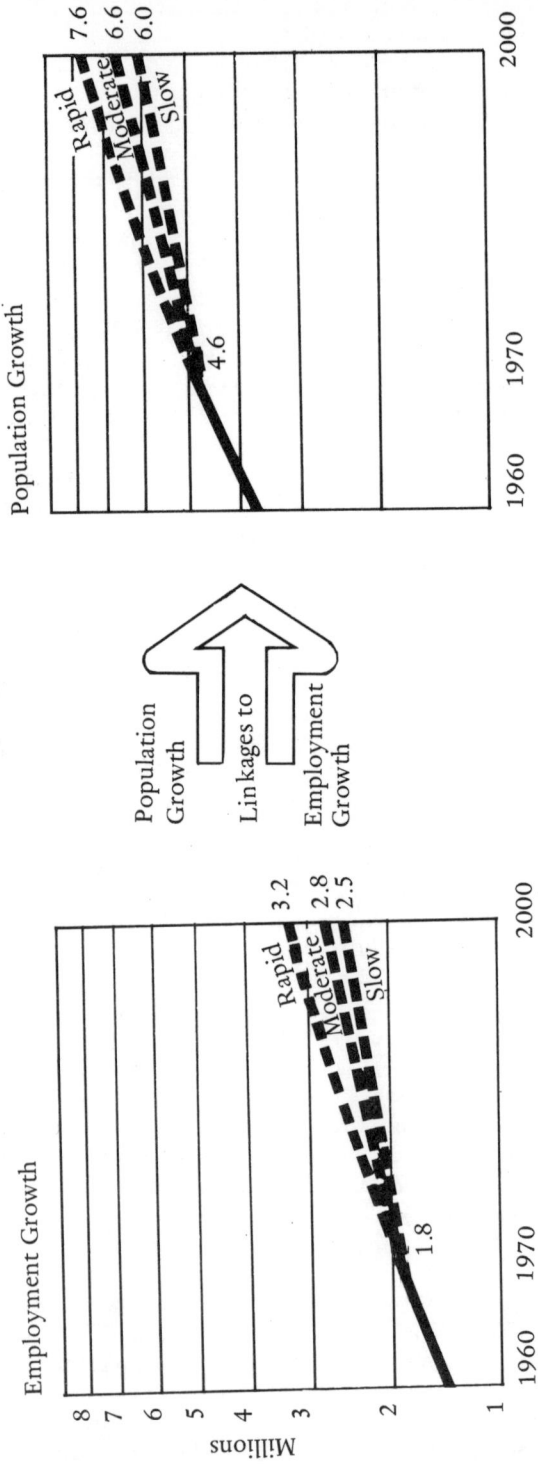

	1970	Alternative Year 2000, Projections		
		Slow Growth	Moderate Growth	Rapid Growth
Total Civilian Employment	1,824,117	2,515,000	2,780,000	3,201,000
Total Population	4,635,988	5,988,000	6,620,000	7,621,000
Projected Average Annual Population Growth Rate (percent)		.86	1.19	1.67
Projected Average Annual Employment Growth Rate (percent)		1.08	1.41	1.89

Source: ABAG staff analysis partially based upon data from the U.S. Bureau of Economic Analysis and from the U.S. Census.

fairly well disperse. Industrial land uses cluster near the ports of San Francisco, Redwood City, Oakland, Alameda, and Richmond and around the San Francisco, Oakland, San Jose, and Moffett Field air terminals.

High residential densities of ten or more units per acre predominate in the older communities, most notably San Francisco, Oakland, Berkeley, Alameda, and Richmond. Suburban tracts, with a medium density of five to nine units per acre, mark the flat portions of the Baylands and Santa Clara Valley inland from the industrial area in a residential belt nearly continuous from South San Francisco to Pinole. Low-density residential concentrations of one to four units per acre characterize the communities of Hillsborough, Woodside, Portola Valley, Menlo Park, Atherton, Los Altos Hills, Saratoga, Los Gatos, Monte Sereno, Alum Rock, Castro Valley, and the Oakland Hills—all found in the foothills surrounding the Baylands.

Eastern Contra Costa County

Eastern Contra Costa County and the Diablo and San Ramon valleys hold a major concentration of population. Urban development has focused on the Diablo Valley, which encompasses the communities of Concord, Walnut Creek, Pleasant Hill, Martinez, and Clayton, where the population in 1950 totalled 30,000 residents; it now exceeds 200,000, in a bedroom community with low and medium residential densities. The Naval Weapons Station at Concord, the Exxon refinery at Benicia, and the Shell and Phillips 66 refineries at Martinez occupy extensive acreages in the northern part of the valley. The narrow San Ramon Valley south of Walnut Creek retains a low-population-density rural atmosphere. Alamo, Diablo, Danville, and San Ramon, once separate, now virtually interconnect. Growth pressures are beginning to affect the San Ramon Valley, but considerable open space still remains on the valley floor, particularly at its southern end.

Another urban area in eastern Contra Costa County, located along the estuary at the confluence of the Sacramento and San Joaquin rivers, includes the towns of Antioch, Pittsburg, West Pittsburg, and Shore Acres, with a combined population of 62,000. Steady urban expansion has gradually linked these communities. Several major manufacturing plants have located along the shore.

Livermore Valley

Although considerable agricultural land still surrounds the communities of Livermore and Pleasanton, residential homes are rapidly filling the Livermore Valley in Eastern Alameda County. The valley's population stood at approximately 60,000 in 1970.

Marin County

The eastern urban corridor of Marin County extends from the Marin Headlands to Novato and constitutes another Bay Area population center. Numerous residents commute to white-collar jobs in San Francisco. The county is primarily residential, with little industry. Its communities remain oriented toward low- and medium-density residential areas. San Rafael and Novato are the two largest, and fastest growing, cities.

A series of transverse ridges jutting into the Bay mark Marin's topography, and flat, easily developed land is at a premium. Consequently, residences nestle into the hills overlooking the Bay, most notably at Sausalito and along the Tiburon peninsula, or concentrate in the small valleys and rolling hillsides that extend into the Marin Mountains. The county's topography has helped preserve the identity of individual communities, with intervening open space.

The Northern Valleys

These valleys have retained their original agrarian flavor. Growth has been largely confined to existing population centers, although in recent years the trend toward sprawl has accelerated. In Sonoma County, the Cotati-Petaluma area, Sonoma Valley, Valley of the Moon, and Alexander Valley form a network of flat and gently sloping land extending from San Pablo Bay to Mendocino County. Petaluma, as the dairy and poultry center of the Bay region, contrasts with orchards and vineyards in the Sebastopol area and the regional urban center of Santa Rosa. Grazing areas dominate the Sonoma Valley and Valley of the Moon, although increasing acreages are devoted to vineyards. Orchards and vineyards constitute the major land use in the Alexander Valley located in the northern part of the county.

Because of Sonoma County's attractive rural qualities, its towns and environs increasingly attract commuters, retired residents, and country farmers. A number of Petaluma's residents work in Marin County. Sonoma State College, moreover, has spurred development in the relatively new communities of Cotati and Rohnert Park. Development activity has also increased throughout the Valley of the Moon, now undergoing sporadic urbanization. Around Santa Rosa, in particular, and Healdsburg, Sebastopol, and Petaluma to a lesser extent, a very low-density residential pattern has emerged. Numerous small farms and ranchettes of two to ten acres dot the landscape.

Vallejo, at the mouth of the Napa River, and Napa, 15 miles inland, constitute the two major cities of the Napa Valley, with populations of 66,000 and 36,000 respectively. Medium residential densities prevail within the limits of both urban areas. The industrially zoned areas between Napa and Vallejo include a number of plants, notably Kaiser Steel, and the authorities expect that Napa Municipal Airport will attract important industry to the area.

Immediately north of Napa we find a low-density rural residential area of small farms, and to the east, the large Silverado Country Club, which give way to predominantly agricultural lands in the north Napa Valley, famous for its vineyards. Growth pressures have yet to impinge upon the small northern towns of Yountville, St. Helena, and Calistoga.

The Coast

With the exception of San Francisco and the northern peninsula, the coastal zone has remained largely undeveloped. Daly City, entirely urbanized, and Pacifica, easily accessible to San Francisco, have become "bedroom" communities. Pacifica, an incorporation of several small preexisting communities, is still growing along the coastal axis, while hillside subdivisions now begin to extend into the western slopes of the Santa Cruz Mountains. The small communities of Moss Beach, Montara, El Granada, and Half Moon Bay have not displayed significant growth, but the planned extension of the coastal freeway and the provision of additional water supplies will probably stimulate growth to the north and south. Along the mid-Peninsula coast, valuable agricultural lands, yielding such specialty crops as brussel sprouts and cut flowers, will thus be lost.

Isolation from the remainder of the region has precluded primary coastal urban development north of the Golden Gate. Most of the Marin County coast is being acquired for national recreation areas, while several recreational subdivisions including Sea Ranch, Bodega Harbor, and Jenner Bay are located along the Sonoma County coast. Recreation-oriented growth pressures will likely increase there and in the Point Reyes-Inverness area. However, livestock grazing presently remains the principal land use activity along the North coast.

The Central Valley

This area encompasses the eastern section of Contra Costa and most of Solano counties, with intensive agricultural production in the northern section of Solano County between Vacaville and Davis, in the Suisun Valley, and in Contra Costa County. Grazing land dominates the Montezuma Hills area. Fairfield and Vacaville are the principal cities in the valley region, with populations of 47,000 and 22,000 respectively. Fairfield's limits extend from Travis Air Force Base, its major employment center, to 13 miles southwest of Cordelia, where the Ford-Astor Corporation intends to develop a new community. The rich farmlands of the Suisun Valley lie between Cordelia and the outskirts of Fairfield. Vacaville continues to expand under heavy growth pressures, while Rio Vista, Dixon, and Brentwood remain small agricultural communities.

The Coast Ranges

The several units of the Coast Range form the backbone of Bay Area open space. Its vegetation includes redwood, conifer, and riparian broadleaf forests, chaparral, oak woodland, and open grassland. Grazing is the major land use activity, but commercial timber cutting also takes place. Lafayette, Orinda, and Moraga, communities east of Oakland in the Berkeley Hills, represent the major urban development in the Coast Ranges where homes are expensive and topography dictates low density. To the north, the great recreational popularity of the Russian River area has encouraged several resort communities, and many urban residents own summer homes in and around Rio Nido, Guerneville, Monte Rio, and Occidental.

Elsewhere in the Coast Ranges, individual home sites, lot splits, and subdivisions appear to be spreading, particularly in small valleys and along its narrow canyons. Green Valley Country Club northwest of Fairfield, Crow Canyon in Alameda County, Kings Mountain and Skylonda in San Mateo County, and Woodacre in Marin County, for example, have counterparts along the major scenic highways, as Skyline Boulevard and Highway 17 above Los Gatos.

ESTIMATED POPULATION GROWTH OF BAY REGION

Various agencies estimate population growth for the Bay Area to range between 5.4 and 9.6 million persons by the year 2000 (see Figure 3).[4] The State Department of Finance, we note, seems to have made the most reasonable estimate of 7.5 million people by 2000 A. D., or approximately 2,865,000 more persons than in 1970 (see Table 4).

TABLE 4

Population Projections, 1975-2000
(in thousands of persons)

County	1975	1980	1985	1990	1995	2000
Alameda	1,130	1,206	1,289	1,368	1,436	1,499
Contra Costa	614	686	772	850	921	986
Marin	227	259	296	333	368	401
Napa	88	102	124	147	171	192
San Francisco	698	708	714	716	713	713
San Mateo	582	613	645	677	700	719
Santa Clara	1,216	1,384	1,518	1,758	1,931	2,100
Solano	172	199	239	287	342	405
Sonoma	235	275	320	370	426	481
Nine-county total	4,962	5,432	5,917	6,506	7,005	7,496

Source: "Provisions Projections of California Counties to 2000," Department of Finance, Population Research Unit (September 15, 1971).

The northern counties will claim a proportionately greater share of the region's growth, assuming that existing urban land at higher densities will accommodate one-third of the additional population increase between 1970 and 2000 and that an individual needs 0.2 acres, or 3,200 persons per square mile. Raw land for urban use in the next 30 years will require an estimated 382,000 acres, or almost 600 square miles.[5]

NOTES

Unless otherwise noted, information contained in this chapter is derived from U.S. Census Data.

1. Mel Scott, *The San Francisco Bay Area, A Metropolis in Perspective* (Berkeley: University of California, 1959).

2. Association of Bay Area Governments, *Preliminary Regional Plan for the San Francisco Bay Region* (1966), p. 7.

3. Security Pacific National Bank, "San Francisco Bay Area Report: A Study of Growth and Economic Stature of Nine Bay Area Counties," Economic Research Division (1971), pp. 5 and 6.

4. Association of Bay Area Governments, "Formulation of Regional Growth Policy for the San Francisco Bay Region," Issue Paper No. 2 (1972), p. 2.

5. California State Department of Finance, Population Research Unit, *Provisional Projections of California Counties to 2000* (September 15, 1971).

CHAPTER

2

IMPACTS OF
URBANIZATION ON
THE ENVIRONMENT:
THE ROLE OF
OPEN SPACE

Bay Area urban growth patterns have generated important environmental and land use problems, including urban sprawl, congested transportation corridors, loss of agricultural and other resource lands, environmental degradation, and hazards to public safety.

URBAN SPRAWL

Low-density residential growth, typifying the expansion of suburban communities, often results in the rapid absorption of land, creating urban sprawl. The process begins with random "leapfrogging" of development beyond built-up areas, either because of high land costs, speculative withholding of land, or inadequate parcel sizes for large housing developments. This developmental process, once established, tends to be self-perpetuating.

Experts believe that the major undesirable effects accompanying urban sprawl derive from inefficient land use. Low-density residential configuration dictates decentralization and duplication of commercial facilities, as well as large land commitments to support a variety of transit modes. Agricultural areas surrounded by residential subdivisions then become committed to urbanization, meanwhile lying fallow because agricultural enterprises become unprofitable.

A "leapfrog" pattern increases community services costs because of the extension of sewer and water lines, roads, police and fire protection, and school services in undeveloped lands. For example,

> where it will cost about $30 per household to furnish homes in town with water, it will cost about $80 to provide water to the outlying developments; since the water rate will be uniform, the townspeople have to make the most of the added cost.[1]

Urban sprawl also promotes the absorption of small towns into contiguous metropolitan areas. A report on metropolitan open space has noted that:

because of the lack of boundaries, definitions or edges . . . a kind of invisible Berlin Wall is all that separates two cities. . . . Loss of visual community means loss of some of the citizen's community identity, loyalty, pride and political responsiveness. . . . In a democracy, . . . a key loss.[2]

Rapidly growing urban areas generate transportation needs that strain existing facilities, creating congestion and safety problems. Low-density suburban development increases dependence on the automobile, thus requiring more land for roads and parking. Population dispersion over a wide area further reduces the feasibility of efficient alternative modes of travel. A *Fortune Magazine* article a few years ago emphasized that

if one failure stands out above all others in leading us to our present state of affairs, it is that we haven't paid adequate attention to what might be called the "demand side" of the transportation equation. The physical arrangement of where people live, work and play has a momentous impact on their demands for travel . . . nearly every American city has concentrated on increasing the supply of highways, rather than controlling the demand for them by strict zoning and land use planning.[3]

The reverse impact of transportation systems on urbanization plays an equally important role. Highways, railroads, airports, and mass transit not only generate but also influence development patterns. The Bay Area Simulation Study (BASS), for example, indicates that 9,000 more dwelling units would be created in Marin County by a full freeway system than possibly would occur without it.[4]

The construction of a highway, or even a mass transit line such as the Bay Area Rapid Transit System (BART), frequently triggers a chain reaction (see Figure 4). A new highway provides access to low-cost land in fringe areas that is developed into low-density residential and commercial uses. Increased traffic congestion soon results in an inefficient transportation system; new or enlarged highways and freeways are built, and so the cycle continues, markedly illustrated by sections of the Junipero Serra Freeway and Highway 101 in San Jose.

Urbanization claims 375 acres of California's agricultural land every day.[5] Since 1945, for example, agricultural acreage in the Santa Clara Valley has declined by 50 percent and its dollar volume has dropped 28 percent in the last decade.[6] Urban development threatens specialty crops (prunes, plums, artichokes, brussel sprouts, strawberries, and grapes) grown only in certain climatological areas. In 1962, the county produced 43 percent of the state's and 39 percent of the nation's brussel sprouts crop. Yet,

in a recent publication of the San Mateo County's Soil Conservation District, . . . federal and state water agencies anticipate that the expansion of urban development will progressively move southerly along the coast so that by 2075, half of the county's prime agricultural crop land will go out of production.[7]

FIGURE 4

Transportation and Development Relations

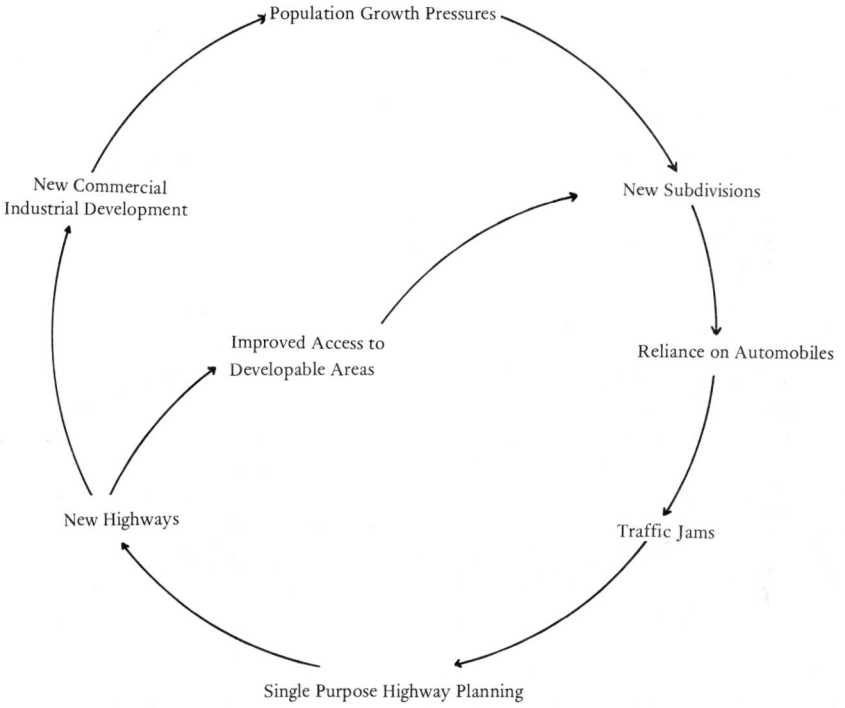

Population Growth Pressures

New Commercial
Industrial Development

New Subdivisions

Improved Access to
Developable Areas

Reliance on Automobiles

New Highways

Traffic Jams

Single Purpose Highway Planning

As urban densities invade agricultural areas, many farm practices, such as pesticide spraying, must be abandoned. Vandalism, theft, equipment transportation costs, crop losses from increased air pollution, and, perhaps most important, higher property taxes increase costs, especially for the small farmer, rendering farming uneconomical in urban areas. The retention of agricultural lands consequently remains an important goal of open space preservation efforts.

> The simple facts are that while it is not imperative for industry and subdivisions to occupy the best farmland, it is imperative that these lands be reserved for agriculture. There is little or no point in attempting to farm second-rate soil.[8]

Permeable soils, known as aquifers, are essential to maintain agricultural land in a prime state. These recharge areas, which significantly contribute to the replenishment of groundwater supplies, must be considered in open space planning.

COASTLINE

For the 4.8 million people in the nine Bay Area counties, the 246 miles of ocean coastline from Gualala to Ano Nuevo Point comprise a unique natural resource, providing significant recreational opportunity. More than 6 million persons visit the coast each year.[9] Recreational activities include sailing, surfing, swimming, fishing, diving, hunting, sunbathing, hiking, horseback riding, and camping. The coast, biologically unique with a wide variety of shoreline habitats ranging from exposed rocky coast to sandy beach and sheltered estuary, reflects an unusual diversity of marine plants and animals.

Urban development, recreational subdivisions, highways, and power plants threaten California's coastal lands. A growing demand for development along the coast suggests that

> the same features which contribute to the uniqueness of our coast also make it very desirable for development, and particularly in the South Coast, where the pressure to "build, build, build" has been tremendous. Nor is the threat restricted to Southern California. In the north, second home recreational subdivisions are proliferating along the accessible parts of the coast. In one 50-mile stretch between Dillon Beach in Marin County and Del Mar Point in Sonoma County, 33 miles are occupied by subdivisions without even minimum public access beyond mean high tide. In the Half Moon Bay area of San Mateo County, developers are poised to suburbanize most of the coast—awaiting only the provision of domestic water.[10]

In some cases, urbanization affects coastal areas by limiting public access to beaches and estuaries and destroying visual amenity. Careless construction practices and illogical land use adversely affect the coastal areas and its ecology. Recognizing that new coastal lands cannot be created, in November 1972,

California voters passed the Coastal Zone Conservation Act, establishing the Coastal Zone Conservation Commission and six Regional Commissions to review all applications for development within the permit zone, basically an area 1,000 yards inland from mean high tide. Terminating in 1976, the act additionally provides that the central commission submit to the legislature in 1976 a master plan for the preservation, restoration, and enhancement of the coastal zone.

Indiscriminate urbanization has lost or damaged outstanding natural resources and historic sites in California. Marshlands and estuaries, in particular, have been diked and filled, streams have been "undergrounded," and redwood forests have been ravaged. Urbanization has destroyed some Bay Area archeological sites,[11] replaced such historic sites as the Mills Mansion in Millbrae, and threatens other historic and natural locales.

Urban development, with its concentration of business, industry, and population in relatively small areas, inevitably contributes to degradation of the environment. Not only are air, land, and water often polluted, but rising noise levels and the loss of visual amenity adversely affect man and his environment.

PUBLIC SAFETY

In the interests of public safety, urban development in the Bay Area requires careful attention to geologic hazards. Dr. William Pecora has observed:

> Our environmental problems are deepening because of the effect of urban growth and it is high time we applied some "preventive" geology. . . . It is after an earthquake occurs, or a hill slide—after the handwringing—that the realization dawns that application of basic knowledge of terrain and its geology and hydrology might have averted disaster and high economic loss.[12]

The San Francisco Bay Region Environment and Resources Planning Study has recently identified extensive potential landslide areas in all nine Bay region counties.[13]

> Landslide costs for nine bay counties during the 1968-69 winter season were at least $25,000,000, of which about $9,000,000 was direct loss or damage to private property, mainly by lower market value; $10,000,000 to public property, chiefly for repair or relocation of roads and utilities; and about $6,000,000 of miscellaneous costs that could not be easily classified in either the public or private sector. The data used to compile these costs are incomplete, so that the total cost could be many times greater.[14]

Urbanization in geologically unstable areas increases the possibility of landslide movement. Excavation, cut and fill, and the addition of water through domestic uses tend to increase soil movement. Various methods to stabilize landslide-prone slopes exist: partial or total excavation; diversionary drainage; planting

FIGURE 5

Historically Active Earthquake Faults

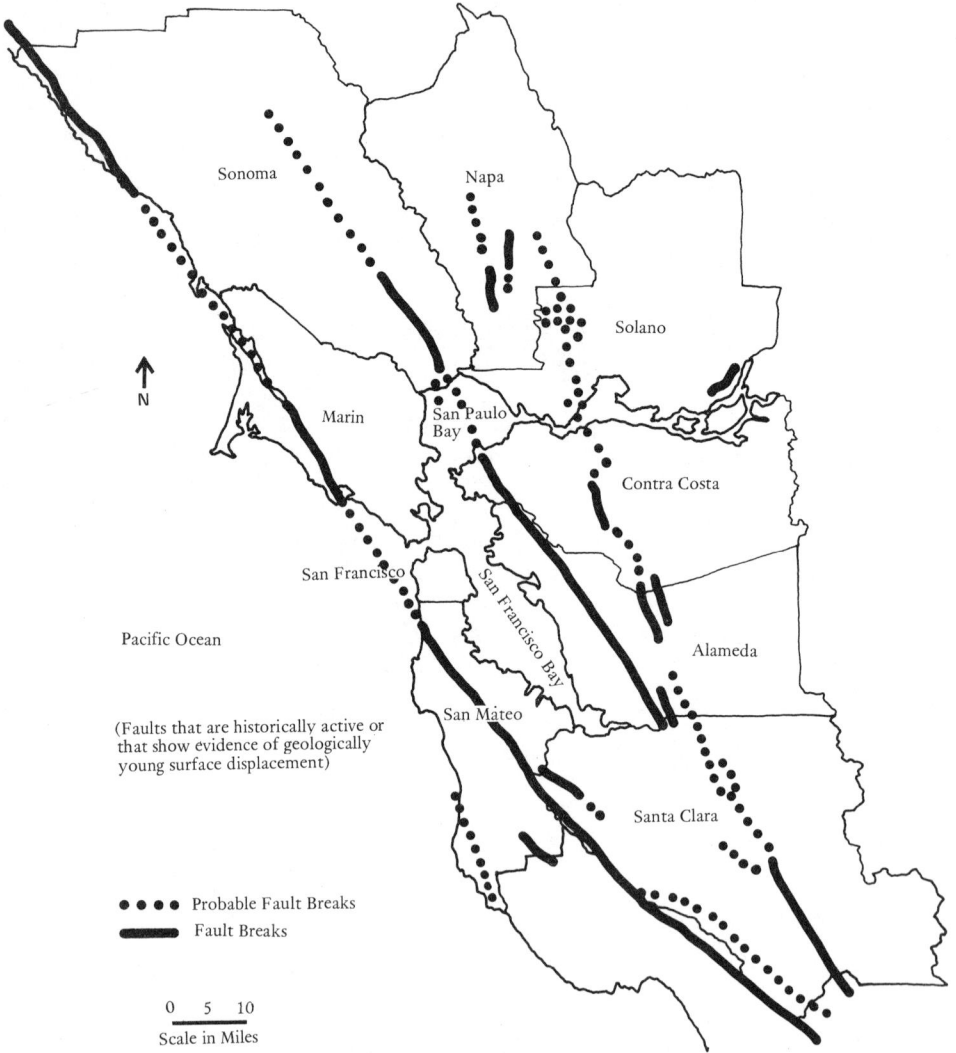

Sonoma

Napa

Solano

N

Marin

San Paulo
Bay

Contra Costa

San Francisco

San Francisco Bay

Pacific Ocean

Alameda

(Faults that are historically active or
that show evidence of geologically
young surface displacement)

San Mateo

Santa Clara

●●●● Probable Fault Breaks

━━━ Fault Breaks

0   5   10
Scale in Miles

Source: USGS (United States Geological Survey) and California Division of Mines and Geology, materials.

28

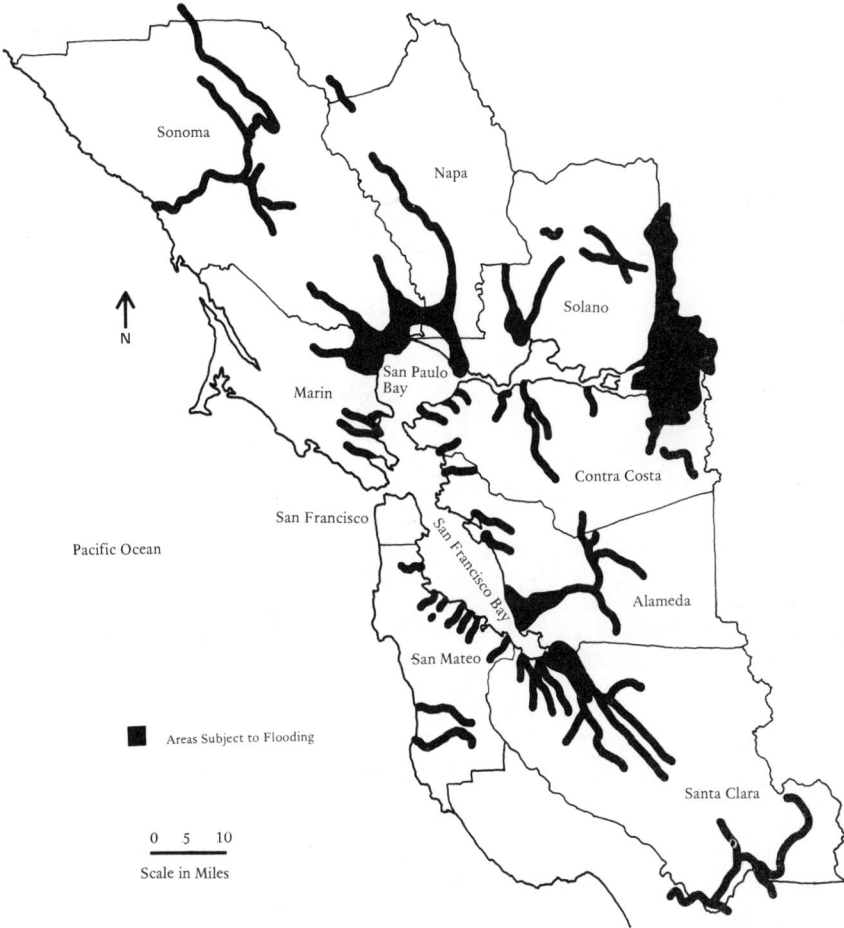

FIGURE 6

Flood Hazards

Sonoma

Napa

Solano

N

Marin

San Paulo
Bay

Contra Costa

San Francisco

San Francisco Bay

Pacific Ocean

Alameda

San Mateo

Santa Clara

Areas Subject to Flooding

0   5   10

Scale in Miles

Source: California Division of Mines and Geology.

29

vegetation; and constructing bulkheads, cribwalls, buttresses, piles, and special structural foundations. Although impractical, "nondevelopment" in landslide-prone areas represents the most effective means of reducing landslide damage.

The area's earthquake potential has received wide publicity. The famed San Andreas Fault, the Hayward and Calaveras Faults, and numerous smaller ones interlace the region. Urbanization has frequently ignored these natural hazards. Entire communities, for example, Foster City, have been built on fill.

Occasional or recurrent flooding in urbanized areas often causes loss of life and extensive property damage. Urbanization increases the potential for downstream flooding and flood damage, due to increased runoff.

> During winter storms, creeks that are normally dry suddenly fill with rushing torrents. Streams nearer the Bay swell with the surge from their many tributaries. Water that once would have been absorbed by the ground is now deflected off roofs and streets into drainage channels and streams. As urban development spreads, the volume of water thus diverted into streams constantly increases.[15]

However,

> because of the apparent economic advantages of floodplain lands in urban areas, their use will probably intensify in the future. A blending of the control of excess flows and the managed use and development of flood plains can be expected, generally, to provide an optimum program to reduce flood losses.[16]

Chaparral-covered hillsides and dense eucalyptus groves represent the greatest Bay Area fire hazards, although modern fire prevention practices, including controlled burning and adequate fire fighting capability, provide some protection. Nevertheless, a public policy of restricting development in high-fire-hazard areas combines the safest and least expensive means of wildfire damage to urban structures.

RECREATIONAL NEEDS

Continued regional growth requires adequate space to meet rapidly accelerating demands for recreation. Neighborhood parks, community-city parks, and conveniently located regional parks must provide outdoor recreational experiences in a natural setting. Parks for specialized recreational pursuits should also be available throughout the entire region.

FUNCTIONS OF OPEN SPACE

The relationship of urban development and land resources, suggesting a number of functions that open space can serve, generally concerns the fulfillment of human psychological needs and the preservation of the environment's physical integrity. Open space that helps maintain mental and emotional well-being recognizes the human need for communion with nature. Open land provides necessary escape from real and imagined urban discomforts. A historian remarks that to preserve natural beauty is to preserve

> a main source of spiritual well-being and inspiration on which our ancestors thrived . . . we are literally "children of the earth" and removed from her spirit wither or run to various forms of insanity. Unless we can refresh ourselves at least by intermittent contact with nature, we grow awry.[1 7]

Open space also provides visual relief from the urban environment. Present open space features such as San Bruno Mountain, major ridgelines, creekside habitats, and San Francisco Bay, if developed, would upset the area's existing visual balance.

Increased leisure time, coupled with greater economic freedom, has engendered a rise in outdoor recreational activities. Community and regional parks with recreational facilities, golf courses, campgrounds, lakes, reservoirs, beaches, nature areas, bikeways, and scenic highways now have become essential. Open space, protecting water quality and natural vegetation, is an atmospheric purifier through the photosynthetic process and also serves the positive planning functions of guiding efficient urban expansion and aid in preserving community identity.

ECONOMIC VALUE OF OPEN SPACE

The positive attributes of open space help ensure urban environmental quality, and advocates suggest these benefits warrant a strong open space preservation program. Nevertheless, commitment of government agencies to such programs often depends upon firm evidence that open space preservation is economically viable. Bay Area studies present major references for the economic consideration of open space. Commissioned by People for Open Space, "An Economic Analysis of a Regional Open Space Program"[1 8] evaluated the costs and benefits of three comprehensive programs for the nine-county Bay Area. It advocated public purchase of all land designated as permanent open space. A second study considered public purchase of some open space in conjunction with zoning restrictions; and the third study, regulation with compensation (see Table 5) concluding that

> a regional open space program—even a program as comprehensive as that proposed by ABAG—would not impose a major financial burden on Bay Area open space lands—would cost no more than $10 per person per year and the net costs would be considerably less. The *total acquisition cost* is less than the combined total of BART and the Bay Area freeway system expenditures over the past 10 years . . . the proposed open space program would produce dramatic savings in governmental and utility costs resulting from concentrating urban

TABLE 5

Summary and Comparison of Alternatives and Present Value Benefit-Cost Ratios
(millions of dollars)

	Total Benefits	Total Costs	Present Value Benefit-Cost Ratio	Comments
1. Total Public Acquisition	$1,527	$2,151	.71:1	Lowest benefit-cost ratio, but all land would be owned in fee and have highest asset value for public. Acquisition costs could be higher, due to major public acquisition.
2. Acquisition Plus Zoning A. Acquire in stages	$1,289	$1,720	.75:1	Same benefit-cost ratio as Alternative No. 1. Lower costs because of use of zoning and limited purchases in areas with little pressure, but staged acquisition may well be more costly in long run because of rapidly accelerating land costs. May be most practical solution. Asset value high. Also, will eventually have to keep acquiring additional land in face of development pressure.

B. Acquire all in near term	$1,336	$1,228	1.08:1	Benefits almost exactly equal to costs. Near term acquisition brings costs of this alternative below No. 2. Other factors the same. Will face problems of continuing pressure to break zoning; alternative will be to acquire additional land.
3. Compensable Regulation				
A. Permanent open space	$1,217	$1,400	.87:1	Slightly higher ratio than acquisition plus zoning. Payment of compensation over time requires present value, but asset values and revenues considerably lower than Alternatives No. 1 and No. 2.
B. Acquisition plus zoning	$1,217	$ 804	1.5:1	Most favorable benefit-cost ratio. However, may encounter legal questions in drawing line between zoning and compensable regulation. Also problems of pressure on zoning in future as described in 2B above.

Source: Development Research Associates.

development and preventing suburban sprawl. The projected difference between the cost of serving the growth patterns that would
result *without* an open space program and the more compact pattern
with open space is approximately $300 million for municipal services
and $835 million for gas, electric, and telephone utilities over a
30-year period. These two savings . . . would offset the costs of
preserving open space under the "purchase plus zoning" alternative. . . .[19]

The Livingston and Blayney study, originally aimed at creating an "Environmental Design" for development of Palo Alto's extensive foothills,[20]
found that if the costs of schools and other municipal services were added, the
total government investment would exceed any tax revenues that residential
land uses could produce, except from the most expensive homes. It concluded
that the most economic environmental design would be no design at all,
recommending that a substantial portion of the Foothills be preserved as open
space.

A rebuttal, prepared by Real Estate Research Corporation for the Associated Home Builders of the Greater East Bay, contended that the Foothills
study oversimplified its economic analysis, ignoring many of the indirect
benefits accruing from residential development.[21] Other reports concerned
with economic growth implications have reached more positive conclusions
regarding costs and benefits of residential construction.[22]

NOTES

1. The Editors of Fortune Magazine, *The Exploding Metropolis* (Garden
City, N.Y.: Doubleday, 1959), p. 123.

2. Eckbo, Dean, Austin & Williams, *Open Space: The Choices Before
California* (San Francisco: Diablo Press, 1965), p. 132.

3. Robert De Maree, "Cars and Cities on a Collision Course," *Fortune*,
February 1970, p. 126.

4. Marin County Planning Department, *Can the Last Place Last?* (1971),
p. 35.

5. John A. Prestbo, "Shrinking Farm Lands: Cities' Sprawl Stirs Fears of
Acreage Shortage," *Wall Street Journal*, July 20, 1971, p. 1.

6. Ibid.

7. San Mateo County Regional Planning Committee, *The Physical Setting of San Mateo County* (1968), p. 84.

8. William H. Geyer and Peter Hanauer, *Preserving Agricultural Land in
Areas of Urban Growth: A Look at the Record*, prepared for the use of the
Assembly Interim Committee on Agriculture and the Advisory Committee on
Land Problems (May 20, 1964), pp. 16-17.

9. Association of Bay Area Governments, *Ocean Coastline Study*
(1970), p. 52.

10. California State Environmental Quality Study Council, *Final Report*
(1972), p. 38.

11. Bert A. Gerow and Roland W. Force, *An Analysis of the University Village Complex with a Reappraisal of Central California Archaeology* (Stanford, Calif. 1968).

12. "Mounting Danger to Homes: Floods, Quakes, and Slides," *U.S. News and World Report*, December 15, 1969, p. 78.

13. Fred A. Taylor and Earl E. Brabb, *Map Showing Distribution and Cost by Counties of Structurally Damaging Landslides in the San Francisco Bay Region, California, Winter 1968-1969* (San Francisco Bay Region Environment and Resources Study, U.S. Geological Survey and U.S. Department of Housing and Urban Development, 1972).

14. Ibid.

15. San Francisco Bay Conservation and Development Commission, *Flood Control* (San Francisco: BCDC, 1967), p. 1.

16. U.S. Water Resources Council, *The Nation's Water Resources* (1968), p. 5-2-8.

17. George Macaulay Trevelyan, quoted by Conrad Wirth in *The Crisis of Open Land* (Wheeling, W. Va.: American Institute of Park Executives, 1959), p. 11.

18. Development Research Associates, "Economic Analysis of a Regional Open Space Program" (San Francisco: People for Open Space, 1969).

19. People for Open Space, "The Case for Open Space in the San Francisco Bay Area" (1969), p. 12.

20. Livingston and Blayney, *Open Space v. Development: Foothills Environmental Design Study*, (Palo Alto; 1971).

21. Real Estate Research Corporation, "Economic Analysis, Foothills Environmental Design Study," (Palo Alto, Calif., 1972); Associated Home Builders of the Greater East Bay, Inc. (Berkeley: April 1972).

22. See generally, "Growth Cost—Revenue Studies," Associated Home Builders of the Greater East Bay, Inc. (Berkeley: 1973).

3

METHODS OF
PRESERVING
OPEN SPACE

ACQUISITION

Acquiring a legal interest in land represents the most effective, but costly, method of preserving open space. Acquired interest in property, held in public trust in perpetuity, has traditionally created parks, beaches, and other recreation and conservation areas.

Fee Simple Purchase

Perhaps the most traditional method of public land acquisition has been outright government purchase of privately owned land. Unlike the use of eminent domain, a government agency must successfully negotiate a sale with the landowner, just as in an individual private transfer of land ownership. Payment for the property usually approximates full market value. State and local governments can normally purchase land for any purpose in the public interest.

The advantages of fee simple purchase for open space purposes include simplicity, preservation in perpetuity, and complete control of present and future land use. But increased costs for maintenance of open space areas and potential liability problems constitute disadvantages. Fee simple purchase represents the most expensive means of acquiring land. Because of limited public funds for park and open space acquisition, its exclusive use precludes the preservation of sufficient acreage to achieve open space objectives. Cost disadvantages often sway government agencies to eschew fee simple purchase, unless legal or political constraints on the intended public use dictate full fee acquisition. Many local governments nonetheless tend to rely on this procedure, believing it alone guarantees permanent open space.

Installment Sale

This involves payment and segmented acquisition of a land parcel during a period of years. The purchase price, fixed upon signing the sales contract, does not affect the actual title transfer, which may occur later, sometimes not until the last payment. Installment sale forestalls depletion of acquisition funds and permits immediate reservation of land parcels.

Because the land price is set at the time of the agreement, thus not subject to inflation, it usually reduces the acquisition cost. The landowner in turn benefits by realizing significant tax benefits in extending his capital gains. An undesirable aspect of installment sale concerns the delay of title transfer, thus postponing development for park purposes.

Purchase and Leaseback

Purchase and leaseback to the original landowner, or another person, secures full title to open space land, reducing the overall cost of acquisition. By allowing funds for acquisition to be derived from bonds repaid by the lease revenue, this technique incurs no additional public tax liability and the property is permanently secured as open space with no maintenance cost to the administering agency.

That the government agency might experience difficulty in obtaining a satisfactory lease to meet bond requirements constitutes a potential disadvantage. Local governments cannot presently take land for such purposes through condemnation proceedings. Whether this application of eminent domain would meet judicial acceptance remains uncertain. Purchase and leaseback involve government in private enterprise by creating a landlord-tenant relationship between the government and the lessee. But the power of eminent domain may be necessary to ensure the viability of any large purchase-leaseback program.

Purchase of Surplus Public Land

Purchasing public lands declared surplus by other governmental agencies secures permanent open space. State and federal governments have established procedures to designate and dispose of surplus lands—park land, for example— often available at substantially reduced prices. This limited method of acquisition, however, depends on fortuitous circumstances.

Tax Foreclosures

An alert park or open space agency can occasionally purchase full title to open space land at less than market value by successfully bidding on tax deeded lands publicly auctioned by the State Controller's Office. Additional savings can derive from specific legislative changes authorizing park and open space agencies to bid prior to public disposal, although the availability of more than a few acres of undeveloped parcels is rare. The City of Philadelphia has established an excellent program to provide urban miniparks on tax delinquent property.[1]

Condemnation

Condemnation is the process by which local agencies acquire essential land when voluntary sale cannot be negotiated with its owner, and it derives from the legal power of eminent domain, the sovereign right of the state to appropriate private property for public use without the landowner's consent. A condemnation suit must be filed by the appropriate agency following independent assessments of the property value and normal legal procedures; then an appropriate court determines the amount of required compensation. Upon compensation, the land goes to the condemning agency. Condemnation proceedings enjoy the advantage of residual power when owners of parcels essential for park or open space refuse to sell or demand a price greater than the agency is willing to pay. However, the proceedings, time-consuming and costly, can engender understandable animosity among those who resent government intrusion in private affairs. Authorities thus consider the power of eminent domain a matter of last resort.

The U.S. Constitution implies, and California's Constitution specifically authorizes, the power of eminent domain for state agencies and municipal corporations supplying vital public services. Not absolute, it constitutionally limits taking private land for a specific public purpose. The California Constitution explains that "private property shall not be taken or damaged for public use without just compensation having first been made to, or paid in court for, the owner. . . ."[2] Consequently, procedures mandate that eminent domain proceedings bring just compensation. A recent California case, *Klopping* v. *City of Whittier,* typifies the complexity of just compensation laws, sustaining the plaintiff's cause of action for inverse condemnation due to loss of rental income from the property when the city unduly delayed after announcing its decision to condemn the land.[3]

The requirement of a public purpose, on the other hand, allows great judicial interpretation, particularly in condemnation to obtain nonpark open space. The California Constitution and the California Civil Code include "public interest" parks and fish and wildlife conservation, but not for open space. In the absence of adjudication by the courts, it appears that open space satisfies the major judicial criteria for establishing a "public purpose." Article 28 of the California Constitution (the tone of legislation on open space) and local open space plan pronouncements seemingly provide ample evidence for the necessity to preserve open space and the existence of a justifiable public purpose. The traditional criteria that a physical public use of the property be demonstrable within a reasonable time after condemnation has been loosened gradually to imply that the underlying purpose of the use must serve the public interest.[4]

Gifts and Bequests

Through a gift or bequest of privately owned land, government agencies can obtain full title, often with substantial tax savings to the donor who normally may claim it as a charitable contribution. Cities and counties may receive gifts and bequests of land for park or open space purposes, regardless of their jurisdictional boundaries. Land may be either transferred outright to a public park or open space agency or it may be donated to a private conservation organization to hold or eventually transfer to a public agency. Where no public or private agency suits the landowner's perceived needs, he may create an agency, or trust, with appropriate purposes and management responsibilities.

Property may also be given outright to a public or private agency, with no restrictions. Or the gift may be conditional by binding covenants and restrictions in the deed at the time of transfer. In the latter case, the landowner may specify that the land be used for certain purposes, that is, a wildlife sanctuary, nature study areea, scientific research facility, or demonstration farm. He may, on the other hand, simply restrict the land to permanent open space uses. He may also provide for incremental conveyance of the property during a specified period, reserving a life estate in the property, even though he no longer holds title to it, but permitting him to use the land during his lifetime. Similarly, he may include covenants in the deed allowing him to lease back the donated land at a nominal cost for a specified number of years. Finally, he may establish a "reverter clause," reconveying title of the land to him, or to his heirs, if other conditions of the gift are not sustained.

Governments face disadvantages attendant to gifts of land. First, an active program encouraging land gifts requires staff time, expertise, and money, with no guarantee that the program will succeed. Secondly, landowners sometimes donate property that fails to conform to the overall agency acquisition program. Particularly when its sole purpose is park acquisition and development, obtaining and maintaining open space parcels may divert the agency from its overall mission. Most governments have encouraged land donations from property owners whose land is being sought for a park project. Under these conditions, authorities sometimes suggest that a donation of half the property and the sale of the remainder would approximate, or even exceed, the net profits. The sale of the entire property as a charitable contribution offsets resultant capital gains tax.

Less-Than-Fee Purchase

This procedure entails the purchase of specified interests or rights of land at less than full fee, without actually gaining title to the property. It may be secured by easements, purchase and return, and leaseholds and licenses. Easements constitute the most common method of establishing by purchase, or by dedication, a lesser interest in property. Consisting of a legal description of the property and the specific rights and conditions defining the lesser interest, the deed similarly records the provisions of the easement.

Easements may be affirmative or negative. An affirmative easement entitles its owner to question the rights of the owner of the fee, for example, by providing public access for fishing and hunting, as in Wisconsin, or by requiring that a road, building, or other facility be maintained in a certain condition. Affirmative easements generally do not provide open space, with the exception of a "flowage" easement permitting its possessor periodically to flood his lands. The more important negative easement limits landowner rights. A negative easement, for example, might prevent the owner's obstructing the natural flow of a stream, building certain types of structures, or felling trees. The advantages of easements include substantially reduced purchase costs in land remote from urban areas, retention of private land on the tax rolls, avoidance of maintenance and liability costs, and a greater degree of protection for open space.

One easement disadvantage centers on the fact that eminent domain does not include less-than-fee acquisition for open space. Air space easements for airport flight pattern approaches and highway right-of-way easements, however, may be condemned. Substantial doubt exists whether courts would uphold such condemnation actions. Public acquisition of development rights has, as a result, become more difficult. The value of urban land largely reflects its development potential, and the cost of purchasing development rights thus approximates the acquisition cost. If the assessment of land subject to easements does not reflect its reduced market value, the resulting taxes could be burdensome. Lands for which open space easements have been obtained must therefore be preferentially assessed according to use, rather than comparative sales. Most state and local agencies have thus hesitated to utilize open space easements on the regular basis, preferring the more reliable full fee acquisition.

Dedication of Easements

In contrast to easement purchase, local agencies may also negotiate the dedication of open space easements with private landowners, a technique similar to contractual agreements under the Williamson Act. Voluntary easements run for a period of not less than 20 years.[5] Open space easements have the advantage of applicability to parcels ineligible under the Williamson Act. More easily understood and administered, they particularly pertain to golf courses, private recreation areas, and smaller open spaces.

Leaseholds

An agreement with a property owner to lease his land for a definite time defines leaseholds. The park or open space agency obtaining a leasehold from a private landowner makes annual rental payments in return for usage privileges, normally for park and recreation purposes. Leaseholds may also obtain the property owner's guarantee that he will not develop his land during its term. Thus, when desirable open space land comes under immediate threat of development, or defensible open space zoning is inapplicable, and when acquisition funds are unavailable, a leasehold becomes advantageous.

Licenses

Licenses allow a private property owner, for example, to license publicly all or certain portions of his land for specific purposes. Typical licenses for public access or recreation allow landowners to cancel them.

ZONING

Zoning is "the legislative division of the community into areas in each of which only certain designated uses are permitted, so that the community may develop in an orderly manner in accordance with a comprehensive plan."[6] Experts recognize zoning as the most useful and widespread legal measure available to local government for the orderly development and transitional use of land. Zoning, applicable without the landowner's consent or compensation, may prohibit specific land uses without affecting title to land. The zoning ordinance sets forth uniform regulations concerning land use in zone districts and a map delineating the district boundaries in which regulations apply. When consistent with the policies of the general plan mandated by the California legislature in 1970, the local zoning ordinance may help achieve a logical, orderly development pattern. Although the traditional zoning objective has separated incompatible uses, protection of property values, and the prohibition of nuisance tendencies in residential areas, it has encompassed an equally valid means for maintaining open space.

Limitations

The need for comprehensive land use controls remained unrecognized until 1900. Land use adjudication depended previously on common-law nuisance principles, allowing governments to abate land use for activities commonly accepted as nuisances in a manner to benefit the community. With the increase of urbanization, however, new problems emerged that confounded traditional approaches. The first comprehensive zoning ordinance, adopted by New York City in 1916, incorporated a concept not widely accepted until 1926, when the Supreme Court upheld a zoning regulation in *City of Euclid* v. *Ambler Realty,* which held:

... with the great increase and concentration of population, problems have developed, and constantly are developing, which require
and will continue to require, additional restrictions in respect of the
use and occupation of private lands in urban communities.... In a
changing world it is impossible that it should be otherwise.[7]

The so-called Euclidian zoning that swept the country at municipal and
county levels in the ensuing years has since expanded beyond its originally
narrow confines. Floating zones, cluster zones, planned development zones,
and combining zones represent examples that provide more flexible administration of land use regulations. Some jurisdictions have recently utilized zoning to
protect open space features.
    The courts, recognizing two basic principles in determining the legal limits
of the police power in zoning cases, have held that the objective of the
regulation must be a proper goal of governmental concern. A "police power"
regulation must promote the general health, safety, and welfare of society, by
preventing land use activities threatening the well-being of others or by
requiring activities enhancing the social, economic, and physical environment as
determined by government. The courts, rarely eliminating a regulation because
it fails to promote a governmental goal, have hesitated to second-guess
legislative determinations of society's general health, safety, and welfare.
Therefore, a regulation defining purpose and bearing a distinct relationship to
stated planning goals will probably remain valid. Several California cases have
ruled that the protection and conservation of natural resources promotes health
and safety, thus serving a public purpose. Courts have found "arbitrary,
discriminatory, or confiscatory" regulations unreasonable and, hence, invalid,
in words embodying historically developed doctrines emanating from the
federal and state constitutions.[8] These doctrines insist that the regulatory
measures must bear a reasonable relation to the desired goal. In practice, a case
rarely rests on these grounds, particularly with respect to a regulation designed
to implement open space plans.[9] Open space regulations generally promote
several goals and, with careful planning, can be closely linked to ecological
considerations.
    Another doctrine holds that similarly situated property owners must
receive like treatment. If an Exclusive Agricultural (AE) zone applies to one
portion of a jurisdiction, but not to another, and if both sections possess
similar physical characteristics, the regulation's legality would be subject to
serious question. Restrictive zoning regulations may be considered confiscatory
if they excessively diminish land value. That a regulation cannot substantially
devalue property generally remains the key issue in most zoning cases,
particularly regarding open space. The concept of extending the costs of
acquiring public benefits for the public is closely related. The court may
determine, in other words, that the public should assume the burden of the
costs by eminent domain, rather than placing the burden on property owners.
    Some decisions have upheld zoning that greatly reduced property value,
the earliest being *Hadacheck* v. *Sebastion* in 1915 when a prohibition against a
brickmaking operation in Los Angeles reduced the value of the land from
$800,000 to $60,000.[10] In *Consolidated Products Rock Co.* v. *City of Los*

Angeles, a California court upheld a similar ordinance, while acknowledging that the property was rendered virtually useless, asserting the

> very essence of the police power as differentiated from the power of eminent domain is that the deprivation of individual rights and property cannot prevent its operation once it is shown that its exercise is proper and that the method of its exercise is reasonably within the meaning of due process of law.[11]

Cases concerning the prevention of land use activity potentially endangering the surrounding community's health and safety, as opposed to court tests of regulations promoting public benefit such as open space, often have almost imperceptible differences. Some experts maintain that these regulations entail dichotomous elements and to treat them separately is fallacious. Unfortunately, very few California cases have concerned ordinances designed to promote public benefits. In those cases available for analysis, however, it remains unclear whether property owners should pay for the benefits accruing to the community or whether they should share through public acquisition.

In one frequently cited case, the New Jersey Supreme Court ruled against a regulation prohibiting the dredging and filling of a wetlands area, holding that the public uses of flood water detention and open space "are necessarily so all-encompassing as practically to prevent the exercise by a private owner of any worthwhile rights or benefits in the land. So public acquisition rather than regulation is required."[12] In a similar Maine case, the court found that

> the benefits of [wetlands] preservation extend beyond town limits and are statewide. The costs of its preservation should be publicly borne. To leave appellants with commercially valueless land in upholding the restriction presently imposed is to charge them with more than their just share of the cost of this statewide conservation program, granting fully its commendable purpose.[13]

Some specialists reason that it is patently unfair to impose substantial cost on individuals when a feasible alternate system exists to accomplish the desired goals.[14] While other cases suggest that zoning for public benefits such as open space falls beyond the scope of police power, they have not established a definitive constitutional boundary in open space zoning. Judicial interpretations of the police power vary considerably. California courts have traditionally set the pace in expanding police power. The landmark case, *Consolidated Rock,* placed the question of "taking" of secondary importance to the purposes of the regulation, a view substantiated in a parallel case, *Hammer* v. *Town of Ross* in 1962, indicating that "even if the reasonableness of the regulation is fairly debatable, the legislative determination will not be disturbed."[15]

Although applicable to the prohibition of specific operations, that is, rock quarrying, that caused demonstrable harm, an identical justification pertains to more direct forms of open space zoning. The California Supreme Court has stated:

... the elimination of open space in California is a melancholy aspect of the unprecedented population increase which has characterized our state in the last few decades. ... [open space] statutes which further the underlying policy expressed in the constitutional section [Article XXVIII of the California Constitution] must be upheld whenever possible to effectuate its salutary purposes.[16]

An appellate court upheld a state regulation facilitating preservation of the natural character of the San Francisco Bay by denying a permit for filling operations. The court, discounting arguments that the action constituted a "taking," declared:

It can be said that refusing to allow appellant to fill its bay land amounts to an undue restruction on its use. In view of the necessity for controlling the filling of the Bay ... it is clear that the restriction imposed does not go beyond proper regulation such that the restriction would be referable to the police power.[17]

Large Lot Zoning

Large lot zoning, also known as estate or minimum lot zoning, may be used to preserve open space or provide an open space atmosphere. Discouraging high-density development by restricting homes on parcels of less than minimum acreage, it often applies to commercial, agricultural, and residential districts, in effect, representing a specific restriction accompanying a zoning ordinance. Large lot zoning may be divided into preservation of open space in residential areas and the limitation of unsightly or environmentally damaging uses in open space areas. A minimum of one or two acres, required by many suburban communities, is the most common application of large lot zoning. The open space character of an area depends upon the total acreage of the zoned area, natural landscape features, parcel configuration, residence location, and the nature of the area development.

Lots including a ranch-style house, corral and stables, sheds and other accouterments of country living, tend to replace open space with a low-density rural community. Lot size relative to open space considerations depends upon the specific character of a given area and the goals of the planning jurisdiction. Large lot zoning finds its widest application in rural area residential zones where land, zoned for four to five acres to accommodate the increasingly popular "ranchette," preserves a low-density rural atmosphere, protects property values, and limits taxes.

Many experts consider large lot zoning an undesirable method of preserving open space:

... large lot zoning does not save open space, it squanders it. By forcing developers to use large lots for little houses, the community forces them to chew up much more of the open landscape than they

have to. Instead of several tightly knit subdivisions, housing will be
spattered all over the place.[18]

Necessitating the costly extension of governmental services and roads,
residential large lot zoning has also received severe criticism as exclusionary.
Lower-income families simply cannot afford a home in an area zoned for large
lots.

The assignation of large parcel restrictions, especially to nonresidential
zoned areas, remains a valuable and perhaps necessary element of open space
zoning. It has thus far not been used extensively, but undoubtedly will increase
in importance as local jurisdictions modernize their zoning ordinances. Large
lot zoning generally strengthens open space zoning classification. For example,
Napa County's establishment of a 20-acre minimum parcel size in Napa Valley
provided an impetus for the preservation of its valuable wine grape industry.

Flood-Plain Zoning

Police power restricts land use subject to flooding and applies to streams
and rivers or low-lying wetlands. Primarily designed to protect the health and
safety of the community and to prevent property loss, flood-plain regulations
may coincidentally provide communities with greenbelts, conserve scenic and
productive natural habitats, and secure land for privately operated recreational
use. The usual distinction between the flood plain, or floodway fringe and the
flood channel, often results in ordinances limited to the "designated
floodway,"[19] essentially preventing building in the stream channel prior to the
construction of a planned flood-control project. California law, encouraging
flood-plain zoning, provides that the "State shall not appropriate money to pay
any cost of lands, easements, or rights-of-way . . . where an appropriate public
agency fails to establish the necessary flood regulations . . . within any area
classified designated floodway."[20]

Regulations for a flood plain, usually based on a complicated study
indicating the area inundated along a stream course under specific flood
conditions—for example, a 100-year flood pattern—permit most types of
development, subject to requirements imposed on the developer, such as raising
elevation, or diking and leveeing to protect structures from flooding. Another
regulation limits development in the flood plain to projects that flooding would
not damage, including parking lots, used car lots, golf courses, driving ranges,
drive-in theaters, fairgrounds, warehouses for storage of material impervious to
major damage, railroad switching yards, temporary structures, parks, and
agriculture. A stronger variation precludes all but defined open space uses,
recognizing that urban structures will increase flood damage in downstream
urbanized areas.

Regulations may divide the flood plain into zoning districts based on
flood hazard, thus the open space value depends upon the size of the flood
plain and the types of restrictions and their enforcement. Flood court cases
have usually established a police-power use protecting health, safety, and the

general welfare.[21] Whether regulations can prevent an individual building in a hazardous flood-plain area remains unclear. Although adequate constitutional grounds exist for preventing development where the public may unwittingly purchase property without full knowledge of flood hazards, a fully cognizant individual enjoys the right to risk life or property damage.[22]

Exclusive Agricultural Zoning (AE)

Exclusive agricultural zoning prevents development of fertile open land a community wishes to maintain in agriculture. It may be used in areas with especially prime agricultural soils or on land producing specialty crops not grown elsewhere in the same quantity or quality. It can protect the public from the high economic costs of urban sprawl by preserving agricultural land as open space. A clear distinction exists between agricultural zoning and AE zoning. The former, usually unintensive use zoning, typically permits single-family homes on one- or two-acre lots, while the latter limits use to agricultural production with necessary supporting facilities. AE restrictions, usually including a description of both a minimum parcel size and permitted zone uses, may be imposed by ordinance or by voluntary landowner-local government commitment.

In the only major test of California AE zoning, a superior court upheld a Napa County ordinance for the Napa Valley.[23] Recent statements and actions of California courts seemingly incline to uphold AE zoning. Moreover,

> the reciprocal benefits accruing to farmers from exclusive agricultural zoning are important in determining the validity of the application of such [exclusive agricultural] zoning. If the reciprocal benefits are minimal, as would probably be true if the sole or chief purpose of such zoning is to preserve open space, there is a possibility of adverse court reaction.[24]

Cluster Zoning

Also known as density zoning, cluster zoning involves regulations that concentrate residences in higher-density clusters to reserve open space in a subdivision development. Differing from other zoning, it permits development and attempts to balance the subdivision and open space, while other zoning forms attempt to preclude urban uses. The cluster zoning ordinance allows the subdivider to reduce the allowable lot area for each residential unit, subject to the limitation that the number of units in the development do not exceed those allowed by conventional zoning. The remaining land is retained as open space.

Cluster zoning ordinances vary. Specific limitations regarding allowable reductions in lot size depend on local preferences. Bonuses allowing a 10 to 15 percent increase in overall density are occasionally provided to encourage permissive or mandatory clustering, as in the Ramapo, New York, ordinance.[25] An important variation, slope-density zoning, links increased density provisions to the extent of slope. Clustering may also be accomplished through planned unit development ordinances that allow for "mixed" uses within a development, a common application in California.

Cluster zoning and Planned Unit Development (PUD), theoretically designed to permit a mixture of uses—single family units, apartments, commercial—in a development, have occasioned confusion. Uses and density are not specified, nor are standards set. The developer who designs his own zoning regulations, submitted to the planning body for approval, has flexibility. Cluster zoning, particularly conducive to large-scale development because it allows the landowner a generous return on his investment, enables a more sensitive subdivision design to scenic, recreational, and aesthetic amenities. It also encourages the developer to respect the topography and natural land conditions to a greater extent than the traditional subdivision design types. Clustering tends to create much more open space than acreage zoning, which often causes scattered development, wasted land and urban sprawl.

If developers plan carefully, open space in adjoining subdivisions may be linked to provide greenbelts. In addition, cluster zoning economizes in building and providing services.

> Only the land best suited to build need be used. Less street mileage is needed than in conventional development, utility lines are shorter and therfore cheaper, children may be closer to schools, and snow plowing, mail delivery, and garbage pickup are all cheaper because routes are shorter.[26]

Cluster zoning regulations may be abused, however, in areas where steep slope or other natural restrictions render land development impractical. The subdivider may purchase property adjacent to land at a lower price and increase densities on the remaining property. Methods to protect open space in a cluster from future development include outright dedication to the community, public ownership, dedication of development rights to the community, or retention in common ownership by covenant among the subdivision's residents. The latter may be achieved by creating a homeowner's association, with levies administered to its members, by a trusteeship established by the developer and enforced by covenant, or by creation of a special assessment district among subdivision residents to fund the maintenance by the local parks and recreation department.

Some courts have upheld cluster zoning as a valid use of the police power. *Chrinko et al.* v. *South Brunswick Township Planning Board* (1963) ruled it was unnecessary for the state zoning enabling law to make specific provisions for density zoning. The New Jersey Court asserted that "such an ordinance reasonably advances the legislative purpose of securing open spaces, preventing overcrowding and undue concentration of population and promoting the general welfare."[27]

California courts have also sustained the cluster concept, although cases thus far have centered on PUD ordinances. *Orinda Homeowners' Committee* v.

the Board of Supervisors of Contra Costa County, a case involving almost a pure cluster zone application of the ordinance, upheld the legality of a PUD zoning.[28]

SUBDIVISION REGULATIONS—ADDITIONAL REQUIREMENTS

The police power enables local government to establish building and housing codes and subdivision regulations. The only aspect of police power directly related to open space is the local government authority to require exactions of land, or fees in lieu thereof, to meet the need for public improvements generated by a subdivision. Exactions permitted by local governments include the requirement that subdividers, as a condition of approval for a final map, either dedicate land, provide funds for the acquisition and development of parks and schools, or provide access to ocean coastline, lakes, reservoirs, rivers, and streams. Mandatory dedication has occurred in nonsubdivision cases with approval of building permits, variances, and zoning changes,[29] if related to the purpose for which approval has been sought.[30]

The courts have upheld subdivision exactions as a legitimate use of police power.[31] The principal judicial criteria hold that the exaction be in the reasonable public interest. In a 1971 landmark case (*Associated Home Builders v. City of Walnut Creek*), concerning park dedication requirements, the California Supreme Court decided that the dedication of land and payments in lieu thereof, even though not used solely for purposes benefiting the subdivision in question, constituted a reasonable exercise of the police power:

> We see no persuasive reason caused by present and anticipated future population growth on the one hand and the disappearance of open land on the other to hold that a statute requiring the dedication of land by a subdivider may be justified only on the ground that the particular subdivider upon whom an exaction has been imposed will, solely by the development of his subdivision, increase the need for recreational facilities to such an extent that additional land for such facilities will be required.[32]

However, in *Selby Realty Co.* v. *City of San Buenaventura,* a lower court granted the plaintiff's cause of action for inverse condemnation when the city required a street dedication prior to issuing a building permit for an apartment house.[33] In a widely criticized decision, the court accepted the plaintiff's contention that, if he dedicated the required land, insufficient space would be left to build the apartments. Rather than invalidating the dedication requirement, the court granted inverse condemnation, with potentially far-reaching consequences regarding park dedication. Park dedication ordinances, like all subdivision exactions, contribute to escalating housing costs, a major concern of both the homebuilding industry and the home buyer.

TAXATION OF OPEN SPACE

Open space taxation plans, designed to remedy inconsistencies in public policy concerning land assessment according to "full cash value" and "highest and best use," generate development pressures at variance with open space objectives of local general plans. In an approach involving the assessment of open land according to its present use rather than its market value, preferential assessment usually results in the substantial reduction of taxes, at least near urban areas. They include mandatory or selective preferential assessment. Preferential assessment has been applied in several states: New Jersey, New York, Florida, Pennsylvania, Oregon, Maryland, Hawaii, and California. Selective assessment, the approach favored by some, includes significant variations. We find the most effective tax concessions to protect open space in those states that impose a restriction on the development of land in return for tax benefits. The Williamson Act in California has provided a model for many states.

Tax Deferral

Tax deferral involves postponing payment of taxes on the property's market value restricted to open space uses in excess of its open space value. Deferred taxes, due when the land converts to a "higher use" within a stated period, remains unavailable in California.

OPEN SPACE ACQUISITION FINANCING

The ability of public agencies to pay for open space is a key factor in its preservation. General obligation bonds represent the most common way of financing major state and local acquisition and development programs. Government entities must retire the bonds with interest in 20 years, or more. A specified portion of the property tax rate raises funds for bond retirement, or in the case of state bonds, general fund appropriations are used. Obligation bonds avail large amounts of money for land acquisition, thus avoiding speculative increases in its value.

Revenue Bonds

Income from the financed project retire revenue bonds, generally used for public golf courses and parks that generate significant revenue. Sometimes they are used for the purchase and leaseback of open space. In addition to the immediate availability of funds, revenue bonds advantageously require only a simple majority vote and do not incur a tax liability. In some cases, however, revenues may not be sufficient to meet the retirement schedule.

Special Tax Rate Allocations

This "pay-as-you-go" method used by local governments provides a constant source of funds for park and open space acquisition. Established by a charter amendment or ordinance, it includes an additional tax levy approximating $.05-.10 per $100 of assessed valuation and provides a constant level of funds during the acquisition period. However, it limits acquisition by the year-to-year availability of funds, resulting in greater costs from speculative increases in land value.

General Fund Appropriations

Appropriations from the operating income of the governing county represent a less certain means of "pay-as-you-go" financing. Congressional authorization usually funds large federal projects in this manner. Occasionally a state will also authorize special acquisition projects. In the absence of other financing programs, local agencies rely on year-to-year budget appropriations to support designated acquisition projects. Because funds must compete with a host of other budget items, this is the least desirable method of paying for open space. The local level of funding, usually inadequate, amounts to ad hoc financing.

Self-Sustaining Funds

Money for open space acquisition from untapped sources of revenue find excellent examples in the Federal Land and Water Conservation Fund and the California Environmental Protection Fund. Self-sustaining funds, however, supply only a small fraction of acquisition funds because of the paucity of taxable sources.

Development Taxes

Some local governments have used a development, or "bedroom," tax as a revenue source for municipal parkland acquisition. Based on the number of bedrooms per dwelling, it reflects potential users of park facilities and, as a one-time tax imposed with the filing of a building permit, it sometimes tends to exclude low-cost housing rather than provide park funds.

NOTES

1. Ira Michael Heyman and Roselyn Rosenfeld, "Open Space Handbook" (unpublished), p. IV-B-1-10.

2. California State Constitution, Article 1, Section 14.

3. *Klopping* v. *City of Whittier*, 1972; 2 Cal 3rd 39, 104 Cal Rptr 1.

4. Gordon C. Rhea, Carl R. Schenker, Jr., and Stephen L. Urbanczyk, *California Land Use Primer, A Legal Handbook for Environmentalists* (Stanford Environmental Law Society, 1972), pp. 39-40. See also, Stanley Weissburg, "Legal Alternatives to Police Power: Condemnation and Purchase, Development Rights, Gifts," in *Open Space and the Law*, ed. Francis W. Herring, (Berkeley: University of California, Institute of Governmental Studies, 1965), pp. 39-40.

5. California Revenue and Taxation Code, Section 422.

6. Gerald Bowden, "Open Space and the Police Power in California," in *Final Report*, California Legislature, Joint Committee on Open Space Lands (1970), p. 65.

7. *City of Euclid* v. *Ambler Realty*, 272 U.S. 366, pp. 386-87.

8. Ira Michael Heyman, "Open Space and the Police Power," in *Open Space and the Law*, op. cit., pp. 8-10.

9. Heyman and Rosenfeld, op. cit., p. 1127.

10. *Hadacheck* v. *Sebastian*, 239 U.S. 394 (1915).

11. *Consolidated Rock Products Co.* v. *City of Los Angeles*, 57 Cal 2nd 515; 20 Cal Rptr 638, 370 P. 2nd 342; *Appeal Dismissed*, 371 U.S. 36 (1962); Bowden, op. cit., p. 80.

12. *Morris County Land Improvement Co.* v. *Township of Parsipanny-Troy Hills*, 193 A2d, 233 (1963), pp. 241-42.

13. *State of Maine* v. *Johnson*, 265 A2d 711 (Me., 1970), cf. *Potomac Sand and Gravel Co.* v. *Mandel* (Md. Cir. Ct., February 25, 1972), 2 ELR 20101.

14. Heyman and Rosenfeld, op. cit., p. 42.

15. *Candlestick Properties, Inc.* v. *San Francisco Bay Conservation and Development Commission*, 11 C.A. 3rd 557; 89 Cal Rptr 897; referring to *Hammer* v. *Town of Ross*, p. 571.

16. *Associated Home Builders etc., Inc.* v. *City of Walnut Creek*, 4 Cal 3rd 633, p. 639.

17. *Candlestick Properties*, op. cit., p. 572.

18. William Whyte, *The Last Landscape* (Garden City, N.Y.: Doubleday, 1970), p. 4.

19. "Designated floodway" is officially defined as the channel of a stream and that portion of the adjoining flood plain required to reasonably provide for the construction of a project for passage of the design flood including lands necessary for construction of project levees. California Water Code, Section 8402 (f).

20. California Water Code, Section 8411.

21. See, generally, Dunham, "Flood Control via the Police Power," 107 *U. Pa. Law Review*, 1098 (1959); Note, "Flood Plain Zoning for Flood Loss Control," 1 50 *Iowa Law Review*, 552 (1965); Benchert, "Constitutional Law-Zoning-Flood Plain Regulations," 4 *Natural Resources Journal* 445

(1965); R. M. Anderson, *American Law of Zoning* (1968); U.S. Water Resources Council, D. A. Yangger and J. A. Kusler, "Regulation of Flood Hazard Areas to Reduce Flood Losses" (1970).

22. Heyman and Rosenfeld, op cit., p. 17.

23. *Napa Valley United Farmers* v. *County of Napa*, Opinion of Judge Charles J. McGalorick, Superior Court of California, February 18, 1971, No. 24961.

24. Heyman and Rosenfeld, op. cit., p. 28.

25. Charles E. Little, *Challenge of the Land* (New York: Open Space Action Institute, 1968), p. 47, wherein is quoted the Ramapo Ordinance: "The town board has determined to empower the planning board to mandate the use of density zoning for a subdivision plot whether or not the applicant has consented to the use of density zoning."

26. Ann Louise Strong, "Open Space for Urban America" (Washington, D.C.: U.S. Government Printing Office, 1965), p. 36.

27. *Chrinko et al.* v. *South Brunswick Township Planning Board*, 77 N.J. Super. 594, 187 A 2d, 221 (1963).

28. *Orinda Homeowners' Committee* v. *the Board of Supervisors of Contra Costa County*, 11 Cal. App. 3d 773 (1970).

29. *Southern Pacific* v. *City of Los Angeles*, 242 Cal. App 2d 38; 5 Cal Rptr 197.

30. California Government Code, Section 68909.

31. *Ayres* v. *City of Los Angeles*, 34 Cal. 2d 31, 206 P. 2d (1949).

32. *Associated Home Builders*, op. cit., pp. 639-40.

33. *Selby Realty Co.* v. *City of San Buenaventura*, 1972; 28 Cal App 3rd 624; 104 Cal Rptr 866.

All levels of government, as well as the private sector, have a vital interest in the allocation of land resources and consequently have become involved in important open space activities.

At this point an important theme needs reemphasis. The basic relationship between open space and urban development suggests that addressing those development forces which erode open space is no less important than seeking positive programs for its preservation. In other words, a discussion of the problems associated with governmental efforts to secure open space should also include measures to provide for more rational, orderly growth and development. Consequently, the ensuing analysis has not separated the broader aspects of land use planning and regulation from their more specific application to preserve open space.

4

GOVERNMENT AND PRIVATE INFLUENCES ON OPEN SPACE PRESERVATION

THE ROLE OF THE FEDERAL GOVERNMENT

Federal involvement in open space preservation has been essentially limited to acquisition and management of federal parks and open space lands, management of the federally owned lands and financial planning, and technical assistance to state and local governments. These programs have had a substantial impact on the United States, and particularly the Bay Area. The federal government has become increasingly involved in the promotion of intergovernmental coordination. And Congress has given serious consideration to direct federal participation in comprehensive planning and land use regulation.

Acquisition and Management of Parks and Open Space

Direct federal involvement in preserving open space occurs through maintenance and expansion of a system of national parks, forests, wildlife refuges, and other public open space lands.

The National Park Service, National Forest Service, Bureau of Sport Fisheries and Wildlife, and Bureau of Land Management administer the programs, although Congress retains the basic responsibility for special projects. Three of these agencies have substantial holdings in the Bay Area.

National Park Service

Created in 1916, the National Park Service acts to conserve unique scenic, natural, and historic lands. It manages 271 national parks, monuments, seashores, lakeshores, recreation areas, and historic landmarks totaling 30 million acres. Point Reyes National Seashore in Marin County is the Bay Area's only major federal park of the 4,300,000 acres of national park lands. Authorized in 1962, it preserves almost the entire Point Reyes peninsula, a ruggedly beautiful and diverse natural area 30 miles from San Francisco. Less than 500 acres of a total 64,546 remain to be acquired. In 1972 President Nixon authorized the 34,000-acre Golden Gate National Recreational Area (see Figure 5). In addition to the transfer of a number of local, state, and federal holdings (Muir Woods National Monument, Alcatraz Island, Forts Barry, Cronkite and Baker, Mt. Tamalpais, Angel Island, Marin Headlands State Park, several state beaches, and Lincoln and Aquatic parks), it authorized the acquisition of 16,000 private acres. With Point Reyes, the Golden Gate National Recreation Area will provide an uninterrupted 40-mile greenbelt of outstanding natural beauty from the northern tip of Point Reyes Peninsula to the Golden Gate. No other region in the United States can claim more than 150 square miles of federal parks so close to the heart of a major urban area.

Bureau of Sport Fisheries and Wildlife

The Bureau of Sport Fisheries and Wildlife, responsible for preserving and enhancing the benefits associated with wildlife and its environment, administers a national network of migratory bird and game refuges of approximately 30 million acres in more than 320 refuges. Most funds for acquisition derive from the Land and Water Conservation Fund and revenues from the sale of migratory bird hunting stamps. The Bureau also recommends measures for the enhancement of, or mitigation of damage to, fish and wildlife resources at federal water development projects.

The California wildlife refuge system encompasses almost 200,000 acres, of which 68,000 acres represent land acquired by the bureau. Most refuges are located in the central valley along the major route of the Pacific flyway. The two major federal Bay Area refuges are the Farallon National Wildlife Refuge (211 acres) and the San Pablo Bay National Wildlife Refuge. Established in 1970, it consists of 2,000 acres of upland and marsh and 7,800 acres of tideland along North San Pablo Bay between Vallejo and Black Point.[1]

In 1972, Congress authorized $9 million for acquisition and $11 million for development of the San Francisco Bay National Wildlife Refuge, which is along the South Bay in Alameda, Santa Clara, and San Mateo counties. Totaling 22,000 acres, of which more than 14,000 consists of upland, salt marsh, and salt ponds, it represents a major addition to the Bay Area's permanently preserved open space. However, the $9 million necessary for acquisition has yet to be appropriated. Future expansion of the National Wildlife Refuge System in the Bay Area remains uncertain.

Bureau of Land Management

The Bureau of Land Management administers public land, public laws, mineral leasing laws, revested timber lands, and grazing districts for 480 million acres of public lands in the 12 western states. Operating primarily as a land disposal agency during the westward expansion of the continental United States, the Bureau of Land Management has emphasized resource conservation and management of the public domain since the passage of the Classification and Multiple Use Act in 1964. It has designed a program to integrate and analyze resource and land use information for multiple-use planning purposes. It holds approximately 53,000 acres of generally remote grazing and timber land in five Bay Area counties,[2] 90 percent of which will remain in the public domain. Small, difficult to manage, isolated parcels with poor public access comprise the other 10 percent designated for disposal. Approximately 1,000 acres in Sonoma County constitute the only large concentration of Bay Area public land designated for disposal. The bureau seeks, whenever possible, to exchange, rather than sell, lands classified for disposal because proceeds from public sale revert to the U.S. Treasury.

For those lands slated to remain in the public domain, the bureau has also prepared comprehensive land use plans for livestock grazing, recreation, timber, wildlife habitat, minerals, energy, and land tenure uses. The bureau has prepared a plan for part of its large holdings in Napa County and will complete others in the next few years. State and local agencies can acquire bureau lands for $2.50 an acre under the Resources and Public Purposes Act, if the land is used for public park purposes specified by the act. Organization toward retention and management of the public domain currently characterizes a period of major change in planning methods in the Bureau of Land Management. Consequently, most of its lands in the Bay Area will remain open space.

Management of Other Federal Lands

Other federal agencies own and operate parcels of land in the Bay Area, many of which have significant open space value. The Department of Defense, by far the most important nonresource-oriented federal agency in the Bay Area, holds more than 40,000 acres at some 35 installations.[3] Other federal holdings of open space include an additional 5,703 acres.

Permanent preservation of those undeveloped federal properties as open space has received only indirect attention. The major consideration of most federal agencies has centered on creating buffer zones surrounding ammunition dumps, airport runways, radio facilities, and high-security installations. Excepting the land around the future Warm Springs Reservoir in Sonoma County, the Army Corps of Engineers and the Bureau of Reclamation have made no commitment for the management of lands surrounding project reservoirs, preferring rather to transfer ownership or management responsibility to other agencies.

The President's Legacy of Parks program, however, has generated a major effort to identify federal properties which may be assigned to state and local agencies for park development. The program directs the General Services Administration to identify by way of annual surveys, all federal properties exceeding the needs of federal agencies. After federal agencies receive notification regarding the status of the lands, and if unclaimed, they become officially "surplus." The Bureau of Outdoor Recreation then contacts state and local park and recreation agencies concerning the property's potential use for park purposes. Public Law 91-485 enables interested agencies to acquire the land, in most cases, for nothing. Thus, more than 200 parcels covering more than 26,000 acres of surplus land have been converted for park purposes, in the Bay Area, including three parcels from Camp Parks to the East Bay Regional Park District, City of Pleasanton, and Valley Community Services District; 76 acres of Nike Battery site 08-09 in Contra Costa County to the East Bay Regional Park District; and small portions of other Army properties to San Rafael and Marin Counties.

Technical and Financial Assistance
to State and Local Government

The financial and technical assistance provided for planning and preservation represents a third important area of federal involvement in open space. Among the numerous federal grant programs, many of which indirectly provide open space funds, (for instance, landscaping and highway beautification grants), two assume major importance: the Land and Water Conservation Fund administered by the Department of Interior, and the Open Space Grant Program, administered by the Department of Housing and Urban Development.

The Land and Water Conservation Fund, created in 1965, provides funds for the preservation of natural resources. Approximately one half of these helps purchase federal recreation areas; the remainder goes to state and local agencies on a matching-fund basis. Revenue sources include income from the sale of surplus federal property, special boating fuel taxes, sale of entrance permits at federal recreation areas, and offshore oil revenues. Since 1965 this has provided more than $13 million for land acquisition, including $9 million to state and Bay Area local agencies (see Table 6).

The Housing Act of 1961 created an Open Space Grant Program that provides matching grants for acquisition of urban land for recreation, conservation, and historic preservation. Since its inception, local agencies in the San Francisco Standard Metropolitan Statistical Area have received $14.5 million (see Table 7).

The Housing and Urban Development program provides funds to local and regional planning agencies for preparation of comprehensive plans. In recent years, environmental and resource plans have received high priority for federal funding in California. Federal technical assistance for open space planning and preservation has been limited essentially to the publication of documents and occasional conferences, with minimal direct assistance to local agencies. The U.S. Geological Survey and the Department of Housing and Urban Development, however, have embarked on a joint research and demonstration study in the Bay Area to develop effective interpretation and presentation of geological information so that urban planners can respond more efficiently to environmental considerations.

TABLE 6

Disposition of Land and Water Conservation Grant Funds, 1965-72

County	City		County		East Bay Regional Park District		State		Total		
	Acquisition	Development	Acquisition	Development	Acquisition	Development	Acquisition	Development	Acquisition	Development	Grand Total
Alameda	218,484	226,989	–	–	862,996	255,000	–	867,000	1,081,480	1,348,989	2,430,469
Contra Costa	51,000	37,230	–	–	–	249,900	–	341,011	51,000	628,141	679,141
Marin	–	–	267,750	166,200	–	–	734,400	–	1,002,150	166,200	1,168,350
Napa	–	–	–	–	–	–	–	–	–	–	–
San Francisco	399,640*	537,303	–	–	–	–	–	–	399,640	537,303	936,943
San Mateo	331,500	–	472,556	9,912	–	–	313,650	538,535	1,117,706	548,447	1,666,153
Santa Clara	1,731,856	569,699	721,650	–	–	–	669,478	–	3,122,984	569,699	3,692,683
Solano	121,742	–	174,420	101,490	–	–	2,091,000	–	2,387,162	101,490	2,488,652
Sonoma	–	–	–	108,936	–	–	–	–	–	108,936	108,936
Total	2,854,222	1,371,221	1,636,376	386,538	862,996	504,900	3,808,528	1,746,546	9,162,122	4,008,905	13,171,327
Statewide total											52,530,761

*Acquisition and development.

Source: California State Department of Parks and Recreation (Sacramento: State Publication, 1972).

60

TABLE 7

Disposition of HUD Open Space Land Grants, 1963 to June 1972
(in thousands)

	City			County			East Bay Regional Park District			Others[b]			Total			Grand Total
	Acquisition	Joint Tenancy	Development	Acquisition	Joint Tenancy	Development	Acquisition	Joint Tenancy	Development	Acquisition	Joint Tenancy	Development	Acquisition	Joint Tenancy	Development	
Alameda	2,740	1,194	1,086	–	–	–	–	–	–	598	242	89	3,338	1,436	1,175	5,949
							1,787	445	20				1,787	445	20	2,252
Contra Costa	1,773	333	210	–	–	–	–	–	–	–	–	–	1,773	333	210	2,316
Marin	104	–	46	260	–	–	–	–	–	–	–	–	364	–	46	410
San Francisco	150	225	–	–	–	–	–	–	–	–	–	–	150	225	–	375
San Mateo	276	118	330	2,356	53	–	–	–	–	142	–	–	2,774	171	330	3,275
Solano	27	–	–	–	–	–	–	–	–	–	–	–	27	–	–	27
Total	5,070	1,870	1,672	2,616	53	–	1,787	445	20	740	242	89				14,604

[a]Figures for Santa Clara, Sonoma and Napa counties not included.
[b]Others includes water districts, junior college districts, school districts, BART.
Source: U.S. Department of Housing and Urban Development (Washington, D.C.: U.S. Government Publication, 1972).

Comprehensive Planning

Present federal land use planning generally exists in single-purpose efforts of separate agencies. Yet the federal government influences the country's growth patterns by Federal Highway Administration programs, grants to state and local governments, policies of federal mortgage insurance and loan agencies, water and power development projects, administration of pollution control laws, and other related activities. At present, concerted effort has been made to correlate these programs with comprehensive national growth and land use policies.

Land Use Regulation

The federal government has generally adhered to the constitutional principle of states' rights and has remained uninvolved with the direct regulation of private land development. Nevertheless, in at least two instances, direct federal involvement in development control became a matter of serious consideration. In its 92nd session the Senate amended a major water pollution bill requiring the Environmental Protection Agency (EPA) to review all federally assisted projects in the Tahoe Basin, including any residential development utilizing federal financing or loan guarantees. If EPA determined that the project posed an environmental hazard, it would be required to make public the finding and refer it to the executive branch. Although the amendment passed the Senate, a Senate-House conference committee struck it from the bill.[4]

In order to meet air quality standards adopted in the Clean Air Act, EPA has proposed establishing federal zoning and building permit guidelines, to be enforced by local governments that fail to establish their own system to control sources of air pollution.[5] Such regulations would not apply in this area, because the Bay Area Air Pollution Control District adopted a permit system in 1972. These proposed measures indicate increasing interest by the federal government in regulating land use resources. However, state and local governments must take the initiative in effecting sound land use controls.

THE ROLE OF STATE GOVERNMENT

The role of state government in land use and open space preservation resembles that of the federal government. Long-standing state programs include the acquisition and management of park and open space land and financial and technical assistance to local governments. In recent years, the state has initiated a more concerted effort to plan comprehensively for conservation and development of the state's resources. The state plays a key role by its broad legal powers regarding local government.

Acquisition and Management of Parks and Open Space

The principal California agency in park and open space preservation is the Department of Parks and Recreation, but the Department of Fish and Game, the Division of Forestry, and several other state agencies also have important responsibilities concerning open space.

Department of Parks and Recreation

Public law requires the Department of Parks and Recreation to maintain a statewide recreation plan that includes a continuing analysis of the state's need for recreational areas and facilities, to encourage participation at all levels of government and private enterprise in the development and operation of recreational facilities, and to acquire, design, develop, operate, and maintain the state park system in securing and preserving elements of the state's outstanding landscape, culture, and historical features, thus providing for the meaningful and constructive use of people's uncommitted time.[6]

California enjoys one of the largest and most diverse state park systems in the United States. It included 63 state parks, 32 recreational areas, 36 historical units, 4 wayside campgrounds, 16 scenic, natural, and scientific reserves, and 60 state beaches, for a total of 211 units with more than 794,000 acres of state-owned lands in 1972. An additional 81,500 acres, leased from other entities, also serve park and recreation purposes.[7] Of this land, 28 park units totaling 57,883 acres are in the Bay Area.[8] The most recent additions to the state park system in this area are the 4,100-acre Annadel Farms Park in Santa Rosa and the expansion of Mt. Tamalpais (1,300 acres), Sugarloaf Ridge (480 acres), and Coyote River parks (175 acres).[9] Acquisitions for the 1972-73 fiscal year and scheduled for 1973-74 include expansion of holdings at Annadel Farms, Bothe-Napa, Sugarloaf Ridge, Bodega Bay, Montara Beach, Mount Diablo and Mount Tamalpais state parks.[10]

Practically all state-owned land represents full-fee acquisition; scenic or conservation easements around existing parks has found little use. State bond issues—$250 million in 1964 and $60 million in 1970, for general park acquisition and development of recreational facilities along the State Water Project—have been a principal source of funds in recent years. No projects for recreational development on state water project lands, however, are included in the Bay Area. The 1964 Bond Act has been almost entirely allocated for projects. Current revenues for park acquisition come from the short-term Bagley Fund, specifically established for conservation purposes, and from federal grants from the Land and Water Conservation Fund.

Balancing the preservation of outstanding natural areas and the provision of outdoor recreational opportunities in a natural environment, with the development of intense recreational facilities in and adjacent to population centers, continues to be the State Park Program's central issue. The California Outdoor Recreation Resources Plan,[11] although recognizing these needs, does not specify programs for meeting them. However, the department has prepared

a California Coastline Preservation and Recreation Plan detailing coastal resources with significant natural and historical recreational values for inclusion
in a comprehensive park system.[12]

Department of Fish and Game

Within its responsibility to preserve, protect, and restore fish and wildlife
resources in California, the Department of Fish and Game has acquired almost
120,000 acres of wildlife area. Since 1947, projects to expand fish hatcheries
and provide fishing and hunting access have been the primary function of the
Wildlife Conservation Board, an adjunct to the department. Wildlife areas
comprise more than 90 percent of the 37,000 acres acquired by the board in
the last 25 years.[13] Grizzly and Joyce islands, the only two state-owned game
management areas of significant size in the Bay Area, are located in Suisun
Marsh in Solano County. They have 8,600 and 1,887 acres respectively.

The Department of Fish and Game also administers the ecological reserve
program, instituted in 1972, which provides for the purchase of lands with
unique ecological values, including land purchases to protect rare and endan-
gered species, rare plant and tree species, critical wildlife habitats, and areas
with unique ecological systems. The Environmental Protection Fund derived
from the sale of personalized license plates has supplied $594,000 for the
program's first year of operation.[14] Among the areas identified for acquisition
are West Marin Island in Marin County and Pescadero Marsh in San Mateo
County.[15]

Division of Forestry

The State Division of Forestry currently owns and operates several state
forests and conservation camps on approximately 75,000 acres. Primarily
experimental forests for research and conservation purposes, they are also open
to controlled commercial harvesting and public recreational use. Los Posadas
State Forest of 796 acres in Napa County, Loughry State Forest of 68 acres in
Santa Clara County, and Black Mountain Conservation Camp of 488 acres in
Sonoma County constitute the only significant Bay Area open space lands
administered by the division. Gifts and special appropriations from the State
Forest System do not exist. The State Board of Forestry claims that no more
land will be acquired until existing areas have been developed.

Although these programs have contributed significantly to the preservation of open space in the Bay Area and throughout California, they suffer
financial constraints. If the 1974 State Park-Bond Act passes, $250 million
additional funds will be available, although most will be directed to acquisition
and development of state and local parks rather than general open space.
Moreover, state projects are generally oriented toward nonurban areas where
acquisition costs are not exorbitant. These conditions suggest the need for a
new source of state funds that will provide substantial revenues for the
acquisition of nonpark open space lands, particularly those near urban areas
where preservation needs are critical.

State Lands Commission

The State Lands Commission, created in 1938 and comprising the lieutenant governor, controller, and director of finance, enjoys exclusive jurisdiction over the state school lands and ungranted tide and submerged lands in California's navigable waterways. Disposal policies of the legislature or various agencies prior to the creation of the State Lands Commission have depleted these lands, once a substantial part of the public trust in California.

How much land California owns today is uncertain. The State Lands Division, serving the commission staff, has not ascertained the boundaries of its offshore and tidelands holdings. By 1970, boundaries had been legally established for only 63 miles of a total 6,939 miles of shoreline.[16] Estimates indicate the state owns approximately 609,000 acres of school lands, including 1,100 acres in Contra Costa and Napa counties, about 2,500,000 acres in a three-mile-wide belt of submerged property in the Pacific Ocean off the coast, and between 750,000 and 1,000,000 acres of river and lake property.[17]

The legislature has recently moved toward more efficient management of state lands, with the requirement that the commission inventory and identify land possessing unique environmental values and adopt regulations necessary to assure their permanent protection. It has also declared a moratorium on further grants of state lands until the inventory is complete, required that an Environmental Impact Report (EIR) be prepared prior to the approval of any lease or permit on state tidelands, and has told existing and proposed recipients of state lands to submit a general plan for land use. Lack of funds, inadequate planning capabilities, and a large and complex body of law limiting flexibility, however, currently inhibit the commission in discharging its responsibilities.

State Reclamation Board

The State Reclamation Board manages a flood-control, drainage, and reclamation program in the watersheds of the Sacramento and San Joaquin rivers. It controls 207,000 acres of valley lands, but only those in Solano County are part of the Bay Area. In Solano County, 1,141 acres north of Rio Vista are owned in full fee for disposal of wastes from the Sacramento River. An additional 13,500 acres in the southern reaches of the Yolo Causeway, subject to flowage easements, preclude permanent development. As long as the Sacramento Valley by-pass system is necessary to divert flood waters, these lands will remain permanent open space.

University of California

The University of California owns approximately 48,000 acres of land in the state, most of which are research and field stations with open space value. Important Bay Area holdings include 3,762 acres on Mt. Hamilton surrounding Lick Observatory, Russell Evergreen Tree Farm and Richmond Field Station in Contra Costa County, Bodega Marine Reserve in Sonoma County, Wolfskill

Experimental Laboratory in Solano County, and San Mateo County Congressional Lands near Butano Park.[18] Approximately 987 acres of the Davis campus in Solano County, 75 acres on Mt. Sutro at the San Francisco campus, and 890 acres on the hills above the Berkeley campus remain predominantly undeveloped.

The university has designated only the Bodega Marine Reserve as permanent open space, but long-range plans indicate most outlying research facilities and field stations will be maintained as open space. Because planners envision only a few additional buildings around the three campuses of the region, these lands will be maintained as open space in the foreseeable future.

Other State Agencies

Other state agencies own Bay Area open space land, including the Department of Mental Hygiene with 2,730 acres at three institutions; the Department of Corrections, 1,400 acres at San Quentin and Vacaville; the Department of Veteran Affairs, 2,300 acres at Yountville; and the Department of Youth Authority, 267 acres in Marin County. No long-range plans to retain lands as permanent open space currently exist, and, in fact, a reduction in number and acreage of these facilities appears probable. The present administration has declared surplus more than 1,000 acres around mental institutions and plans to close all of them eventually.

In such cases, property disposal goes through an elaborate bureaucratic procedure, somewhat paralleling federal treatment of surplus lands. Other state agencies, and then local governments, receive the option to purchase, for 50 percent of market value, land declared surplus by the legislature upon recommendation by the Department of General Services. Failure by governmental agencies to take advantage of these options results in a public auction. For example, the Valley of the Moon Recreational District purchased 143 acres at Sonoma State Hospital for a park. At present, a State Senate Committee is investigating surplus property procedures to determine how they can be improved.

Technical Assistance

Several state departments and agencies offer technical assistance to local governments. The Department of Water Resources assists in the preparation of flood plain management plans. The Department of Conservation helps in flood prevention, water management, recreation, fish and wildlife development, and pollution control. The Division of Mines and Geology provides data on geologic hazards and mineral resources. The Council on Intergovernmental Relations assists in establishing or enhancing the comprehensive planning process, the coordination of intergovernmental planning activities, and the obtaining of federal grants. The Parks and Recreation Department supplies technical assistance on recreational matters. The Department of Fish and Game helps identify and protect wildlife habitats.

Despite a large reservoir of data and expertise among state agencies, local governments have not widely utilized their services. A League of California Cities report states:

> Most examples of state technical assistance relate to programs or services provided by a state agency for the state, which assistance may also be available to cities. In many cases it is very informal . . . offered almost on a cooperative basis. . . . Oftentimes it is highly specialized and relates more directly to services provided by a specific city department. It is not uncommon for state programs of technical assistance to be limited to providing information and advice on the interpretation and implementation of state laws and standards of interest to cities. . . .
>
> Additionally, limited use of technical assistance by city officials may reflect the fact that many of the technical assistance services are not publicized, and are really only an adjunct of a service actually being provided for and by another level of government or someone else. In some cases, technical assistance is only available on a cost basis; and this can be a deterrent. . . . There is little available in terms of technical assistance that [cities and counties have] found to be comprehensive in nature or related to the broad community planning and management concerns . . . on a daily basis.[19]

Financial Assistance

Two state programs provide financial assistance to local agencies for open space preservation. The Department of Parks and Recreation distributes state bond revenues, according to predetermined formula, to cities and counties for purchase and development of park lands. The State Bond Act of 1964 has granted more than $45 million to local agencies. An additional $90 million, including $19.4 million for Bay Area cities and counties, will be available in 1974 if the proposed bond issue passes.

The Department of Education has made available $345,000 from the Environmental Protection Fund (the personalized license plate program) for local school districts to develop conservation education programs and assist in acquisition and development or use of lands with high ecological value.

The State Planning Function

State government's most important role in open space preservation probably lies in its comprehensive planning for the conservation and development of the state's resources. The California state planning function may be viewed as developing policies and long-range plans to define goals and guide local agencies in the preservation of open space resources, and as promoting improved governmental coordination.

Statewide policies and plans for open space have been limited to several specific plans prepared by single-purpose state agencies. They include the California Outdoor Recreation Resources Plan and the California Coastline Preservation and Recreation Plan (Parks and Recreation), Scenic Highways Plan (Public Works), Comprehensive Ocean Area Plan (Navigation and Ocean Development), California Protected Waterways Plan (Resources Agency), and the California Fish and Wildlife Plan (Fish and Game). The Fish and Wildlife Plan and the Recreation Resources Plan, for example, deal with open space only incidentally. Other plans, while identifying specific areas with open space that should be preserved, fail to treat open space resources comprehensively.

Recognizing this apparent state planning vacuum, the legislature created the Office of Planning and Research (OPR) in 1970 to develop long-range goals and policies for open space preservation and resource management. In 1972, OPR submitted its Environmental Goals and Policy Report, now under revision, which delineated several broad environmental goals and policies and included an environmental resources protection plan. Stipulating that the state should be concerned only with resources of statewide interest, the plan describes 16 environmental resources categories, most of them directly relating to open space preservation. It identified broad areas of statewide interest and potential critical concern for each environmental resource, considering open space within a 40-mile radius of metropolitan areas as potentially critical.

Following the expected adoption of the environmental goals and policy report by the state administration late in 1973, the Office of Planning and Research will prepare maps detailing the geographic areas—Environmental Resources Areas—of potential critical concern. It will also develop guidelines for each environmental resource, identifying incompatible uses that could destroy or significantly damage an area's significant qualities. Plan revisions and the formal designation of critical areas will follow public hearings. The plan will propose that local governments be mandated to amend their general plans, including those areas of critical state concern designated in the Environmental Resources Protection Plan. Local open space plans and those areas in the Metropolitan Open Space Study will be included. If any land use proposal falls within a designated area of critical concern and is listed as an incompatible use in the development guidelines, local governments will be required to notify the state, which then would either provide advisory assistance, take legal action, or move to acquire the land.

The California government is presently at work on legislation necessary to implement the plan. One version establishes an administrative nine-man environmental protection commission, four cabinet members and five public members, empowered to ensure that local governments include areas of statewide critical concern in their general plans. The present administration version, however, avoids the commission approach in favor of an unspecified implementing entity without enforcement provisions.

Regulation of Land Use

California presently has no direct involvement in land use regulation on privately held property. However, it has extended significant land use regulatory authority to independent, nonlocal government entities through creation of the Tahoe Regional Planning Agency, the San Francisco Bay Conservation and Development Commission, and the State and Regional Coastal Commissions.

THE REGIONAL ROLE

No single Bay Area governmental entity presently holds primary responsibility for regional planning needs. Rather, nine regional councils and commissions exert varying degrees of authority concerning comprehensive pollution abatement, transportation planning, and development control. Only three, however, play an important role in open space preservation: the Association of Bay Area Governments—primarily a planning and coordinating agency in an advisory capacity, the San Francisco Bay Conservation and Development Commission, and the regional coastal conservation commissions. A fourth entity, the San Francisco Regional Water Quality Control Board, together with its parent agency, the State Water Resources Control Board, exerts indirect land use control by declaring moratoria on sewer connections in the absence of adequate water treatment facilities.

Association of Bay Area Governments

Created in January 1961 and the fifth oldest council of governments in the nation, the Association of Bay Area Governments' (ABAG) founding recognized that the physical, economic, and social well-being of the region depends on mutual cooperation and coordination among the plans, policies, and services of Bay Area governments. A contractual agreement among member cities and counties acting under the authority of the California Joint Exercise of Powers Act established the formal organization of ABAG. It now includes 7 counties and 84 cities in the Bay Area, each of which designates one of its elected officials to the ABAG General Assembly, a legislative body meeting several times a year to consider regional policy issues. An executive committee consists of 34 members selected from the General Assembly.

The ABAG originally aimed to serve as "a forum for discussion and study of metropolitan area problems of mutual interest and concern to the counties and cities of the San Francisco Bay Area and for the development of policy and action recommended."[20] Since 1963, when the state recognized it as a Bay Area regional planning agency, ABAG has encompassed regional planning and review functions of local government applications for federal grants. In addition, ABAG coordinates programs of local agencies. Membership dues, special assessments, and grants in funds and services from other regional agencies and the state and federal governments finance ABAG's programs.

Regional Planning

This planning program attempts to coordinate regional growth. Principal plans prepared by ABAG to date include the Preliminary Regional Plan, Regional Plan 1970:1990, Phase II Regional Open Space Plan, and Regional Ocean Coastline Plan. The Preliminary Regional Plan published in 1966 included land use, bayshore, transportation, refuse disposal, and open space elements.[21] Significantly, it represented the first metropolitan area plan in the United States that included an open space element; in this case, approximately 1.75 million acres. Following its publication, a long period of review by cities and counties ensued, culminating in 1970 with adoption by ABAG. It included policies and a physical land use map that provided spatial dimensions to regional development and open space,[22] expanding the permanent open space system to approximately 3.4 million acres, while amply providing land to accommodate population growth anticipated by the year 2000.[23]

The Phase II Regional Open Space Plan, prepared in 1972, primarily responded to a federal requirement that obliged regional clearinghouses to maintain an open space program for continued open space grant funds from the Department of Housing and Urban Development. The plan reestablished and confirmed the target for open space preservation outlined in the 1970 regional plan. The Phase II Plan related resource and natural characteristics to help set priorities for open space reservation and also presented two alternative five-year model programs, one based on current levels of state and federal grants of $25 million during five years, the other based on a doubling of grant funds. Both recommended open space zoning of 201,830 acres in priority areas.[24]

The Regional Ocean Coastline Plan, prepared in 1972, classified the coastal zone into growth policy areas and open space areas, the latter with either high open space values or severe hazards to public safety. It called for limited growth throughout the coastal zone. Within the growth policy areas, it permitted no new construction, restricted development to existing settlement areas, but allowed some growth, subject to careful siting and design to satisfy environmental and open space parameters. The Regional Ocean Coastline Plan provided a potential model for the Regional Coastal Commissions.[25]

The current planning programs center on a growth policy for the San Francisco Bay region. In 1972, the General Assembly of ABAG proposed a policy to limit regional population growth urging official agencies to plan for a population of no more than 5.5 million people by 1980, or a 1.7 percent annual increase based on the population at the time of 4.6 million.[26] The February 1973 adoption of an amendment to the policy, which recognized that "efforts to guide population growth may require efforts to redirect economic growth in some areas requiring full allowance for each jurisdiction's specific problems," somewhat softened its firmer stand.[27] However, at a meeting of the ABAG General Assembly in October 1973, a growth resolution was passed, charging ABAG to study the consequences by the year 2000 were growth limited to 6.0-7.5 million people. The current population in the nine-county area stands at about 4.8 million: it will probably reach 5.5 million by 1980.

The Phase III Open Space Study now being prepared by ABAG will provide a master recreation plan for the East Bay Regional Park District—the prototype for a nine-county recreation plan—and an implementation plan for regional nonpark open space. The latter will emphasize the use of open space regulations by Bay Area planning agencies and the proper regional role in the implementation process. Two other programs, the regional housing element and a more specific policy for implementation of the coastal zone plan, are presently underway.

Since the federal government designated ABAG as a regional "clearing-house," it reviews requests for federal and state project funding in conformance with federal laws and adopted regional plans: Circular A-95 of the Federal Office of Management and Budget has established review procedures, known as the "A-95 review process." ABAG also examines Environmental Impact Reports required by the National Environmental Policy Act and California Environmental Quality Act. The project review system ensures coordination of the planning activities of local, state, and federal agencies.[28] ABAG, formally reviewing all planning programs, also screens projects potentially conflicting with the open space provisions of the 1970 regional plan.[29]

The A-95 review process enables regional councils of government to prod recalcitrant local agencies in implementing regional plans. In effect, a negative evaluation by ABAG essentially vetoes federal funding, although federal agencies have sometimes approved projects despite regional objections. Because ABAG comprises local representatives, their hesitation to follow a policy possibly applicable to their jurisdiction in the future is understandable. More-over, whether such a policy could be administered without jeopardizing other equally important regional goals remains doubtful.

Technical Assistance

Technical assistance to local and regional agencies represents less visible function of ABAG. The association has, in some cases, entered into Memoranda of Agreement for long-range studies. In other cases, "pass-through" agreements, providing staff-to-staff-level information exchanges, have provided assistance. ABAG lacks the resources to supply technical data or assistance on a regular basis; consequently, city and county officials have not always turned to it for technical assistance.

Coordination

Implementing regional objectives remains the primary obligation of local governments, but ABAG has the responsibility to coordinate the often-conflicting policies of more than 100 independent decision-making entities. In its present limited capacity as an advisory agency, voluntary coordination represents the only means by which ABAG may achieve its open space goals, a formidable task. The State Environmental Quality Study Council believes that ABAG-type organizations

> lack any authority to implement an on-going regional planning effort other than by gentle persuasion of local government. Should a

county or city hold fast to a development policy which conflicts
with regional policies and plans, the Council of Government is
powerless, and the implementation of regional objectives
thwarted.[30]

Despite this limitation, ABAG has significantly contributed to Bay Area
regionalism, dramatized regional problems, suggested through its planning program a methodology to solve them, and provided a catalyst in recognizing the
importance of the Bay Area's open space resources. ABAG has also fostered
greater cooperation among Bay Area cities and counties.

San Francisco Bay Conservation and Development Commission

The San Francisco Bay Conservation and Development Commission
(BCDC) comprises 27 members, 20 representing federal, state, and local
agencies, and 7 representing the public. Created in 1965 as a temporary study
commission for investigating and developing solutions to the complex problems
of the Bay, upon its own recommendation, 1969 legislation made it permanent.[31] BCDC's jurisdiction includes San Francisco, San Pablo, and Suisun
bays, all sloughs of the Bay system, certain creeks and tributaries, and a
100-foot strip of land inland from the Bay. It also enjoys limited jurisdiction
over the filling of salt ponds and managed wetlands, such as those areas diked
off from the Bay and used for salt ponds, and duck hunting preserves.
Protecting the integrity of the Bay for its use and enjoyment by future
generations represents the primary purpose of BCDC. In effect, it preserves
outstanding open space resources. BCDC has permit authority in all Bay
dredging and filling, as well as regulation of land use within the 100-foot strip
of land surrounding it. In its nine-year existence it has forestalled large-scale
filling of the Bay, but it has approved filling for water-oriented purposes
consonant with the San Francisco Bay plan objectives.

Regional Coastal Conservation Commissions

In 1972, California approved an initiative proposition establishing a state
and six regional commissions to protect coastal zone resources.[32] Like BCDC,
the coastal commissions hold limited geographic area responsibility, with planning responsibility in the area three miles out to sea, inland to the top of the
nearest coastal mountain range, and permit authority in the area 1,000 yards
from mean high tide. The commissions exist only for three years, during which
they must prepare a comprehensive, coordinated, and enforceable plan for the
orderly, long-range conservation and management of the natural resources of
the coastal zone. Furthermore, they must ensure that any development in the
permit area during the study and planning period will be consistent with the

objectives of the proposition. The state commission consists of 12 public members appointed by the legislature and the governor. Membership on the six regional commissions varies from 12 to 16, with half representing local and regional commissions and the other half representing the public.

THE ROLE OF THE PRIVATE SECTOR

Individual and corporate economic initiative, fundamentals to an area's growth, shapes land use patterns. Decisions of the private sector regarding the siting, design, and landscaping of private facilities are critical to the overall aesthetic quality of the urban environment. The private sector—business and industry, land developers, recreational enterprises, private and quasi-public organizations, and private conservation organizations—contributes importantly to open space preservation.

Business and Industry

Business and industry, of course, can provide much-needed open space within the urban environment. Larger industrial plants, for example, may be set apart from other urban uses by open space "buffer" zones. Open space areas, by careful landscaping and planting, may reduce the often unpleasant visual impact of the factory. The August Busch Corporation's planned brewery in Fairfield represents a case in point.

Parks atop the roofs of business offices constitute an excellent method by which private corporations may contribute significantly to much-needed open space in urban core areas. The 3.5 acre Kaiser Center Rooftop Park in Oakland, completed in 1960, one of the largest parks of its kind in the world, allows more than 60 percent of the land occupied by the Kaiser buildings to be covered with planting.[33] Parks may be established on top of underground parking facilities in business or commercial areas, for example, at Union Square in San Francisco.

Land Developers

Allocation of open space and provision of other amenities improves the marketability of a subdivision. Although developers would logically incorporate those features in a subdivision design, they have generally not designated open space as a major subdivision feature. The great success of the standard post-World War II subdivision has inhibited experimentation with innovative planning techniques. According to the *Architectual Record*,

Builders who have done very well . . . selling suburban sprawl argue that "We give buyers what they want." What's wrong with the

argument . . . is that with rare exceptions there have been no alternatives for buyers—there . . . have been no communities with planned
open space, with pleasant clusters of single-family houses . . . and
pleasant groupings of garden apartments and condominiums. . . .[34]

Planners have generally prodded developers to increase open space in the
subdivisions and planned unit development designs. Many communities have
ineffectually used local ordinances permitting design flexibility. Woodlake
Apartments in San Mateo, Sycamore in Danville, and San Marco and Rossmoor
in Walnut Creek incorporate more than 25 percent of open space in their
designs, and others have open space ranging from 10 to 25 percent.[35] Recently
approved developments in Petaluma, San Rafael, and Concord dedicate even
greater amounts.

Private Recreational Facilities

Golf courses and country clubs are prime examples of private sector visual
and recreational open space. The Bay Area includes almost 100 private golf
courses with 10,000 acres of open space. Picnic and camping areas, riding
academies, dude ranches, and other private recreational facilities abound.
    Most owners of golf courses and other recreational areas have not perma-
nently committed their land to open space. Voluntary restrictions on development in return for use-related assessment may prolong their existence as an
open space resource. Large private wilderness areas have a new trend in private
recreation parks. An outgrowth of the recreational subdivision boom of the
1960s, these areas are open only to members, purchasers of an undivided
interest in the park.[36]

Private and Quasi-Public Institutions

A number of private and quasi-public institutions own land in the Bay
Area. Churches, Boy Scouts, Girl Scouts, YMCA, and YWCA, all examples of
quasi-public institutions, own and operate campgrounds, day camps, retreats,
and other open space areas in the region. Development, in the main, does not
threaten these areas. Stanford University, with almost 90 percent of its 8,100
acres in a natural state, represents a valuable open space asset in the heavily
populated San Mateo peninsula. The university's Board of Trustees, responsible
for campus land use decisions, makes them on an ad hoc basis, as the
need for development arises. It recently decided not to expand an existing
475-acre industrial park and to preserve, by scenic easement, 90 acres of
undeveloped land.[37] The only additional campus park designated as
permanent open space is the 960-acre Jasper Ridge Natural Preserve. Other
Bay Area private colleges—Mills College in Oakland, College of Notre Dame

in Belmont, St. Mary's College in Lafayette, and Pacific Union College in northern Napa County—include significant open space.

Private Conservation Foundations

Among the conservation organizations, the Nature Conservancy stands out because of its efforts to protect valuable wildlife habitats. First chartered in 1951, the Nature Conservancy acquires significant natural areas, and often plays a "tic-tac-toe" real estate game by covertly purchasing small scenic acreages in the path of development, now estimated at 1,435 acres within the Bay Area in the last decade, thus effectively blocking development several times larger.[38] Nationwide, it has protected over 400 separate areas in more than 40 states—a total of approximately 109,000 acres, one-third of which it owns and manages.[39]

The Nature Conservancy also acquires open space lands for eventual transfer to public agencies and private institutions for park and open space purposes. Thus, it often purchases land at a comparatively low price. Covenants with "reverter clauses" cover these lands, carefully protected from uses inconsistent with the organization's purposes. It presently owns 3,359 acres in the Bay Area that will be turned over to the federal government. Membership dues—it has 25,000 members nationwide—and contributions from individuals and foundations provide the funds for these activities. The organization also has an excellent program to encourage gifts of land for conservation purposes.

The Sierra Club Foundation, National Wildlife Federation, and National Audubon Society also undertake occasional fund-raising projects to protect threatened open space. With the help of other groups, the Audubon Society purchased the 885-acre Audubon Canyon Ranch and 756-acre Richardson Wildlife Refuge in Marin County. Among local conservation groups, the Marin Conservation League and the Committee for Green Foothills actively participate in several fund-raising projects to preserve open space areas.

NOTES

Unless otherwise cited, data in this chapter is derived from personal communications with federal agency officials.

1. U.S. Department of Interior, Bureau of Sport Fisheries and Wildlife, *San Pablo National Wildlife Refuge* (January 1971).

2. California State Lands Commission, State Lands Division, *Public Land Ownership in California, 1971* (June 1971), pp. 4-5.

3. Ibid. pp. 11-16.

4. Leo Rennert, "House Senate Unit Drops Tunney Plan for Tahoe," Sacramento *Bee*, September 15, 1972, p. 1.

5. "EPA Soon May Set Zoning Guidelines," Sacramento *Bee*, November 17, 1972, p. B1.

6. California· State Department of Finance, *Governor's Budget, 1973-1974* (1973), p. 878.

7. California State Department of Parks and Recreation, *Statistical Report, 1971-1972 Fiscal Year* (1972), p. 16.

8. Ibid., pp. 4, 10.

9. Ibid., and California State Department of Parks and Recreation, *Statistical Report, 1970-1971 Fiscal Year* (1971), pp. 6, 12.

10. *Governor's Budget*, op. cit., pp. 888-98.

11. California State Department of Parks and Recreation, *California Outdoor Recreation Resources Plan* (January 1972).

12. California State Department of Parks and Recreation, *California Coastline Preservation and Recreation Plan* (August 1971).

13. California State Department of Fish and Game, Wildlife Conservation Board, *Summary of Wildlife Conservation Board Projects* (June 30, 1972).

14. *Governor's Budget*, op. cit., p. 761.

15. California State Office of Planning and Research, *Environmental Goals and Policies* (March 1, 1972), p. 29.

16. Sedway/Cooke Associates, *Regional Ocean Coastline Plan for the San Francisco Bay Area, Phase II*, prepared for the Association of Bay Area Governments (July 1972), p. 25.

17. Michael Harris, California State Lands Commission, *Public Land Ownership*, pp. 18, 39-40.

18. University of California Physical Planning Department, *Summary of University of California Land Areas* (Berkeley, July 1, 1972) (mimeo.).

19. League of California Cities, "Planning and Management in California Cities: An Assessment of Legal Impediments and Technical Assistance" (Sacramento, 1971), p. 40.

20. Association of Bay Area Governments, *Preamble to Bylaws.*

21. Association of Bay Area Governments, *Preliminary Regional Plan for the San Francisco Bay Region* (1966).

22. Association of Bay Area Governments, *Regional Plan 1970:1990 San Francisco Bay Region* (1970).

23. Planning Policy Committee of Santa Clara County Urban Development/Open Space Subcommittee, statements of Rudy Platzek, Planning Director of ABAG in minutes of the meeting of November 8, 1972.

24. Association of Bay Area Governments, *Regional Open Space Plan, Phase II, San Francisco Bay Region* (Summary) (1972).

25. Sedway/Cook Associates, op. cit. p. 25.

26. William Moore, "ABAG Votes to Limit Bay Growth," San Francisco *Chronicle*, November 11, 1972, p. 1.

27. "ABAG Alters a Former Firm Stand," San Francisco *Sunday Chronicle and Examiner*, March 4, 1973, *This World* section, p. 5.

28. Association of Bay Area Governments, *Project Review Policies and Procedures* (1971), p. 1.

29. Association of Bay Area Governments, *Regional Open Space Plan, Phase II*, op. cit., p. 11.

30. California State Environmental Quality Study Council, *Final Report* (1972), p. 43.

31. California State Government Code, Sections 66600-66661.

32. California Coastal Zone Conservation Act of 1972 (Proposition 20), to be codified at Cal. Pub. Res. Code, Section 27000 et seq.

33. Mildred F. Schmertz, ed., *Acquisition, Conservation, Creation and Design of Open Space for People* (Washington, D.C.: American Institute of Architects, 1970), p. 78.

34. Walter F. Wagner, "Alternates to Suburban Sprawl: New Processes, New Involvement," *Architectural Record*, November 1970, p. 9.

35. Lee A. Syracuse, "Innovative Residential Development in California," *Building Our Community*, no. 4 (no date); Home Builders Association of Contra Costa-Solano Counties.

36. Robert Hollis, "Camping for $1,800," San Francisco *Sunday Examiner and Chronicle*, December 3, 1972, p. 1.

37. "Open Space Agreement on Stanford Land," San Francisco *Chronicle*, March 7, 1973, p. 2.

38. Gerald D. Adams, "The Open Space Explosion," *Cry California*, Fall 1970, p. 28.

39. President's Council on Environmental Quality, *1st Annual Report* (1970), p. 218.

5

THE ROLE OF
LOCAL GOVERNMENT
IN OPEN SPACE
PRESERVATION

Although the activities of federal, state, and regional agencies constitute an important element in providing adequate open space in and around urban areas, the basic responsibility* for the direction of regional growth and development belongs to the local government. It alone must decide how much land will be converted to differing urban uses, where and when to provide essential urban services, and the desirable environmental amenities. Local government, in short, makes the land use decisions that shape urban patterns.

The 7,000-square-mile Bay Area includes 9 counties and 92 cities, each with an understandable provincial interest in the management of its environment. The region's physical form thus results from the land use decisions of 101 separate governmental entities, all trying to preserve identity and integrity in a metropolitan environment. More than 500 special districts, most of them with single-purpose functions, including education, water supply, sewage treatment, mosquito abatement, street lighting, and park development, overlay this geographic jigsaw of political jurisdiction. Some special districts, notably schools and utilities, can significantly influence urban development. Park and recreation and water districts, with watershed lands, also become directly involved in the open space preservation effort.

The local government capability to resolve metropolitan problems has long absorbed the attention of students of governmental affairs. Debate has focused on local efforts to plan and regulate land use. Many remain convinced that "local government is not strong enough to control development in the face of the pressures from large landowners and developers."[1]

Visible evidence supports this observation throughout the metropolitan area in the sprawl and monotony of development, blight of commercial areas, lack of open space, subservience to the automobile, and deterioration of the natural environment. Critics of local government assert that

present methods of long range planning and regulating land use have been unable to protect communities from the unnecessary direct and indirect costs which result from [man-environment] conflicts and against the lowering of environmental quality".[2]

In the emerging age of environmental awareness, however, local governments have begun to confront the consequences of their land use decisions. But, given the nature and scope of environmental, social, economic, and other complexities, does local government in its present form have the capability of effectively meeting the many needs of the urban community through planning and management? To answer that question, the basic problems associated with local land use control and open space preservation must first be identified, and subsequently the Bay Area governments' response to these problems.

Planning and land use control related to open space has focused on several criticisms of local government. They include failure to provide for orderly urban expansion, inadequate containment of rural development, poor consideration of open space and environmental quality in the planning process, failure to implement plans, poor control of new development, and inadequate programs for acquisition of parks and open space.

STATUTORY AUTHORITY OF LOCAL AGENCIES TO REGULATE AND ACQUIRE OPEN SPACE LAND

Charter and General Law Cities

Two categories of municipal government exist in California. Enabling laws govern general law cities, as well as counties. They must have express authorization through the State Constitution, or statutes, to act. Charter cities, on the other hand, have exclusive authority in matters that the courts have held to be "municipal affairs," and only their charter and the state and federal constitutions limit them. The Bay Area includes 21 charter cities such as Santa Rosa, Napa, San Francisco, Oakland, San Jose, Redwood City, and Gilroy.

Whether the California Government Code applies to charter cities as well as general law cities presently remains unclear. Although in previous years California specifically exempted charter cities from government code provisions, it now tends to include them under new legislation. Little divergence exists in practice between charter and general law cities regarding land use planning and regulations.

Land Use Planning

The principal government code provisions affecting land use management by general law cities may be found in the Planning, Zoning, and Subdivision Map Acts. Present planning law,[3] although extremely flexible in general local planning procedures, involves basic requirements. For example, cities and counties must have a planning agency, a planning department, a planning commission, or the legislative body itself, to develop and maintain a general plan. This body must develop specific plans and review the city's capital improvements program. The planning commission must comprise at least five and not more than nine members. Local authorities determine details of organization, term of office, and appointment procedures. Each planning agency must prepare, and the legislative body must adopt, a comprehensive, long-term general plan for the physical development of the jurisdiction, including land use, housing, conservation, open space, seismic safety, scenic highway, and noise elements. The agency may also submit plans for areas within the jurisdiction, including all regulations, conditions, programs, and proposed legislation necessary for the systematic implementation of each general plan element.

Zoning

The Zoning Act permits legislative bodies to regulate land use.[4] Although not identifying specific permissible zoning categories, it required cities and counties to adopt an open space zoning ordinance by June 30, 1973. In addition, the legislature has authorized creation of a Board of Zoning Adjustments and a Board of Zoning Appeals, or a zoning administrator, to hear and consider applications for conditional uses and variances. Variances cannot be granted for the use of a property parcel not expressly authorized by the appropriate zoning regulation. The legislature also provided that zoning comply with the adopted general plan by June 30, 1973.

Subdivision Control

The Subdivision Map Act applies to the division of all land into five or more lots and sets forth city requirements in regulating and conditioning the subdivision.[5] Local agencies cannot approve subdivisions causing substantial environmental damage or public health problems. The Map Act permits local agencies to require dedication of land, or payment in lieu thereof, for certain public purposes, including streets, schools, and parks. Local agencies may regulate the division of land into four or less lots, but they cannot impose standards exceeding those in state statutes.[6]

Williamson Act (Land Conservation Act)

In 1965 the California legislature authorized cities and counties to make contracts with landowners to maintain land in agricultural or compatible uses through passage of the Williamson Act.[7] Before entering into a contract with a landowner, a local agency must establish agricultural preserves limited to definite agricultural or compatible uses. These parcels are generally 100 acres or more, although smaller plots are permissible for land with unique characteristics. All preserves must be consistent with each government's local plan.

Contracts are voluntary, run for a period of ten years, and provide that land be maintained as open space in return for assessment according to its current use, rather than cash value. Providing a tax break for the owner and open space for the city or county, the government or landowner does not need to renew the contract when it expires. It may also be cancelled upon the owner's petition if consistent with the act and in the public interest. Each city or county deals with contractual procedures.

Acquisition

State law, explicitly placing open space preservation in the public interest, enables local government to purchase land for open space and scenic purposes. It also allows local agencies to acquire lesser interests in property through purchase of scenic or open space easements; to purchase and leaseback to its original owner, or other persons, any property that limits use of the land to open space considerations; and to accept gifts, grants, bequests, and other conveyances of open space lands.[8]

Local governments have the power of eminent domain, "taking" land for public use, such as parks, if "just compensation" is made to the landowner.[9] Whether local agencies can use eminent domain to obtain land in full fee or less-than-fee interest for nonpark scenic and open space use remains questionable. But, local governments may "incur indebtedness," most commonly by the sale of general obligations bonds. However, the California Constitution requires that the indebtedness incurred by a local agency through sale of municipal bonds in any one year cannot exceed its revenues for that year unless the electorate approves by a two-thirds vote.[10] The total indebtedness cannot exceed 15 percent for cities and 5 percent for counties of their total assessed valuation.[11]

THE FAILURE TO PROVIDE FOR
ORDERLY URBAN EXPANSION

Urban sprawl and irregular patterns of Bay Area city boundaries clearly reflect local governments' lack of success in adequately controlling urban growth. Some experts attribute this to a laissez-faire approach by local governments, finding a rationale in the traditional American belief that private enterprise forms the basic decisions regarding the timing and location of urban development. Local officials have directed more attention to the design of the development, its conformity with the community's character, and its economic contribution, rather than whether additional development should occur.

Local governments, therefore, have generally accommodated urban development, annexing unincorporated land and providing services for residential subdivisions and commercial or industrial facilities often without comprehensive planning. Many have thus reluctantly recognized the influence of urban infrastructure on development patterns utilizing the extension of improvements and services. Perhaps unwittingly, local governments have also devised general plans encouraging sporadic and irrational development. The general plan, theoretically expressing meaningful community growth policies, manifests weakness when local authorities attempt to achieve flexibility in the planning process. The consensus of specialists maintains the general plan should provide a framework of policies with guidelines for community development, rather than specific designations of land use on a parcel-by-parcel basis.

Most general plans attempt to project urban development for 20 years. The resulting plan usually specifies desirable mixes of land use and residential densities surrounded by a "greenbelt" of open space. This traditionally has encouraged private developers to seek lands throughout the entire area planned for urban expansion. Local officials inevitably receive a subdivision proposal for the periphery of planning area, which may be premature yet conforms to the general plan. If approved, tax and speculative forces ensue that further encourage peripheral development. As development proceeds in a random pattern, the entire planning area becomes essentially committed to, even if not ultimately required for, urbanization. Pressures on the periphery of the planning area often threaten to obliterate the open character of land designated as greenbelt in the general plan.

Another problem in local planning centers on population forecasts underpinning policies. In many communities throughout the Bay Area, plans based on population projections made during the 1960s now appear unrealistic in light of present growth trends.[12] In some, such as Half Moon Bay, anticipated growth strikingly conflicts with regional and state objectives, resulting in an unnecessary or undesirable commitment of land by local governments to urban development and further reducing the likelihood of compact urban growth with the concomitant maximum use of open space resources.

Inadequate attention to open space factors in new development siting has plagued local agencies. The standard post-World War II subdivision, with its curvilinear street pattern, uniform lot sizes, set-back lines, and housing design has typically failed to provide aesthetic or functional open space as part of the overall design. Local agencies have permitted these subdivisions to proliferate, resulting in critical shortages of urban open space.

Making land conform to the subdivision rather than designing the subdivision to conform to the natural environment has become quite common. Land has often been graded and subdivided with apparent abandon. The well known miles and miles of monotonous homes lining Daly City's hills is an extreme but highly visible example.

The problem, critics contend, lies with permissive treatment of new development by local government.

Most plans and regulations have been devised for flat areas with little or no attention paid to the topographic diversity and related problems of drainage, erosion, street grade, and utilities. Geologic problems—an integral part of every hillside location—have largely been ignored.[13]

The abstract nature of political boundaries, including uneven environmental standards enforced by cities and other government agencies, complicates the problem. Bay Area local government has responded to past regulatory deficiencies with new techniques and ordinances designed to help protect the environmental integrity of new development. Grading requirements, soils and geological reports, and utility undergrounding now constitute standard features of subdivision ordinances. Several communities have created architectural boards to ensure that new development will enhance, rather than blight, the visual environment. In providing more open space within developing urban areas, park dedication provisions, cluster zoning, slope-density ordinances, and environmental impact reports for private projects have assumed particular significance.

Park Dedication

Although state legislation in 1965 permitted local governments to enact a "dedication of land, the payment of fees in lieu thereof, or a combination of both, for park or recreational purposes" as a condition to the approval of a subdivision,[14] Bay Area cities and counties began to make widespread use of the provisions only within the last five years. More than half of the cities have adopted a park dedication ordinance or a similar provision that many communities regard as their principal means of obtaining land for local parks.

Cluster Zoning

Cluster zoning enables a developer to increase residential density on a portion of his land and preserve the remainder as open space without increasing the overall density. Either a separate ordinance applicable to residential development, or the general provisions of the Planned Unit Development Ordinance, permitting maximum flexibility in designing new developments, can provide clustering.

In the Bay Area, development results from planned development provisions adopted by 90 percent of the communities. However, negotiations with the developer usually determine the open space area; the ordinance frequently omits specific standards for clustering. Only a few communities—Morgan Hill, Cupertino, San Rafael, Los Gatos, and Martinez, for example—have separate cluster zoning provisions, applying only to residential areas, which may or may not include density bonuses awarded for clustering. Few developments involving cluster zoning have resulted in dedication of large amounts of open space. However, Pacheco Ranch in Novato, where 350 acres of a total project area of 700 acres will be dedicated as open space, represents an outstanding exception. The Hoffman Company in Concord plans to dedicate two-thirds of a 300-acre hillside tract as open space. Development projects that provide more than 65 percent open space have received approval in Petaluma.

Most efforts to utilize clustering concepts for the provision of open space have not been notably effective. Development in several cities has not been on a scale sufficient to permit significant clustering. In others, developers have hesitated to try innovative techniques, and the public has opposed increases in density, particularly with townhouses and condominiums. This combination has often limited the designation of open space in new developments. We note that where planned developments have been approved, 10 to 20 percent of open space generally separates building units. Many cities, however, are presently striving for greater use of clustering concepts to implement open space planning, particularly in hillside areas.

Slope-Density Zoning

The slope-density ordinance is another innovation increasingly utilized by local governments. Although highly technical and subject to several variations, it employs a gradient, relating slope to lot size. As the slope increases, the permitted lot size increases. The gradients vary widely in each community, ranging from upper limitations of 40 percent slope of one-half acre in San Rafael, to two acres in Saratoga, to a proposed nine acres in portions of Santa Clara County. Some ordinances also include density regulations that encourage clustering of hillside development. The city of Pacifica, on the other hand, has adopted an ordinance providing decreasing building coverage as the slope increases. For example, at 35 percent slope or greater, only 10 percent of the land could be developed. The potential problem of high-rise construction proposals on that allowable 10 percent for development remains unresolved.

Environmental Impact Reports

The California Supreme Court ruled in 1972 that the provisions of the California Environmental Quality Act, requiring Environmental Impact Reports (EIRs) for public projects, apply to private projects significantly affecting the environment.[15] An investigation of the environmental consequences of such development proposals may lead to local agency consideration of potential impacts, thus motivating developers to design projects with greater amounts of open space and reducing desolation of the natural landscape.

LOCAL AGENCY FORMATION COMMISSIONS

Although local governments bear the major responsibility for the direction of urban growth, they must operate within the framework of various inter-locking agencies designed to aid their decision-making processes. Recognizing that local governments have had difficulty in adopting and enforcing policies that ensure orderly urban development, the California legislature in 1963 required the creation of a Local Agency Formation Commission (LAFCO) in each California county, except San Francisco County.[16] Each LAFCO com-prises two county supervisors, two city councilmen, and a public member. The legislature mandated them to discourage urban sprawl, encourage organized formation of local agencies, and

> to make studies and obtain and furnish information which will contribute to the logical and reasonable development of local govern-mental agencies so as to advantageously provide for the present and future needs of each county and its communities.[17]

Generally staffed by the county, each LAFCO must initially review all proposals for incorporation, annexation, and consolidation of cities and special districts, subsequently conditionally approving, disapproving, or approving them with reference to the county's orderly growth. In recent years, LAFCOs have received additional responsibilities, including a directive that they estab-lish "sphere-of-influence" boundaries for each city within the county.

LAFCO Role in Open Space Preservation

Empowered to approve or deny annexations to both cities and special districts, LAFCOs can greatly influence the pattern of new urban development, particularly with decisions based on urban infrastructure plans. By refusing to permit the extension of services in areas designated as open space, they can also restrict urban development. LAFCOs, however, do not have authority in all new development. If a proposed subdivision lies within, or is coterminous with, an existing special district, services may be provided to the development without its approval.

The influence of LAFCOs on development patterns has, of course, varied considerably among Bay Area counties, some of which strongly support an-nexation requests. In Solano County, for example, this tendency, linked to a strong policy that urbanization be contained in existing cities, has led to substantial annexations of land for urban development by Fairfield and Vaca-ville. In other counties, LAFCO has assumed a stronger role in questioning the appropriateness of new development, making its decisions accordingly. Bay Area LAFCOs have generally succeeded in eliminating annexation wars and defensive incorporations, curbing the proliferation of special districts, reducing irrational strip annexations, and promoting more efficient and economical urban growth. LAFCO has permitted leapfrog development, however in most counties.

Primary concern has converged on the capability and efficiency of local government to provide necessary services. LAFCO usually has not approved a proposal if it is not orderly, logical, or economical; creates islands, corridors, or unincorporated territory; or duplicates other services. Open space considerations in themselves generally have not influenced LAFCO decisions.

Spheres of Influence

In 1971 the state legislature amended the Knox-Nisbet Act, requiring each LAFCO to designate a sphere of influence for each city and district under its jurisdiction. Sphere of influence legally means "a plan for the probable ultimate physical boundaries and service area of a local governmental agency." The act directed each LAFCO to consider for each agency the projected future population growth, the types of development occurring or planned for the area, the maximum possible service area, the range of services that could be provided, the present and probable future service needs, and the existence of social and economic interdependence between the agency and area surrounding it.[18] All but one of the eight Bay Area LAFCOs have begun to establish service areas to accommodate urban growth for the next five to ten years. Santa Clara, Contra Costa, and Napa counties have made substantial progress, but only Santa Clara County has integrated LAFCO plans into an overall plan.

Cities have generally indicated their entire general plan area, or more in some cases, when asked to identify their service areas. Urban service area boundaries will often approximate indicated urban areas in city and county general plans. Alameda County's LAFCO has, in fact, opted to identify ultimate service area boundaries. Thus, for the short term, restraint in the location of new development may be limited. On the other hand, the very task of designating urban and nonurban areas forces LAFCOs to consider open space. LAFCO decisions consonant with the service area boundaries will, in effect, serve as an urban limit line beyond which development will be prohibited and open space resources presumably preserved. LAFCO action on annexation proposals can be tied to an overall plan, rather than made on an ad hoc basis, thus setting a method of evaluating the effectiveness of LAFCOs in controlling the spread of urban development.

LAFCO in Perspective

LAFCO presently has the power to implement an adopted open space plan by denying city and special district annexations and preventing urban development of open space lands. Uncertainty, nonetheless, exists concerning specific criteria for the suitability of annexations vis-a-vis open space preservation. Although some have forcibly argued that LAFCOs have a mandate to protect open space values,[19] commissions thus far have hesitated to take a positive stand. The recent effort to designate urban service area boundaries for cities and special districts will undoubtedly stimulate more direct involvement. It should be kept in mind, however, that the local composition of the commissions, the designation of more than sufficient land for urban expansion within a short time frame, and legal limitations preclude a guarantee by LAFCOs that future Bay Area urban development will be a compact and orderly process.

An Example of LAFCO: Santa Clara County

Santa Clara County, a sprawling metropolitan area, has initiated a major campaign to achieve orderly growth. It has proposed an urban development and open space (UD/OS) plan recognizing that "open space resources can be preserved only by controlling urban development and that the course of urban development can only be wisely planned by considering the need for open space."[20] The plan coordinates future growth policies of the county, its cities, and LAFCO. In 1970, San Jose became the first city in the county to adopt a set of urban development policies. Its planning area, essentially divided into two categories, includes an urban area and an urban reserve area. The urban area has approximately 26,000 acres of vacant land, enough to accommodate an annual growth of 25,000 persons for 15 years. Urban reserve comprises land not needed for development during the next 15 years, permanent open space areas, and lands deemed undesirable for development because of public safety hazards. The policy prohibits development in the urban reserve area except under specifically defined circumstances.[21]

The Santa Clara County LAFCO incorporated these measures into a county urban development policy in 1971. They reaffirmed that urban development should occur within cities and outlined a process by which local governments would identify and categorize suitable land for open space in conjunction with the designation of urban service areas. Most Santa Clara cities, adopting the LAFCO policies, began to define their urban service area boundaries. Policies in the UD/OS plan for staged urban development ultimately depend on the cities for implementation. In addition to San Jose, only Gilroy and Milpitas thus far have adopted policies regarding the timing and location of urban growth.

Milpitas, critically short of education facilities for future growth and with no foreseeable financial relief for its school district, passed an ordinance in 1972 regulating residential development.[22] It prohibits urban residential development unless the school district can adequately accommodate new students without a tax increase. A set formula determines the number of allowable residential units per year, and development proposals may be approved only if they do not exceed the allowable new residential units. Milpitas, having adopted a temporary policy approach to growth, permits the city council to exceed the limit under certain conditions. It represents, nevertheless, a unique attempt to limit growth in terms of a critical facility, that is, schools, to serve the additional population.

Gilroy's growth policies perhaps typify the probable approach of most cities in Santa Clara County. They include staged development to ensure that public facilities do not become overburdened and the evaluation of proposed land for future urbanization before development occurs. If the city cannot provide adequate services, it will declare a moratorium on new development until they can be provided. Implementation of these policies is on a case-by-case basis.[23]

The Petaluma Experiment

The controls enacted by the city of Petaluma in southern Sonoma County represent one of the more innovative approaches to urban development.[24] Faced with a sudden developmental upsurge in 1971, the city council placed a moratorium on building, embarking on a program to develop and implement a new general plan. The city decided that expansion should be slowed to 500 units per year, the average rate of growth during the 1960s. After studies, policy statements, and public hearings, the program devised the Residential Development Control System, adopted in 1972. New development, divided equally in both the east and west sections of the city separated by the Petaluma River, requires residential builders to apply for a development allotment by September in order to be considered during the ensuing year, which begins May 1. A Residential Development Evaluation Board of 17 public and private members reviews applications and considers the capability of water, sanitary sewer drainage, fire, school, and street facilities to accommodate the development. Design quality, provision of open space, and low-cost housing, as well as the extent to which the development would accomplish orderly and contiguous expansion, receive attention. The board rates each factor and establishes a priority list, presented at a public hearing. The city council then dispenses development allotments, beginning with projects receiving the highest rating in each housing category and proceeding until the allotment of 500 units has been fulfilled.

Although the system worked well, according to the city's planning director, some landowners and developers in the area brought suit. In early 1974, a U.S. District Court ruled the "Petaluma Plan" unconstitutional on the grounds that the quota plan violates the constitutional right to travel. The court held that "no city shall regulate its population growth numerically so as to preclude residents of any other area from traveling into the region."[25] Petaluma's mayor has indicated that the city will probably appeal the court ruling once its council reviews the ruling.

Other Bay Area cities, with similar rapid increases in their growth rate, have begun to examine seriously the applicability of the Petaluma approach in their respective communities. Napa, Novato, Livermore, and Pleasanton are considering similar ordinances.

Except for these specific examples, little progress has been made toward establishing definitive policies and mechanisms to limit urban growth. Because of sewer service limitation, a few communities have established moratoria or severely restricted new residential development pending adequate services. The majority of communities lack specific growth policies. Several have indicated that such policies will be adopted as part of their general plan revision programs. Because almost one-third of the 92 Bay Area cities approximate full development, little opportunity exists for expansion.

RURAL DEVELOPMENT

More subtle than the spread of distinctly urban development, yet no less threatening to the preservation of open space, is the increasing rural development in the Bay Area. With the creeping congestion of the urban corridor, more and more people have sought escape in outlying areas. "Scattered development" activity is low density, primarily ranging between lot sizes of one to five acres. More recently, five-acre ranchettes and somewhat larger "country farms" have become popular. The effectiveness of these extremely low-density rural uses in maintaining open space quality depends on several factors.

While the subdivision is the primary vehicle for urban development, the lot split is favored to accomplish low-density rural growth. This process involves the breaking up of an existing parcel into no more than four smaller parcels. Gradual division of a large parcel by successive lot splits until it consists of many small parcels suitable for development represents a common practice. Because the law defines a subdivision as five or more units, subdivision regulations do not apply.

Rural Growth in the Bay Area

Sonoma County has experienced by far the most rural development in the Bay Area. Indeed, the problem in Sonoma is "rural" rather than urban sprawl—the scattering of small half-urban, half-rural developments across the countryside. More than 50 percent of the county's 1970 population resided in unincorporated areas. Rural development, particularly west of Petaluma and Santa Rosa, also surrounds Sonoma and Sebastopol and threatens to fill the Valley of the Moon. The county has recorded almost 3,800 lot splits, averaging between two and four acres, since 1967.

Southern Santa Clara County has experienced a rapid increase in rural development since 1970, with more than 600 lots established in unincorporated areas around Gilroy and Morgan Hill between September 1971 and March 1972. Lot sizes averaged five acres, although they ranged from two to ten acres in some areas. Rural development also represents a distinct threat to the continued viticulture and open space value of the Napa Valley, although building activity has yet to reach the level of Santa

Clara or Sonoma counties, Building pressures have also increased in Solano, Contra Costa, and Alameda counties.

A report on the status of rural development in Alameda County typifying the situation of most Bay Area counties asserts that rural-residential areas have

> been previously established without benefit of a location policy or other comprehensive planning tool. Strip residential zoning . . . are (sic) examples of the previously utilized haphazard approach to the provision of rural homesites. In addition to those areas following numerous residential uses through zoning . . . de facto residential areas have grown by variance. . . . [They] are not in areas planned for eventual development and are not capable of economic provision of residential necessities.[26]

County Response

Bay Area counties have recently begun to limit the spread of rural development, by generally raising minimum lot sizes in agricultural zones. Alameda County in May 1972 established a minimum 100-acre parcel size throughout most of the county nonurban area. A rural residential policy also sets guidelines for the further rezoning of already established rural residential areas, now studied on a case-by-case basis.

In 1968 Napa County established a 26,000-acre exclusive agricultural district, with a minimum lot size of 20 acres for the Napa Valley. More than 20 percent of the county, including a half-mile-wide transition zone around the valley agricultural preserve, was rezoned in 1972 to a five-acre minimum lot size because of increasing low-density urbanization. Early in 1973, the county adopted an emergency interim zoning ordinance that raised parcel sizes to 5 acres in districts zoned rural-residential, 20 acres in those zoned agricultural, and 40 acres in those zoned for watershed protection. This will remain in force until the development of new zoning, following completion of the general plan with an open space element.

Santa Clara County has adopted an interim policy for the rezoning of land in its south county to a minimum of 2.5 acres pending a special area study. Marin County has rezoned more than 90 percent of its central rural corridor—excluding public agency lands—to minimum sizes of 20, 40, and 60 acres. Contra Costa County intends to raise the minimum lot size of its agricultural district to five acres. Solano County has applied agricultural zoning to most of its rural areas. Although San Mateo County's agricultural and forest zones permit one-acre lots, most of these areas are overlaid by a strict slope-density district precluding intense development. Moreover, San Mateo has maintained a strong policy against septic tank disposal systems, which has forestalled rural development to date.

While these changes in zoning display an awareness by the counties of the deleterious effects of possible uncontrolled rural development, they fail to ensure permanent protection of the region's open space resources. Because of the haphazard pattern of past development, many areas have already been committed to low-density development. Thousands of legal building sites, already approved, have yet to be developed. Landowners who claim their land is no longer profitable for grazing or agriculture continue to exert strong pressures for rezonings and variances on land that is indicated as open space in county general plans. In parts of the Bay Area, rural development has accelerated with little or no policy direction from the counties.

Williamson Act

When the legislature passed the California Land Conservation Act, or Williamson Act, in 1965, observers hailed it as a major step forward in the effort to stem the tide of urban sprawl and preserve rapidly disappearing agricultural lands. Since then, 43 of the state's 55 counties have adopted the act and entered some 11,400,000 acres of agricultural and other open space land into ten-year, automatically renewable contracts, providing that land remains in open space use in return for reduced property taxes. Eight counties and four cities in the Bay Area have adopted the act, placing more than 1,071,000 acres in agricultural preserves (see Table 8).[27]

Preservation of Prime Land

Although an explicit objective of the act, critics argue that only about 25 percent of class I and II prime agricultural land in the state, even less in the Bay Area, has come under contract. They claim that tax reductions on high-cash-value crops from certain prime lands are not sufficiently substantial to attract landowners. More importantly, much of the prime agricultural land also has development potential, and landowners have thus been understandably hesitant to restrict their lands to open space use. Conceding this point, advocates claim that subsequent amendments to the act, together with its application by counties, have rendered the original agricultural use distinctions a nullity. Furthermore, they contend that, from an open space standpoint, the aesthetic value of nonagricultural land is perhaps more important.

Prevention of Urban Sprawl

Critics seemingly agree with a study conducted by the University of California that the Williamson Act is "not yet accomplishing its objective of discouraging premature and unnecessary conversion of agricultural land to nonagricultural use."[28] Development does not immediately threaten most land covered by the act. Only a fraction of agricultural preserves repose within the three miles of existing urban areas in the San Francisco Bay Region. Although

TABLE 8

Williamson Act Lands in the Bay Area, 1972

County	Acres Prime Land	Acres Now Prime Land	Total Acres	Tax Revenue Difference
Alameda	6,418.64	137,577.05	143,995.69	235,471.16
Contra Costa	1,285.00	49,024.00	50,309.00	82,564.00
Marin	8,805.00	76,204.00	85,009.00	161,627.00
Napa	5,370.37	55,320.43	60,690.80	1,986.04
San Francisco	—	—	—	—
San Mateo	1,587.12	38,451.98	40,039.10	98,678.00
Santa Clara	15,360.00	270,002.00	285,362.00	438,286.00
Solano	92,828.00	66,106.00	158,934.00	268,020.00
Sonoma	12,538.00	208,861.00	221,399.00	314,904.77
County subtotal	144,192.13	901,546.46	1,045,738.59	1,601,536.97
City				
Fremont	1,867.00	15,545.00	17,412.00	57,098.49
Menlo Park	—	1,991.88	1,991.88	1,717.63
San Jose	65.00	6,220.00	6,285.00	10,633.42
Saratoga	130.00	—	130.00	26,752.00
City subtotal	2,062.00	23,756.88	25,818.88	96,201.54
Bay Area total	146,254.13	925,303.34	1,071,557.47	1,697,738.51

Source: California State Department of Conservation (Sacramento: State Publication, 1973).

more than 100,000 acres have been preserved near urban development, the well-scattered parcels are not sufficiently numerous to limit sprawl. The prospect of a large financial gain upon the sale of farm land for development has provided an effective deterrent to extensive use of the act in urban areas.

Yet, many think the act cannot eliminate the complex economic, demographic, and social problems creating urban sprawl and that its provisions are more appropriately aimed at long-range protection of open space land than immediate restrictions in urban areas.

Voluntary Provisions and Permanence

Some observers have criticized the act because of its voluntary nature, that is, because the landowner cannot be forced to enter into an agreement, only those intending to develop their land within the next 10-20 years are likely to sign a contract. Landowners have embraced the act with caution, doubt, and reluctance in almost every county where it has been implemented. Labeling its temporary nature as a shortcoming, critics note that the restrictions will be removed after ten years, once a landowner files a notice of nonrenewal. After filing the notice, property taxes gradually increase until they approach the full market value of the land at the end of the ten-year period.[29] These conditions lead to a further criticism that land speculators can use the Williamson Act as a holding device, thus enjoying interim tax benefits, and that it tends to discourage permanent open space preservation by allowing speculators to operate leisurely and profitably.

The "temporary" nature of the commitment remains arguable. Advocates contend that the vast majority of landowners have no ulterior motivation for entering into Williamson Act contracts—they do not go into the act for ten years, but forever. That few notices of nonrenewal or cancellation requests have so far been filed supports their claim. The newness of the act, however, makes it impossible to accurately assess the permanence of the open space commitment.

Subsidies to Large Landowners

Critics have also questioned the beneficiaries of tax advantages. Standard Oil, Kern County Land Company, and the Irvine Company, among several owners of large California acreages, have presumably become eligible for substantial tax reductions through the act, while some receive large agricultural price support payments from the federal government. The Nader Task Force, among others, challenged the idea that corporations deserve substantial tax breaks for their land, most of which is not threatened by development, now or in the future. Agricultural and other interests respond that the Williamson Act is an inappropriate vehicle to challenge land tenancy issues. They argue, moreover, that if open space is a "good thing," then the more of it the better: larger land holdings should thus be welcomed.

Impact on Local Finances

The Williamson Act has unquestionably affected local government funding. According to one report,

> On a statewide basis, the average decrease in assessed valuation per acre of land under agreement was $46.49. In the 9-County Bay Area, the average was $74.74, although the individual county averages ranged from a high of $140.07 in San Mateo County to a low of only $33.42 in Napa County.[30]

Tax revenue differences for cities and counties of $14.6 million and $1.7 million in the state and Bay Area respectively have resulted.[31] Statewide, school districts claim losses of $13.3 million in revenues.

> As farm lands go under contract and receive lower assessments, the result in many cases has been higher tax rates ... school districts,

which may not be in a legal position to raise their tax rates, sometimes end up in the worst bind of all.³²

Arguing that tax allocations help distribute the costs of local government more equitably because agriculture demands few local government services, some specialists assert that local agencies should not shoulder the entire tax burden. Consequently, the state has authorized $13 million to help replace lost revenues. Unfortunately, these subventions to local government will not begin to replace total dollars lost. Those favoring this method of preserving open space observe that, despite the cost, it represents the cheapest open space. Land remains in private ownership and use restrictions do not involve legal and political problems associated with zoning. Despite its shortcomings, the Williamson Act has placed large acreages of land in open space use and has been a principal instrument in containing rural and remote recreational development.

OPEN SPACE AND ENVIRONMENTAL QUALITY IN THE PLANNING PROCESS

Although open space considerations have been an element of most local plans for many years, they have only recently become significantly more than concepts. Most local jurisdictions in the Bay Area have seemingly subordinated open space preservation to urban development. General plans have often failed to recognize the need to protect certain lands from urban development. Expansion, apparently, has taken precedence over scenic values, rare plant and animal habitats, greenbelts, and public access.

In striving for planning flexibility, local officials have emphasized goals and policy making rather than precisely delineating open space areas. The general plans of cities and counties have consequently tended to view open space in the abstract. The plan map, a brightly colored representation of the planning area's future physical shape, includes liberal areas of "green" space. A greenbelt encircles the urban area within which one finds appropriately spaced blocks for parks. Allocating different land uses, some insist, constitutes a textbook planning exercise, made with minimal recognition of the extreme variability of the landscape's ability to absorb the physical impacts of differing uses. As urban development pressures build within the community, the general plan specifies no countervailing mechanisms to protect open space needs. In short, the general plans of most communities and counties have leaned toward concentration on the *absence* of development. Designed to guide the area's future growth, the plan normally undergoes continuous pressure for urban development.

Open Space Elements

The California legislature responded to this imbalance in local planning in 1970 by adding to the Government Code the requirement that local governments adopt an open space element. It imposed a deadline of June 30, 1973, for adoption by local governments and made the implementation process mandatory. It reinforced the importance of open space by requiring city and county governments to execute the plan enforcing an open space zoning ordinance. No building permit may be issued, or subdivision approved, and no open space zoning ordinance adopted unless each coincides with the local open space plan.[33]

Local Open Space Plans—Cities

Goals and policies at the local level generally recognize the wide range of functions that open space serves and the need to preserve certain areas in a natural state. However, only a few entirely developed communities, notably Berkeley, Albany, and Santa Clara, have essentially considered their park and recreational areas as open space elements. Implementation programs at present appear rather generalized in most cases.

With few exceptions, existing agricultural land is not designated for preservation as open space within planned urban areas. It is considered green-belt open space in plans of communities adjacent to agricultural areas. Most plans recognize the importance of creeks and streams being preserved in their natural states, and marshes and wetlands are almost invariably identified as open space in local plans. Most city plans attempt to integrate parks and open space areas into a cohesive system through the use of riding and hiking trails, creekside parks, and utility corridors.

Separation of communities by substantial greenbelt areas have been included in the open space plans where physically possible. Fairfield is attempting to reserve an existing greenbelt between its two growth centers. Where cities have already begun to coalesce, for example, Milpitas-San Jose and Pittsburg-Antioch, no noteworthy effort has been made to provide a separating greenbelt. Substantial open space, on the other hand, is specified in currently undeveloped or partially developed areas of communities in, or adjacent to, hillside terrain. Development plans, generally defining the location of open space areas, often include special policies providing that future development in hillside areas be carefully sited to avoid environmental degradation. Many plans also suggest greater use of cluster development principles and park dedication provisions.

Yet, diversity in the physical and political nature of Bay Area communities dictates a varied approach and commitment to open space preservation for which a number of cities have prepared bold and innovative plans. Palo Alto has recommended preservation of its entire hillside area, almost 8,000 acres in natural state, and has begun to implement the plan.[34] Lafayette, nestled in the Berkeley Hills, has proposed a unique mechanism of density transfers to implement a plan that maintains most of the incorporated community in open space.[35] Petaluma plans focus on a buffer zone of public park land between the developed portion of the city and the agricultural greenbelt beyond. Hercules, actually a new community planned by the Hercules Company, promises to consider carefully open space values.[36]

Many cities, however, may maintain that city boundaries define urban uses, and therefore the county bears responsibility for the provision of open space areas. Because most undeveloped Bay Area land falls under the jurisdiction of the counties, their open space plans have become quite important.

County Open Space Plans

Alameda County has proposed a plan indicating the same residential and open areas as in the general plan, but restructuring open areas into four major categories: agricultural open space, both cultivated and uncultivated; preserve areas with irreplaceable nature or environmental resources, primarily those shown as major park and recreation on the general plan; residential canyon open space where larger open space areas intrude into canyons of slope land adjacent to residential lands; and open space corridors consisting of scenic routes and trails and serving to link and provide access between other open space areas.[37]

Contra Costa County, in preparing a ten-year open space plan, has designated urban areas that will remain essentially those in the 1963 general plan. The implementation section, which includes actions by other county agencies and an explanation of open space financing, uses zoning and full fee acquisition for implementation.

Marin County has adopted a new general plan in which the open space element represents a critical feature.[38] It divides the county into three "corridors": eastern urban, inland rural, and coastal recreation. Of the county's population, 90 percent will be located in the urban corridor where the plan designates the preservation of almost 22,000 acres in 13 ridgelands and hill areas identified as "community separators" (see Figure 6). In addition, it recommends preserving 5,500 acres of water-edge lowlands along the Bay and Petaluma River as open space. It identifies more than 22,000 acres in the eastern corridor for future urban expansion to accommodate the county's projected population by 1990. The plan includes preservation of almost the entire inland rural and coastal recreation corridors as open space, either in public or private agricultural ownership. It also delineates conservation zones subject to special protection. Development in these areas would be limited to 10,000 acres in rural villages, 1,800 to be developed between 1970 and 1990, at an average density of one unit per acre.

Napa County adopted a framework plan in late 1973 that recognizes urban areas, suburban areas of one to five-acre lots, and rural areas of five-acre or larger lots. The remainder of the county is identified as open space. It delineates development areas according to county population projections by the planning staff.

San Mateo County adopted its parks and open space element in 1969, identifying almost 50 projects for acquisition, totalling almost 32,900 acres and providing for a parkway and trails system.[39] It indicates most of the Santa Cruz Mountains as open space, but forecasts substantial development along the

Bay coast and mudflats. The county has started to modify the open space element as part of its general plan revision program.

Although final details are not yet complete, a new plan being devised for the coastside mouth of Pacifica and Santa Cruz mountains will classify land as a "development district" for urbanization through 1990 and an urban resources district for temporary and permanent open space (see Table 9). The urban development district will accommodate 40,000 people, or 50 percent more than the population projection of 28,000 for the mid-coastside area. Success in protecting agricultural and open space will depend primarily on the adoption of staged growth policies and the extent of cooperation by Half Moon Bay. Restrictive zoning will be applied to agricultural areas and lands unsuitable for acquisition. Lands of unique aesthetic value, which cannot be reasonably regulated, will be publicly acquired.[40]

Santa Clara County, in the process of adopting its urban development and open space plan, envisions almost 100 policies covering all aspects of open space preservation. Essentially, all land not reserved for urban expansion remains open space either for recreation, agricultural production, grazing and watershed protection, protection of waterlands, or salt production.[41]

Solano County has adopted an interim open space element establishing basic goals and policies and identifying areas requiring protection.[42] Planned

TABLE 9

Tentative Land Classification for San Mateo Coastside Area

Urban Development District	Approximate Acreage
Phase I urbanization area through 1990 (assumed 4 units per acre)	4,000
Urban Resources District	
Land undesirable for urbanization during Phase I (1 unit per 5 acres to 1 unit per 20 acres)	17,000
Land unsuitable for urbanization—hazardous, inaccessible, agricultural preserves (1 unit per 40 acres maximum)	96,000
Exclusive agricultural district (1 unit per 40 acres maximum)	9,000
Public interest lands, public and quasi-public, or restricted use private	28,000
Rural settlements for expansion of commercial services and ancilliary housing	under 1,000
Total	155,000

Source: Status of Coastside Plan, San Mateo County Planning Department, January 18, 1973.

urban areas will not decrease, although reducing the extent of possible industrial expansion will receive consideration in the general plan.

Sonoma County, in the midst of preparing a long-range general plan, has
established a temporary permit procedure for any development in areas defined
in the county's resource inventory as environmentally sensitive, hazardous to
development, or unique.

San Francisco County's open space plan understandably concentrates on
parks and their recreational use.[43] It emphasizes preservation of existing public
open space areas, including the maintenance of an unbroken stretch of natural
public open space along the Pacific Coast from Fort Funston to the eastern
edge of the Presidio. Its policy also covers the improvement and expansion of
neighborhood park and recreation space, the elimination of nonrecreational
uses in park areas, and the provision of usable open space in new residential
development. The plan outlines several methods of implementation. Intense
urban development, high land values, and lack of funds, of course, limit the
amount of open space that can be acquired to supplement the existing citywide
system. Proposals for new parks generally concentrate on the eastern shoreline
and include an 85-acre park at Candlestick Point and a 46-acre recreational
facility at India Basin. Specific additional neighborhood facilities are suggested
for five districts, including Chinatown and the Mission, which are considered
deficient in open space. However, the plan suggests no program for financing
acquisition. The city's award-winning Urban Design Element supplements the
open space plan with policies to promote aesthetic qualities by applying
landscape and design principles to new development and civil improvements.
An ordinance relating open space requirements to height represents one important step toward this goal.

The basic Bay Area pattern of county plans delineates urban areas, with
the remainder as open space. This will differ, of course, from the adopted
ABAG plan regarding direction of open space in several areas, but in general the
individual county plans reflect the regional plan's philosophy. Although implementation programs remain unspecified, the primary vehicle will be zoning,
accompanied by acquisition of certain areas by way of county or district park
programs.

Inadequacies in local plans to protect open space may seem inevitable,
either because of excessively broad scope or narrow perspective. However, any
effort to plan specifically for open space needs marks an important step
forward by local government. Local policies and plans certainly recognize the
value of open space. A balance being struck between open space and urban
needs has begun to specify the desirability of preventing development in certain
areas.

THE FAILURE TO IMPLEMENT PLANS

Although general plans prescribed and mapped land use policies prior to
1970, they did not necessarily mandate the adoption of enforceable restrictions
to control private land by local government. Furthermore, they placed no

demands upon local officials to conform these policies with the general plan. In fact, when confronted with the direct pressures of individual proposals to modify the landscape, local officials have, perhaps understandably, tended to disregard even the best designed plans in favor of political expediency. Long-range capital improvement budgeting and short-range expenditures have often disregarded plan proposals. The zoning map sometimes fails to reflect designated land uses, and zoning changes ignore adopted policies. In more than one community during the last two decades, the general plan has apparently been forgotten or deliberately ignored.

Critics have long cited the use or abuse of zoning as an instrument of land use policy. Numerous books and articles have appeared in which "zoning has regularly and repeatedly been flayed by the cognescenti" for a multiplicity of reasons.[44] In suburbia, some observers have identified zoning as the principal vehicle for the preservation of the status quo, by excluding all but single-family homes from the community and discouraging innovative planning and housing concepts. The vagueness and inadequacy of zoning standards have not lacked vociferous fault finders. The straining of transportation facilities, the separation of people from employment opportunities, the promotion of monotony, the encouragement of bad architectural and site design, and wasteful land use patterns represent only a few of the adverse consequences partially or wholly attributed to local zoning practices.

Perhaps the strongest criticism has focused on the emasculation of zoning as a positive instrument of public policy through indiscriminate granting of variances and rezoning. Although these legal devices were originally intended to provide reasonably flexible administration in zoning, a report to the National Commission on Urban Problems believes that

> in scores of cities "reasonable flexibility" has become excessive looseness. The single-family district that once seemed to be protected from the intrusion of incompatible uses now has a service station on one corner, a medical clinic on another, commercial parking spilling over from the adjacent business district, 10 families living in a converted single-family mansion. . . . The zoning ordinance has become eroded by variance, exceptions, small amendments and even unchecked violations that it is meaningless. . . .[45]

Zoning has not effectively allayed urban sprawl or protected open space. Developers have generally experienced little difficulty in obtaining the requisite rezoning of land from agricultural to urban classifications, except in more or less isolated areas. Those areas immediately outside the planned urban area, where an exception does not appear to violate blatantly the policies of the general plan, remain particularly vulnerable to urban use zoning. However, as the number of exceptions have increased, the plans of many communities have been rendered useless.

Variances and special use permits for nonrural land uses in undeveloped areas have also been obtained relatively easily. Although administrative decisions that fail to follow adopted ordinances are invalid, they are seldom litigated because courts have generally manifested leniency. Zoning ordinances and other implementation techniques are inadequate, but local officials have not convincingly applied them. Some critics assert this lack of conviction does not result simply from ignorance or disinterest. Several factors, they insist, have worked to defeat the implementation of general plans, including property tax pressures, susceptibility to property rights arguments, growth ambitions, land speculation, and political influence.

Recent Trends

Two new state laws have generated renewed attention on efforts of local agencies to implement their general plans. The first was the 1970 legislation requiring incorporation of an open space element in cities' general plans along with implementation methods and adoption of a zoning ordinance. The other, enacted by the California legislature, required that all zoning ordinances must be consistent with the adopted general plans of cities and counties by January 1973.[46] Subject to certain time limitations, a resident of a city or county can force compliance with this provision.

Although not ensuring implementation of open space proposals in local plans, these laws require local agencies to conform to general plan proposals before taking action when considering individual applications for zoning changes. They also provide that zoning districts serve a land-specific interpretation of the policies embodied in the general plan.

More than half the cities and counties, however, had not revised their zoning ordinances by February 1973. Although most had begun a review process, only a few had adopted an open space zoning ordinance. The legislature's failure to indicate the meaning of conformity has generated some confusion among local officials. For example, when the adopted general plan shows an area as urban, but indicates development in 15 or 20 years, the question arises regarding the immediate zoning of the land for residential or industrial purposes, thus intensifying development pressures. Conformity, conceivably, could be achieved by maintaining an open space or agricultural zoning classification for these lands and then applying an overlay zone incorporating the designated future use as well as a time requirement based on criteria such as proximity with existing urban development and public services. Nevertheless, precisely how local agencies will mesh zoning ordinances with their specific plans remains uncertain.

Despite the new laws, councils and boards can avoid the legal requirements by simply amending the plan whenever they wish to enact an ordinance, or allow an unauthorized land use. Fairfield, for example, has amended its general plan to accommodate a brewery in a prime agricultural area designated in the previous draft as a greenbelt. Many local governments have been noticeably deficient in implementing their adopted policies. The present revitalization of the planning process among local agencies in the Bay Area evidences a greater commitment to implementation.

INADEQUATE METHODS FOR
ACQUISITION OF OPEN SPACE

In order to meet the open space goals of the ABAG general plan, which presently recommends almost 6,000 square miles as permanent open space, public agencies must acquire a large amount of land in the San Francisco Bay Area. Although state and federal agencies have maintained active acquisition and management programs, a large share of the responsibility has fallen, and will continue to fall, upon cities, counties, and certain special districts.

Acquisition Programs of Cities and Counties

Local agencies have been comparatively more successful in full-fee acquisition of parks and open space than other metropolitan regions of the country. The counties of San Mateo and Santa Clara and the East Bay Regional Park District in Alameda and Contra Costa counties have made significant accomplishments. Cities have generally responded to the need for local recreation, with a system of neighborhood and community parks, although obvious deficiencies exist in some areas. A number of cities have acquired large tracts of open space within their communities. Yet the degree of public concern and the existing deficiencies in urban and regional open space systems clearly indicate that government efforts still have not fulfilled open space needs. Although financial commitments to open space preservation vary among Bay Area governments, we discern some general observations.

Local efforts have almost exclusively focused on land acquisition for its present or future recreational value. Rarely has land been purchased *primarily* for its open space value. Local financial commitments for park acquisition have generally been directly proportional to the degree of urbanization. To a large extent, less urbanized areas have been unable to raise enough revenue to purchase adequate parks. Demonstrated threats to open space usually have been insufficient to stimulate the necessary public support for park programs.

Most Bay Area agencies do not have a definitive financial program to acquire parks, and appropriations have been made on a year-to-year basis from general revenues. Moreover, local acquisition programs are subject to significant financial constraints. Although the demand for governmental services has rapidly increased, legal and political factors limit taxes and other revenues. Park projects must compete with a host of other urgent community needs and oftentimes have not been accorded high priority. The resistance of local electorates to authorize park bond issues has further impeded local acquisition programs. The availability of matching federal and state grants, however, has been an important stimulus to the allocation of local funds for park acquisition.

Napa Valley—Agricultural Scene

Courtesy Redwood Empire Association

Marin County Scene, 1958

Mt. Tamalpais, Marin County

Courtesy Redwood Empire Association

Unspoiled Seashore, Point Reyes National Park

Francis Drake stopped here during his 1579 voyage. Courtesy Redwood Empire Association.

Mt. St. Helena, and Extinct Volcano, Napa County

Courtesy Redwood Empire Association

San Francisco circa 1967

Courtesy Pacific Gas and Electric, San Francisco, California

Tiburon and Belvedure

Courtesy Pacific Gas and Electric, San Francisco, California

However, within the last few years a remarkable shift in priorities in several Bay Area communities has appeared. As an editorial in the San Francisco *Chronicle* observed following a 1972 general election, the citizens of the Bay Area

> demonstrated an unmistakable upsurge of sentiment in favor of public acquisition and preservation of open spaces for the creation of local and regional parks ... reflect[ing] a growing public concern about overpopulation and a resulting intent to restrain the kind of urban sprawl that has already overrun the peninsula's open fields and orchards and threatens to invade the foothills and the bay shore.[47]

Nowhere has this new commitment been more phenomenal than in Marin County. Since January 1972, voters have

● approved a countywide measure to create a regional park agency and support it with a levy of $.10 per $100 assessed valuation, estimated to raise $800,000 in the fiscal year 1973-74;

● approved by a 73 percent majority a $1.25 million bond issue to acquire a 200-yard-wide, two-mile-long corridor running along the spine of the Tiburon Peninsula ridge;

● approved by a 75 percent majority a $2.25 million bond issue to purchase open space in San Rafael;

● approved by a 96 percent majority a $315,000 bond issue, at a cost of $40 per year for each owner, to buy 285 acres of hillside property in the unincorporated community of Lucas Valley;

● approved a $600,000 bond issue in Marinwood for the purchase of 350 acres of undeveloped land along Highway 101;

● created a special assessment district in the north Marin-Twelve Oak Hill area to purchase 180 acres of land for open space.

Plans are also underway to form county service areas to buy a portion of the north-facing ridge of the Las Gallinas Valley and to establish a community park and preserve, a marsh in the Greenbrae—Kentfield area. A $500,000 bond issue to purchase open space in the City of San Anselmo is the only acquisition proposal to be defeated, failing by 2 percent to gain the necessary two-thirds majority in the April 1973 election.

Other successful elections in the Bay Area during the last year include:

● the approval of a charger amendment in San Matel County to increase the county tax rate by 10 cents in order to raise 31 million dollars to purchase and develop approximately 8,300 acres of land for county parks over the next ten years.

● the creation in a November election by a 2 to 1 margin of a Mid-Peninsula Regional Park District in northern Santa Clara County authorized to levy a 10 cent tax rate to purchase nonpark open space land.

- the approval by an 82 percent majority of a bond issue to purchase a 17-acre park site in Belmont.
- support by the voters of Oakland for the city to double the amount of money spent on parks and open space.

Proposals to establish a special property tax of ten cents per $100 assessed valuation for ten years to acquire, develop and maintain San Mateo city parks, and a bond issue to acquire 20 acres of open space in Millbrae were defeated at the polls.

In addition to authorizing a substantial increase in funds, these measures also represent the first significant commitment of money for the purchase of nonpark open space. Furthermore, in connection with the development of open space plans, several cities have already begun seriously to consider ways in which the necessary additional funds might best be provided to implement their plans. Others have indicated that they will begin such reviews in the near future. That present financial programs are inadequate in terms of proposed plans has been readily recognized by many officials in these communities.

Whether this realization will result in the continued acceleration of local acquisition programs cannot now be foreseen. The greatest response at the community level has so far come from upper-middle-class suburban communities, with a greater interest in open space and a greater ability to pay for it. In less prosperous communities, important economic and political constraints to the intensification of open space acquisition efforts will continue. In the less urbanized counties of Solano, Napa, and Sonoma, widespread, although gradually decreasing, opposition to significantly expanded programs will also continue inadequate in terms of proposed plans has been readily recognized by many officials in these communities.

The East Bay Regional Park District

The East Bay Regional Park District represents an outstanding example of an existing local park and open space program. A tax-supported district governed by an elected board of directors, the only one of its kind in California and one of the very few in the United States, operates under special provisions of the State Public Resources Code. The district, formed in 1934 in eastern Alameda County, has since expanded to include most of Alameda and Contra Costa counties. It currently serves 1 million residents, covering an area of 955 square miles.

Its original charter obliges the district to provide regional recreation areas for active recreational, regional parks, including not less than 500 acres of land and offering a network of continuous trails and open space, designated as land left totally untouched. Many newer parks, including Las Trampas, Briones, and Sunol, classified as "urban wilderness areas," have a minimal amount of development and use planned primarily for hikers and day campers.[48]

In 1936 the district opened its first parks, Tilden, Temescal, and Robert Sibley, comprising almost 4,400 acres. Today it owns or operates 22 parks

TABLE 10

Water Agencies in San Francisco Bay Area

Agency	Type	Approximate Land[a] Holdings (acres)	Status of Recreational Use	Location of Holdings
San Francisco Water Department	County department	63,200	Limited	San Francisco, Alameda, Santa Clara, San Mateo
East Bay Municipal Utility District	Special district	27,800	Open to public[c]	Alameda, Contra Costa
Marin Municipal Water District	Special district	18,400	Open to public[c]	Marin
North Marin County Water District	Special district	650	Open to public, developed park	Marin
City of Napa Water Department	City department	5,550	Open to public[c]	Napa
Vallejo Water Department	City department	5,700	Restricted	Napa, Solano
San Jose Water Works	Private company	7,500[b]	Restricted	Santa Clara
California Water Service Company	Private company	1,200	Restricted	San Mateo
Total		130,000		

[a]Includes reservoir acreages.

[b]Total land holdings; approximately 7,000 acres of watershed, reservoir lands.

[c]Picnicking, fishing, hiking, and horseback riding only, except Milliken Reservoir of Napa City where organized camping

Source: Data supplied by the water agencies and compiled by the editors (1972).

exceeding 29,000 acres,[49] much of which forms a string of parks in an outstanding greenbelt along the ridgeline overlooking the populated East Bay urban corridor. Recently the district has begun to acquire and develop a system or riding and hiking trails that will eventually form a network linking many of the area parks.

Most of the district's operating revenues come from a $.10 property tax rate levy which, in 1971-72, provided $4.4 million. Interest, concessions, fees, and grants from other agencies produce roughly $2 million in additional funds. In 1971, the legislature passed a bill authorizing the levy of an additional tax rate of $.05 per $100 assessed valuation, earmarking 80 percent of the additional $2.5 million in yearly revenues provided by the tax increase for land acquisition.[50]

In early 1973, the district made public a recently completed, but as yet unadopted, long-range plan for land acquisition. The plan identifies approximately 60,000 acres at 39 sites for potential expansion of the regional park system and designates 12 of these sites, comprising 28,100 acres, as high priority for acquisition, including the expansion of 6 existing regional parks and 6 new parks. The total acquisition cost for all 39 proposed sites will range from $22 to $40 million.[51]

Water Agencies

Bay Area water service agencies have contributed to local efforts in providing for public open space. Three special water districts, three local water departments under city or county direction, and two private water service companies have acquired, and now manage, approximately 130,000 acres of watershed lands in the region (see Table 10). Most of these lands were acquired several decades ago; at present no plans exist to acquire additional watershed lands.

The East Bay Municipal Utility District has adopted a master plan for its holdings in Alameda and Contra Costa counties that recognizes the open space value of the watershed.

> Lands . . . will be administered as a public trust to preserve and protect the open space characteristics of the lands. Uses permitted will be only those which depend on these characteristics for their enhancement.[52]

These uses include grazing, farming, developed and primitive recreational activity, nature study, and natural reserves.

The San Francisco Water Department has accepted, but not officially adopted, a similar plan for the Peninsula and Alameda-Santa Clara County watershed lands.[53] It stipulates that existing department holdings will be retained and, except for a few small industrial and residential areas in Alameda County, open space uses will be encouraged. The long-term uses for most of the watershed lands include water storage, scenic corridor, ecological reserve, cultivated agriculture, and recreation. The report's concepts represent an un-official, yet generally heeded, set of guidelines for future watershed land use, supplemented by an adopted policy affirming the retention of the Crystal Springs watershed on the Peninsula as permanent open space.

Except for North Marin County water district's Stafford Lake, no similar plans or commitments to open space uses exist for the other watershed lands identified in Table 10, although it is unlikely that they will be lost in the foreseeable future.

NOTES

Unless otherwise cited, data in this chapter is derived from personal communications with local officials.

1. League of California Cities, *Planning and Management*; in *California Cities*; p. 22.

2. Tito Patri et al., *The Santa Cruz Mountains Regional Pilot Study: Early Warning System* (Berkeley: University of California, 1970), p. 56.

3. California Government Code, Planning and Zoning Law, Chapter 3, Sections 65100-65700.

4. Ibid., Chapter 4, Sections 65800-65912.

5. California Business and Professions Code, Subdivision Map Act, Sections 11500-11641.

6. Ibid., Section 11535.

7. California Government Code, California Land Conservation Act, Sections 51200-51295.

8. California Government Code, Section 6953.

9. California Constitution, Article I, Section 14-1/2 and Article 1, Section 13.

10. California Constitution, Article XI, Section 18.

11. California Government Code, Sections 29910.1 and 43605.

12. Association of Bay Area Governments, "Formulation of a Regional Growth Policy for the San Francisco Bay Region," Issue Paper No. 2 (1972), p. 6.

13. Donald R. Nichols and Catherine C. Campbell, eds. *Environmental Planning and Geology* (Washington, D.C.: U.S. Department of Housing and Urban Development and U.S. Geologic Survey, December 1971), p. 76.

14. California Business and Professions Code, Section 11546.

15. *Friends of Mammoth* v. *Board of Supervisors of Mono County*, 8 Cal. 3d 1.

16. California Government Code, Section 54773 et seq.

17. Ibid., Section 54774.

18. Ibid.

19. Michael McCracken, "The Local Agency Formation Commission: An Open Space Trustee?," Stanford Law School (April 1971).

20. Santa Clara County Planning Policy Committee, *Summary of the Draft Urban Development/Open Space Plan for Santa Clara County* (November 1972), p. 1.

21. San Jose City, *Urban Development Policies* (April 1972), pp. 7-9.

22. Milpitas City Ordinance 38-235, Regulation of Residential Development, Sections XI-10-8.01 et seq., December 5, 1972.

23. Gilroy City, *Urban Development Policies* (October 2, 1972), p. 3 (mimeo.).

24. William C. McGivern, "Putting a Speed Limit on Growth," *ASPO Planning* 38, no. 10 (1972), pp. 263-65.

25. "Judge Ousts Petaluma Plan," San Francisco *Examiner*, January 18, 1974.

26. Alameda County Planning Department, *Rural Residential Development Policy—Revised* (January 22, 1973), p. 1 (mimeo.).

27. California Department of Conservation, Division of Soil Conservation, *City and County Entitlements under the Open Space Subvention Act* (1973).

28. Alan Post, "Report on Open Space and Taxation," California State Legislature, December 22, 1971, *Legislative Analyist*, p. 24 (wherein is quoted an article by Hoy F. Carman and Jim G. Polson, *National Tax Journal*, December 1971, p. 455).

29. California Revenue and Taxation Code, Section 426.

30. Duncan & Jones and Ribera & Sue, Inc., *Interim Report—Parks, Recreation and Open Space Program: Phase I*, prepared for Santa Cruz Planning Department (March 1971), p. 72.

31. California Department of Conservation, op. cit.

32. University of California Cooperative Extension, "An Environmental Controversy: The Williamson Act and State Land Use Policy," *California's Environment*, April 1972, p. 3.

33. California Government Code, Section 6590 et seq.

34. Palo Alto Department of Planning and Community Development, "The Open Space Element of the Palo Alto General Plan" (April 5, 1972), p. 19; and Palo Alto City Ordinance No. 2654, *O-S Open Space District Regulations* (June 5, 1972).

35. Lafayette City Planning Department, "Open Space, Conservation Element of the General Plan" (proposed, 1973), pp. 30-32.

36. Planning Research Corporations, *Town of Hercules—General Plan* (April 1972), pp. 34-36.

37. Alameda County Planning Department, *Summary Report on Open Space Element of the Alameda County General Plan* (July 20, 1970), p. 1 (mimeo.).

38. Marin County Planning Department, *A User's Guide to the Marin Countywide Plan* (September 1972).

39. San Mateo County Planning Commission, *Parks and Open Space Element, San Mateo County General Plan for 1990* (March 1967), map and summary.

40. County of San Mateo Planning Department, memo to Board of Supervisors and Planning Commission Re: Status of Coastside Plan (January 18, 1973).

41. Santa Clara County Planning Policy Committee, *Findings and Policies of the Draft Urban Development/Open Space Plan for Santa Clara County* (undated and unpaged).

42. Grunwald, Crawford Associates, *Resource Conservation and Open Space Plan (Phase I) Solano County, California*, prepared for Solano County Planning Department (June 1972).

43. San Francisco Department of City Planning, *Improvement Plan for Recreation* and *Open Space and Programs Recommended for Carrying out the Improvement Plan for Recreation and Open Space* (September 1972).

44. Stephen Sussna, "Land Use Control: More Effective Approaches," Research Monograph No. 17 (Washington, D.C.: Urban Land Institute, 1967), p. 6.

45. American Society of Planning Officials, "Problems of Zoning and Land-Use Regulations," Research Report No. 2, prepared for the National Commission on Urban Problems (Washington, D.C., 1968), p. 25.

46. California Government Code, Section 65860.

47. "Election Upsurge for Open Space," San Francisco *Chronicle*, November 9, 1972, editorial page.

48. Nina Stern, "Regional Parks," *Sierra Club Bulletin*, June 1971, p. 18.

49. East Bay Regional Park District Fact Sheet, 1971-1972.

50. East Bay Regional Park District, *Budget* (July 1972), p. 8.

51. Dale Champion, "Bay Parkland Proposal—60,000 Added Acres," San Francisco *Chronicle*, March 20, 1973, p. 17.

52. East Bay Municipal Utilities District, *The Land Use Master Plan of the East Bay Municipal Utility District* (October 1970), p. 6.

53. Wilsey & Ham & Metcalf & Eddy, *Technical Data: Preservation and Recreation Concepts: Peninsula and Alameda-Santa Clara County Watershed Land*, prepared for the San Francisco Water Department (undated).

6

THE GROWTH ETHIC

A recent *Wall Street Journal* article reported that

in a growing number of states and localities across the country there is serious debate for the first time about whether the spiral of more people, more industry, and more environmental damage should be brought to a halt by moves to slow down economic and population growth.[1]

These debates center on the belief that growth, whether in numbers of people or in economic output, remains essential to progress and prosperity.

The growth ethic has been indigenous to American social and economic philosophy. Manifested in the frontier expansion of the eighteenth and nineteenth centuries, it was nurtured by America's rapid transformation from an agrarian to an industrial nation and reinforced by the wealth and power that the technological age engendered. Unsurprisingly, therefore, a great number of Americans regard growth as a prerequisite of prosperity.

Some scholars maintain that population and economic growth are necessary to facilitate employment, improve the lot of poor and minority groups, provide new jobs, maintain a high standard of living, encourage scientific and technological advances, and supply the financial resources to clean up the environment. Others advocate zero growth, claiming that the above objectives are attainable under stable population conditions within a closed economic system that emphasizes quality over quantity. They further argue that resource depletion and environmental degradation have become so serious that survival itself is at stake.

Ian McHarg, a regional and "ecological planner" with a Philadelphia-based firm, writes,

We have but one explicit model of the world and that is built upon economics. The present face of the land of the free is its clearest testimony, even as the gross national product is the proof of its success. Money is our measure, convenience is its cohort, the short-term is its span and the devil may take the hindmost is its morality.[2]

Perhaps McHarg overemphasizes his point but economic considerations have historically dominated our approach to the use of land reinforced by the growth ethic. Frequent encouragement and acceptance of development in the belief that it was necessary for continued economic solvency and prosperity has been the cornerstone of growth and land use.

Santa Clara County provides an excellent example. In the early 1950s a new administration in the city of San Jose "made no bones about its goal of making San Jose the Los Angeles of the north. It formulated definite goals for expansion and growth without any limits or qualifications [and] ... moved with alacrity to implement them."[3] Other communities in the county responded similarly with their own active growth and expansion activities, and urban areas, afraid larger cities would swallow them, incorporated. Thus, seven new cities were established in Santa Clara County in the 1950s. Conflict and rivalry among them soon developed. It reached a peak following the 1955 enactment of the Agricultural Exclusion Act, which prohibited annexation of exclusive agriculture zoned land without owner consent. Cities rapidly extended their boundaries during the 90 days before the law took effect.[4]

Karl Belser, former planning director of Santa Clara County, concludes:

Under the impression that growth was progress and that any development, regardless of quality, was good, cities competed for unincorporated land, ... promised services that they were unable to render ... and sold out to business and industry by making concessions inimical to the public interest as inducements for development investment.[5]

Of course, the growth ethic was not totally responsible for suburbanization in the Santa Clara Valley. The area's attractiveness to the expanding electronics industry had initiated substantial growth pressures. However, the growth ethic has provided a philosophical framework that has often made controlled, planned urban development virtually impossible. To the extent that the growth attitude dominated the general public and elected decision makers, other public needs, including open space, tended to be put aside. With high receptivity to new development, planning devolved to accommodation, rather than direction, and open space considerations received proportionately inadequate attention.

In the recent past traditional views have markedly shifted. More Americans apparently agree that at some future time it will become necessary to limit population size in order to maintain present living standards. Some communities, moreover, have already begun to cope with this problem. In both 1971 and 1973 Marin County voters defeated a new water supply project based on the reasoning that it would lead to undesirable growth. Marin County now verges on approving a new general plan that would accommodate fewer people than population studies forecast. After receiving a survey indicating that its foothills development was uneconomic, Palo Alto moved to prevent it. Brentwood, a small town in east Contra Costa County, narrowly defeated a 1972 initiative limiting its population to 7,500 people during the next ten years. In several California cities, "growth" has become an election issue that finds successful candidates for city councils frequently advocating more limited, cautious growth. Elections in Cotati, Brentwood, Livermore, Napa, Pleasanton, and San Rafael are only a few examples.

Rather than attempting to halt growth, rational, controlled expansion of urban areas has now emerged. In 1972, for example, the voters of both Livermore and Pleasanton accepted the Save All Valley Environment (SAVE) initiative in the Livermore-Amador Valley. If upheld by the courts* it would block the issuance of residential building permits any time that schools are overcrowded, water rationing is imminent, or sewage treatment facilities are inadequate. A majority of voters thus indicated that the valley's future growth should not occur in the absence of essential services.

Despite these developments, some Bay Area communities strongly advocate growth. Solano County has instituted an active program for attracting business and industry. When San Jose, one of the country's fastest growing large cities, temporarily froze construction because of a recent State Supreme Court decision, its mayor announced, "This is a very crippling blow to our economy . . . because growth is our biggest industry."[6] Other communities in rapidly expanding areas, accepting growth as inevitable, have demonstrated their intention to accommodate it.

PROPERTY RIGHTS

Since 1290, when Parliament "extended to every free man the right to sell his lands or any part thereof without any interference from any intermediate Lord,"[7] private ownership of land has been integral to Anglo-American democratic thought. Our nation's history abounds with examples of the emphasis on private initiative through private ownership. The constitution of California holds that

> all men are by nature free and independent, and have certain inalienable rights, among which are those of enjoying and defending life and liberty; acquiring, possessing, and protecting property; and pursuing and obtaining safety and happiness.[8]

Many persons actually consider private ownership of property the fundamental freedom, the key to our nation's successful development:

---

*The measure was not sustained by the trial court and is presently being appealed.

By this process of making many millions of independent, individual decisions about land use, our economy has progressed to great heights. The property owner has the opportunity to succeed—or fail—on the exercise of his own judgment. . . . In this way, national productivity and resource utilization are improved.[9]

Government considers property rights subject to limitations when it becomes necessary to preserve the public's health, safety, or general welfare. Similarly, government can take an owner's land for public use with just compensation. However, growing population density, mounting demand on limited natural resources, and changing social values have created new and complex problems.

Legal aspects pertain fundamentally to whether a regulation permits the taking of property without just compensation. Although the courts have not clarified this point, the California judiciary appears to support the application by local governments of regulations necessary to insure orderly growth and to protect the integrity of the environment, even though these regulations may infringe on the traditional concepts of property rights. In his analysis of the scope of the police power, Ira Michael Heyman concludes: "Rights in property have been defined and protected by the courts only to the extent that such rights and protections are consistent with social, economic, and political realities."[10]

Property rights arguments also assume great importance in the political arena. When a local governing body considers action on a proposed development or on restrictive land use regulations, the fundamental American constitutional principle that allows a man to do what he wants with his property emerges. Restrictions, such as imposition of an "urban limit line" evoke heated opposition, much of it focusing on the perceived threat to constitutionally guaranteed property rights. Those who purchase land for future development object to any regulation that might prohibit appreciation of the land's value. In many cases, imposition of open space zoning or similar restriction substantially diminishes the value of property at the expense of its owner.

Controls designed to promote a balance between urban development and open space frequently succumb to political pressures generated by landowners whose property rights are affected. The recent controversy over the urban limit line concept for the control of urban growth proposed in the new Sacramento General Plan is a representative case. After months of heated debate between environmentalists and property owners, the limit line approach was deleted from the general plan.[11] Because Santa Clara County is currently considering a similar approach to land use control, the results in Sacramento bear particular relevance.

It appears that local officials often do not utilize such land use controls, perhaps fearing that landowners or developers "will claim 'inverse condemnation,' demand compensation, round-up their lawyers" and begin a bothersome and costly legal battle.[12] Locally elected officials, sometimes holding, moreover, that restrictive land use regulations will not be upheld in court, conclude that the most effective way to preserve open space is by acquisition. Regulatory devices to preserve open space thus can become a highly charged political issue. The success of controls logically depends upon the reasonableness of the regulations, the commitment of elected officials to environmental planning principles, and, above all, the strength of public support.

LAND SPECULATION

Any attempt to institute a workable system of land use controls, balancing urban development and open space, must consider land speculation. The typical process in the conversion of undeveloped land to urban uses begins with sale to a speculator, who holds the land for a certain period or perhaps leases it for agriculture. Eventually he sells to a developer, or to another speculator, for a substantial profit. The developer then builds on the land and markets the individual units.

The relatively small proportion of land in the Bay Area with a suitable topography, the proper locational attributes, and the economical service of water and sewer lines makes it profitable for speculators to hold much of the land with urban use potential. Holdings along freeways, particularly at interchanges; adjacent to airports; and in the vicinity of parks, waterways, and other scenic areas represent the most desirable speculative acreage. The speculator who anticipates development benefits immensely, although he contributes virtually nothing toward enhancing the land's value.

Widespread speculative activity induces certain adverse effects. It undoubtedly contributes to the escalation of open space acquisition costs. Point Reyes National Seashore is a good example:

When Congress authorized purchase in 1962, the total cost was estimated at 14 million dollars. By the time this money was available, however, speculators had driven the cost up double the amount. In 1966, Congress came across with another 5 million dollars but the gap was wider than ever. Total estimated cost [in 1968] was 58 million dollars.[13]

A similar situation prevails, perhaps not so dramatically, in most large open space acquisition projects. Since 1969, nationwide land prices for parks have escalated at estimated rates of 12 to 20 percent per year.[14]

Land speculation also encourages leapfrogging development that results from land close to urban areas being held off the market by owners who anticipate major increases in its value. Of course, speculation is not entirely responsible for urban sprawl; the absence of effective land use controls, developer preferences for cheaper, peripheral lands, and the influence of the property tax have also contributed to leapfrogging development patterns.

Finally, land speculation has been more of a factor in the rising cost of houses than construction costs.[15] During the 1960s, raw land prices advanced at an average annual rate seven times that of the wholesale commodity price index, and almost four times that of consumer prices.[16] Speculative activity presents practical problems for local agencies by limiting the amount of available land within the "ultimate" urban expansion area of each community. Thus, in high priority development areas available land may not be sufficient to meet housing needs. Local government, consequently, hesitates to restrict the land market by designating specific pockets or contiguous areas for initial development.

Land speculation remains an integral part of free enterprise. Existing land use regulations as presently enforced do not significantly curb such speculation.

THE PROPERTY TAX

Importance of the Property Tax

Since early in California's history, the property tax has been an important revenue source, particularly for local government. During 1966-67 it comprised 44 percent of all state and local revenues, 34 percent of all city revenues, 38 percent of all county revenues, and 54 percent of all school district revenues.[17] It raises more than $6 billion annually for cities, counties, schools, and special districts and constitutes virtually the only major revenue source for local government.

This has caused continual increases in property tax rates to meet the enhanced cost for existing services. Critics claim that administration of the property tax can be unfair, citing the fact that similarly situated landowners often pay different taxes because of the difficulty in assessing land and property equitably, despite the assessor's best efforts.[18] Some believe it also discourages renovation of existing structures in larger cities by placing a stiff excise on improvements. The property tax also influences allocation of land resources.

Impact of the Property Tax on Private Development

Farmers and cattlemen in productive agricultural enterprises near urbanizing areas contend that high taxes force them out of business. The process starts when a developer purchases relatively inexpensive outlying farm land for a subdivision. Then assessors must reappraise adjacent property to reflect the current market value as residential land. Faced with an increasing tax burden, some landowners cannot farm profitably. When the opportunity occurs, they sell to developers. More land is reassessed upward, and tax rates rise to meet the community's increased need for new schools and government services, in turn accelerating the trend toward development. A leapfrogging development pattern that further disperses the assessor's impact in a wide area inevitably results.

To help prevent the continuance of this prevalent situation, the California legislature in 1965 enacted into law the Williamson Act. However, only a small number of landowners in the Bay Area's urban fringes have taken advantage of the act. A potentially large profit, subject to favorable capital gains treatment from the sale of land for development, has clearly influenced their decisions. Thus, some experts do not consider the property tax as critical in influencing decisions to develop land.

Impact of the Property Tax on Public Land Use Decision

As a recent commentary on urban problems noted,

Local governments face a situation in which the *demand* for services is generated by forces beyond their control: (1) increased affluence, which leads to rising expectation about the quality of services, and (2) population growth which requires increases in the number of output units of service. At the same time, the supply of services is strongly constrained by legal and political limitations on increasing (property) taxes and other revenue.[19]

Constantly striving to maximize the ratio between taxes received and the costs of urban services, local governments try to encourage land uses that reduce public expenditures and generate high tax-producing revenues. Zoning often reflects these fiscal concerns.

Large-lot Residential Zoning

Common in the Bay Area, large-lot zoning pertains to neighborhoods, or entire towns, such as Atherton, Los Altos Hills and Hillsborough. Assumptions underlying large-lot zoning hold that low residential densities reduce costs for streets, sewers, water supplies, and fire and police protection. It is also assumed that the value of a home increases with lot size, thus generating higher assessed valuation and tax revenues and maximizing the ratio between costs and revenues.

Large single-family lots, of course, offer a pleasant, aesthetic environment that is safe, quiet, spacious, and private. The homogeneity of land uses protects property values but sometimes excludes lower-income groups. With increasing concern for environmental protection, moreover, large lots can minimize adverse impacts in sensitive areas, particularly hillsides.

Industrial Zoning

Local governments actively seek research and development and other "clean" industries in an attempt to secure high-revenue-producing land uses. Questionable land use decisions often result:

Often a major tax producing facility will be lured to a community and given swift approval without careful consideration of its social and physical consequences, service needs or costs to the community.[20]

A recent survey revealed that industrial parks account for 14,167 acres of Bay Area land, of which 8,668 acres remain to be developed.[21] Additional large acreages already zoned or indicated on general plans as industrial indicate some future development.

Rezoning

Rezoning of open space to industrial or commercial uses may also improve the local tax base. A report prepared by the American Society of Planning Officials states:

> An industrialist wanting to build a new plant can be confident that he will be able to get nearly any site he selects rezoned for industry, if it is not already so classified. He need only say to community A, "if you do not rezone this property there is another site in community B." ... The City officials are persuaded to change, not because new zoning appears to produce the best land use pattern for the future, but because they are anxious to get the factory to improve the tax base. ...[22]

Annexation Policies

Annexation policies maximize community revenue resources. Land that will provide substantial tax revenues with relatively small service expenditures has affected annexation proposals, resulting in incongruous and unnecessarily large city boundaries and discouraging rational land use. Since the 1963 creation of LAFCOs, however, planning and economic considerations have influenced annexation proposals.

HOUSING PREFERENCES

More than 90 percent of Americans live in metropolitan areas with limited land to accommodate the pressures of urban growth and still provide for aesthetic, recreational, and resource needs. Logically it would seem that a compact urban form would best achieve the most desirable living environment. The detached single-family home, the trademark of the suburban lifestyle that has come to dominate the urban scene, contradicts this logic. Spread four to an acre, these homes form a monotonous pattern. Spacious yards, of limited functional use, surround the dwelling unit, and the resulting low densities dictate dependence on the automobile, in turn requiring large expanses of parking lots. In short, the single-family home grossly consumes land.

The general American urge to return to the rural lifestyle of an earlier age, providing a clean, wholesome atmosphere and embodying the basic elements of the "American ideal," underlies the popularity of the single-family home. We understandably seek to escape the noise, crime, pollution, crowded schools, impersonalized atmosphere, and hectic pace of the city in favor of the relative quiet, safety, uncrowded conditions, and natural beauty of rural and suburban neighborhoods. The city connotes imprisonment; rural areas convey a sense of freedom.

The automobile has provided the means by which this can be accomplished, yet make jobs and cultural amenities in the central city accessible. Ironically, families have moved into new homes surrounded by countryside, only to find it replaced within a few years by a sea of development with the attendant social problems common to the central city. Home ownership, valued by most Americans, and economically advantageous, provides a sense of security, a private "castle" within which individual pleasures may be freely pursued. In addition to the equity, federal income tax and state property tax laws provide a deduction of property tax payments and mortgage interest rates from taxable income, and a deduction in assessed valuation—$1,750 in California.

The Federal Housing Administration (FHA) and Veterans Administration (VA) loan programs have enabled millions of middle-class Americans to finance their own homes, but they have tended to discourage design improvements, variety, and alternative housing:

> Many of the problems arising from this . . . influence may be traced directly to FHA codes which, in turn, have produced what is commonly called in the trade either "FHA modern" or "Later VA" styles. The blame can be laid squarely on the agencies' desire for standardized procedures.[23]

Builders have only recently provided significant alternatives to the single-family residence. Encouraging signs of a major shift from single-family homes to compact, environmentally integrated types have appeared in the last few years and more apartments, condominiums, townhouses, and mobile homes are being built in California. Apartments accounted for one-third of new California dwelling units in 1971, a 20 percent increase compared with the previous year.[24] Mobile homes sales set a record in 1971, increasing 21 percent from the previous year; and in 1970, 62 percent of all Bay Area building permits covered multiple units, compared with 36 percent in 1966.[25]

New housing developments utilizing these types of accommodations have increased, partially resulting from improved planning. Cluster housing, continuing to gain public acceptance and support, requires an average of 40 percent fewer streets, sewers, and other public facilities. Planned unit developments, also increasing, may incorporate cluster zoning with different housing types and commercial areas.

Second Homes and Second-Home Subdivision

Although the suburban tract home has assumed a lesser share of the total housing market, the second home or vacation retreat has greatly gained popularity during the last decade. Added leisure time, rising incomes and living standards, more and better roads providing access to recreational areas, and more urban living frustrations have caused many people to seek second family homes. In 1971, one out of every ten houses built was a vacation home. During the 1960s, moreover, subdivision of rural areas into second-home lots became a highly popular and profitable enterprise. In California, since 1957, projects have been approved for marketing land for second homes totalling more than 172,000 lots on 341,000 acres.[26]

Concentrated second-home subdivision activity substantially diminishes open space. Because such subdivisions provide increased tax revenues for counties, without generating increased costs for several years, they have until recently faced little government opposition. Proximity to the urban area has limited extensive second-home development in the Bay Area. Only in the Russian River area and along the Sonoma coast do we find a significant concentration of second homes. However, opposition to the promotional and sales practices of many recreational subdivisions, recognition of their adverse environmental consequences, and saturation of the real estate market have combined to curtail the development of new large land projects in the Bay Area and throughout the state.

WEAKNESSES IN THE LOCAL PLANNING PROCESS

An obscure but important problem in rapidly growing communities concerns the disproportionate commitment of time and energy by planning commissions and elected local officials to the processing of subdivision maps, rezoning requests, variances, and building permits. Many local officials find themselves swamped with administrative work and lack sufficient time to consider long-range planning. The planning department, particularly in smaller communities with an insufficient staff to perform administrative responsibilities, encounters similar difficulties. Having to devote time to administrative details seriously constrains the long-range goals of planning and effective land use.

Inadequate Training of Lay Decision Makers

In order to serve effectively on local legislative bodies and planning advisory commissions, a basic understanding of local planning responsibility and procedure is critical. However, in most cases, the lay representatives of these bodies have no prior experience or knowledge of planning and land use regulation complexities. They often lack the time and the desire to familiarize themselves with new planning developments, other than by the gradual accumulation of experience. Yet, they must contend with new planning legislation, more complex land use control and an ever-changing legal system. Insufficient training can engender unwise land use decisions and discourage innovative planning techniques.

Inconsistent Policy Making

Most local boards maintain a tenuous balance between environmental and development-oriented points of view in land use policy. While the philosophical shift occurring with the election or appointment of planning commission members may appear dramatic, the more frequent shifts of individual positions on specific issues generate greater discrepancies in the continuity of land use control policies. Impermanence in land use planning and regulation does not constitute an undesirable factor in the democratic system. Indeed, it remains central to the proper functioning of a representative government. But lack of continuity in land use decisions can complicate policies to effectuate planning goals.

Political Pressures

Political pressures at local and other levels of government often characterize the legislative process. Inordinate influence of special interests, however, can hinder the advancement of development restrictions to promote open space objectives. The extent to which political pressures constrain the advancement of open space objectives partially depends upon the degree of public interest in open space issues. Public apathy in the planning process causes neglect in the decision-making process, often to the detriment of the quality of land use decisions.

NOTES

1. Sanford Sesser, "The Nation Debates an Issue: The Economy vs. the Environment," *Wall Street Journal,* November 4, 1971, p. 1.

2. Ian McHarg, *Design with Nature* (Garden City, N.Y.: Natural History Press, 1969), p. 25.

3. Karl Belser, "The Making of Slurban America," *Cry California* 5, no. 4 (1970): 5. Statements in this article are supported in a 1970 study by the Stanford Environmental Law Society entitled *San Jose: Sprawling City.*

4. Ibid; page 11.

5. Ibid; page 5.

6. Rick Carroll, "San Jose Halts Its Growth," San Francisco *Chronicle,* November 5, 1972.

7. Bertel M. Sparks, "Changing Concepts of Private Property," *Freeman* 21 (1971): 588.

8. California Constitution, Article 1, Section 1.

9. T. D. Barrow, "Private Property and the Coastal Zones" (mimeo.).

10. Ira Michael Heyman, "The Great Property Rights Fallacy," *Cry California,* Summer 1968, p. 33.

11. Lee Moriwaki, "Urban Limit Vetoes; Planners Vote to Drop Idea in Revised County Map," Sacramento *Bee,* June 13, 1972, p. B1.

12. Philip R. Pryde, "New Strategies for Open Space," *Sierra Club Bulletin,* February 1972, p. 10.

13. William H. Whyte, *The Last Landscape* (Garden City, N.Y.: Doubleday, 1970), p. 66.

14. Albert Mayer, "Land as a Public Resource v. Speculative Commodity," *Architectural Record,* June 1970, p. 138.

15. Ibid.

16. U.S. Senate Committee on Interior and Insular Affairs, *National Land Use Policy*, 1972, p. 4.

17. California State Office of Planning, *California State Development Plan Program* (Sacramento: State Printing Office, 1968), p. 251.

18. Dick Netzer, *The Property Tax Case for Federal Tax Sharing* (1969), p. 89.

19. James G. Coke and John J. Gargan, "Fragmentation in Land Use Planning and Control," Research Report No. 18, prepared for The National Commission on Urban Problems (Washington, D.C., 1968), p. 12.

20. California State Office of Planning, op. cit., p. 252.

21. Security Pacific National Bank, "San Francisco Bay Area Report: A Study of Growth and Economic Stature of Nine Bay Area Counties," Economic Research Division (1971), p. 118.

22. American Society of Planning Officials, *Problems of Zoning and Land Use Regulation,* Research Report No. 2, prepared for The National Commission on Urban Problems (Washington, D.C., 1968), p. 35.

23. George Taylor, "The Crisis in Land Use," *AFL-CIO American Federalist,* February 1967, p. 10.

24. "Apartments Led 1971 State Building," Sacramento *Bee,* March 12, 1972.

25. "1971 Mobile Home Sales Set Record," Sacramento *Bee,* February 27, 1972.

26. California State Environmental Quality Study Council, *Final Report* (1972), p. 36.

7

COORDINATION

Numerous public agencies at all levels of government directly and indirectly participate in the complex process by which land resources are allocated. Comprehensive city planning and zoning, acquisition and development of parks and recreation facilities, and air and water pollution control are but a few of the resulting activities.

Serious land use conflicts often arise among government agencies. An environment in which urban land uses integrate with, rather than destroy, environmental and open space resources requires coordination of objectives. Coordination in this context is defined as the incorporation of operable mechanisms and procedures into the government system so that the components of government function in unison. Government agencies have not been notably successful in coordinating their respective land use responsibilities. Important gaps in coordination exist at all levels of government, as well as among the different agencies within each level.

> California agriculture policy seeks to keep farmers in business through the tax provisions of the California Land Conservation Act while federal policy subsidizes the farmers in certain cases for not growing crops. Federal soil conservation policy helps to develop agricultural irrigation and development of farming areas while federal housing policy encourages conversion of the same lands to residential uses. There is no federal policy related to preservation of agricultural lands. State and federal freeway policies encourage urban expansion into rural areas in spite of other policies designed to contain cities. . . . There is no federal policy with respect to coastline development and conservation and therefore no direct action, guidelines or assistance to the states in developing their coastline policies. . . . Notwithstanding . . . expressed state policy on coastal land, the agencies involved have not been able to the present time to resolve conflicting plans and demands on coastal resources.[1]

These gaps in coordination reflect the failure of state and federal agencies to assume a comprehensive view of their respective roles in promoting social and environmental goals or defining the proper relationships between state and federal land use objectives.

LACK OF STATE GUIDANCE TO
LOCAL GOVERNMENT

State government has generally failed to guide local agencies in their use of enabling legislation to accomplish regional and state land use objectives.[2] The Joint Committee on Open Space Technical Advisory Committee comments that "failure to articulate the state's interest in rational land use has allowed the private landowner to unduly control the location and timing of the state's metropolitan growth."[3] Moreover,

a failure on the part of state government to establish land use policies and to take positive action constitutes, in itself, a land use policy. It commits the state to accept present urbanization and growth trends as the basis for determining future needs. Because this course is not founded on any conscious attempt to measure the total costs of growth and rapid urbanization, and to evaluate alternatives, the state is forced to react to crises as these problems accelerate and become apparent.[4]

FRINGE AREA POLICY CONFLICTS

Lack of coordination between cities and counties has caused problems regarding appropriate land uses in fringe areas. On the one hand, counties have seen "a good general plan gradually destroyed by half a dozen competing, rapacious cities hacking off bits and pieces of county land through annexation and doing such a poor job of planning that they cannot even get their road patterns to meet."[5] On the other hand, city officials, often the most experienced with the problems of built-up areas, have no voice in county policy guiding urban development in the fringe areas adjacent to the city. Thus, open space in the fringe areas of some cities has gradually been eroded as a result of county development policies.

REGIONAL VACUUM IN COORDINATION

Although ABAG has defined several important regional objectives and prepared a number of regional plans, cities and counties essentially continue to ignore these recommendations. ABAG recognizes the failure of local planning coordination on a regional scale.[6]

Similarly, each Bay Area regional agency entertains its own conception of an urban growth policy:

> The comprehensive health planning agency defines it in terms of physical and environmental health needs; the air pollution control district defines it in terms of air quality; the water quality control agency defines it in terms of wastewater management; ABAG defines it as an overall land use allocation-regional economy problem; the Bay Conservation agency defines it in terms of the use of the Bay shoreline, and the Regional Transportation Planning Agency defines an urban growth policy as it relates to transportation systems.[7]

LOCATION OF PUBLIC FACILITIES

The siting and routing of public facilities often critically impacts the population distribution and land use patterns of the surrounding areas. Highways, schools, water projects, defense installations, and other public facilities provide important stimuli to growth and development.

A lack of coordination with respect to the planned capacity of sewage treatment facilities and water supply projects, particularly where these are the primary responsibilities of special districts, also exists. Plans of local agencies rarely include these essential services.[8] Locational decisions do not reflect overall governmental population distribution and land use objectives.

GOVERNMENTAL FRAGMENTATION AND COORDINATION PROBLEMS

Geographical fragmentation politically divides a region into a multitude of jurisdictions. In the Bay Area, public policies that determine land use patterns are vested in its 92 cities, 9 counties, and several regional agencies. Together with several hundred special districts, the boundaries of which often overlap, they exercise jurisdictional powers to encourage or discourage growth and to balance development with open space. "The fragmentation of decision making makes it difficult, if not impossible, to formulate a unified, efficient policy for the provision of governmental services."[9]

Not only does the number of discrete government agencies influence land use patterns, their differences make coordination difficult.

> The reinforced differences between cities and their suburbs in the composition of population and the mix of public services, as well as the physical differences of age of stock, etc., lead to different goals

and strategies for each. The exacerbation of differences between cities and suburbs makes technically rational solutions for metropolitan areas less accessible. It is not surprising that there is no single objective welfare function for metropolitan areas.[10]

Despite the important coordination aspect of day-to-day government administration, only a few formalized programs specifically relate to the coordination of land use planning and regulation.

ENVIRONMENTAL IMPACT REPORTING

The federal and state governments in 1969 and 1970 passed legislation requiring government agencies to prepare an environmental assessment for those projects and actions with significant environmental impacts. Both laws require that agencies that have long ignored factors directly relating to their single-purpose missions now consider their activities in the broader environmental context. Unfortunately, poor quality has marked many Environmental Impact Reports (EIRs). The requirements, furthermore, have built mountains of additional paperwork. The environmental impact review system has also tended to obscure the need for agency plans and policies reflecting environmental considerations in advance of the precise location and design of governmental projects.

JOINT CITY-COUNTY PLANNING COMMITTEES

Three Bay Area counties, San Mateo, Santa Clara, and Marin, have created special committees to coordinate the planning programs of each county and its cities. Comprising representatives from each city council and planning commission and the County Board of Supervisors and Planning Commission, these committees advocate the adoption of common land use and plans by each county jurisdiction. Plans first go to the committee where, after public hearings, they are adopted and forwarded to the county. Finally, each city reviews and adopts the county plan with its own planning program. Because of their representation, presumably the committees serve to "legitimize" the plan, making it more acceptable to the cities.

This process, entirely cooperative, does not bind cities to adopt the county plan or modify their existing land use plan to conform. Many observers remain dubious regarding the overall value of a formalized review and adoption process. Others nevertheless believe it represents an important step toward a workable coordination mechanism.

LAFCOs AND SPHERE-OF-INFLUENCE BOUNDARIES

Because of their responsibilities, LAFCOs have increasingly assumed an important coordinating role in urban growth policies. Of course, LAFCOs have the power to deny annexation and incorporation. The preparation of sphere-of-influence boundaries promises to reduce significantly the undesirable aspects of competition between local governments. LAFCO authority is not all-encompassing, however, and many have hesitated to concern themselves with questions of land use.

OFFICE OF PLANNING AND RESEARCH

In 1959 the legislature created a State Planning Office to "prepare, maintain and regularly review a comprehensive long range general plan for the physical growth and development of the state."[11] After ten years, during which a comprehensive plan failed to materialize, the legislature replaced the State Office of Planning with Office of Planning and Research (OPR). OPR was charged with assisting "in the formulation, evaluation and up-dating of the long-range goals and policies for land use, population growth and distribution, urban expansion, open space, resources preservation and utilization, and other factors that shape statewide development patterns and significantly influence the quality of the state's environment."[12] It was also obliged to evaluate departmental programs, coordinate research activities of the state, and assist the Department of Finance in program budgeting. In short, OPR must co-ordinate the activities of the state government influencing land use and the environment.

To date OPR has not assumed a leading role in promoting coordination among state agencies. Its current limited efforts include monthly meetings of the state agencies' planning chiefs to exchange information, the identification of areas of statewide interest and critical concern, and the unadopted Environmental Goals and Policy Report. Funds will become available to develop criteria and review state agency plans and programs in terms of their compatibility with state goals and policies, if the Environmental Goals and Policy Report is adopted.

REGIONAL COORDINATION EFFORTS

With the exception of the A-95 review process, ABAG has concentrated on the preparation of regional plans, rather than the promotion of coordinated policies at the local level. In connection with the development of regional population growth and distribution objectives, however, ABAG intends to work closely with local agencies in an effort to reach a consensus regarding the allocation of regional growth to cities and counties.[13]

Improved governmental coordination together with existing interagency communication channels have not significantly eliminated gaps in co-ordination. Progress to date has resulted from piecemeal changes in the system rather than the design of an overall land resource management role for each government entity.

NOTES

1. Eckbo, Dean, Austin, & Williams, "State Open Space and Resource Conservation Program for California," for California Legislature Joint Committee on Open Space Lands (April 1972), p. 15.

2. Ibid.

3. Citizens Technical Advisory Committee on Open Space Lands, *Final Report*, for California Legislature Joint Committee on Open Space Lands (January 1970) p. 8.

4. Testimony of Norman Emerson, Executive Director of Joint Committee on Open Space Lands before a hearing of Planning and Land Use Committee of California State Assembly (January 19, 1972).

5. California State Office of Planning, *California State Development Plan Program, Phase II Report* (Sacramento: State Printing Office, 1968), p. 202.

6. Association of Bay Area Governments, *Regional Open Space Plan, Phase II San Francisco Bay Region* (Summary) (1973), p. 7.

7. Association of Bay Area Governments, "Urban Growth Policy for the San Francisco Bay Region," Issue Paper No. 1 (1972), p. 5.

8. Sedway/Cooke Associates, *Regional Ocean Coastline Plan for the San Francisco Bay Area, Phase II*, prepared for the Association of Bay Area Governments, July 1972, p. 17.

9. Richard T. LeGates, "California Local Agency Formation Commissions" (Berkeley University of California, Institute of Governmental Studies, 1970), p. 67.

10. John W. Dyckman, "The Public and Private Rationale for a National Urban Policy," in *Planning for a Nation of Cities*, ed. Sam Bass Warner Jr. (Cambridge: MIT Press, 1966), p. 25.

11. California Government Code, Section 65040.

12. California State Environmental Quality Study Council, *Final Report* (1972), p. 41.

13. Association of Bay Area Governments, "Formulation of Regional Growth Policy for the San Francisco Bay Region," Issue Paper No. 2 (1972), p. 11.

PART

ALTERNATIVES

Open space preservation, has been a topic for debate by many public and private groups. ABAG, representing cities and counties, has a planning program aimed specifically at open space preservation. Research sponsored by the University of California, People for Open Space, and other groups has also focused attention on this phenomenon. It is a principal concern of the Bay Area Council in its overall discussion of regional government.

Although many unresolved questions remain, the discussions concerning land use generally and open space specifically have led to certain areas of consensus. With respect to open space preservation, it is apparent from information previously reported that state, regional, and local governments have different roles in the preservation of open space; acquisition is necessary and desirable, but the preservation of all desired open space cannot be attained only by outright acquisition. Furthermore, zoning has sometimes been ineffective, existing tax policy has not always worked to encourage open space preservation, tax benefits do not necessarily contribute to the preservation of open space permanently needed in urban areas, and the activities of government agencies have not always related to a comprehensive program of open space planning and enforcement.

Many individuals and groups recognize that more needs to be done in encouraging open space preservation. Eliminating barriers to effective preservation does not constitute an insuperable task. Proposals designed to provide government with more land use authority, or revisions aimed at changing the impact of present public policies, may offer great possibilities for achieving additional open space, although they may be difficult to implement. Specific proposals have been advanced to rectify current legal deficiencies and, in general, to cope with the remaining issues lacking agreement. However, a number of questions exist. Should local planning be strengthened? And if so, how? What additional regulatory tools can be made available to governmental agencies? How should tax benefit and other incentive programs be improved? What can be done to facilitate the acquisition of open space? What changes in present tax policy are necessary to encourage orderly, balanced land use and development? How can the public be motivated toward the seemingly inevitable goal of preserving open space without resorting to institutional means?

The pragmatic issue confronting the San Francisco Bay Area concerns the optimum coordination of the open space efforts of state, regional, and local agencies. Effective open space preservation will not occur unless government activities are simultaneously related to an overall coordinated program of regulation and acquisition. The emphasis of these conclusions has focused on government activity because of minimal private individual participation. Except in isolated instances, the private sector is virtually uninvolved in open space preservation. This has necessarily mitigated toward increasing intervention by government at all levels. Although this trend is evident and is recognized as an attempt to deal with open space needs, it should not necessarily be accepted as the only vehicle available to preserve open space.

CHAPTER

8

ALTERNATIVES TO
SUPPLEMENT EXISTING
TECHNIQUES

STRENGTHEN LOCAL PLANNING

Any program of local open space preservation rests on an effective planning process, comprehensive in terms of geographic coverage and helpful in resolving problems extending beyond jurisdictional boundaries. Alternatives to strengthen the local planning process and, therefore, to improve the ability of local communities in effectively planning for open space include an improvement of the ability of cities to annex adjacent land areas, an expansion of the authority of LAFCO, and an enhancement of the quality of planning decisions by more formalized training for planning commissions and others in the local planning process.

Annexation

The preservation of open space areas by local agencies depends, in part, on their ability to effect comprehensive land use planning and regulation. One problem pertains to the city's ability to anticipate and plan for growth, or to control it in urbanized unincorporated areas. A recent article summarizes the problem:

> The problems presented for cities by concentrated urban development within contiguous unincorporated areas are both numerous and serious. Residents of urban fringe areas use city services such as parks, libraries, and streets, and in many instances receive police and fire protection without sharing in the cost. Zoning, subdivision and building regulations, and environmental and land use planning in the suburbs affect the city. The nature and density of development in

139

the fringe area may not only be incompatible with contiguous areas of the city, but may determine the ultimate growth and expansion of the city without the ability of the city to control and plan for the direction, nature, and rate of such growth and expansion, and the ultimate allocation of its own resources. . . .[1]

If cities, as the principal regulators of land use in urban areas, are to effect comprehensive planning, some believe they must be able to adjust their boundaries from time to time by annexation. Under existing law, residents of the area initiate annexation proceedings, and once underway, they decide the annexation question. In a recent study of impediments to comprehensive planning, however, the League of California Cities indicates that city officials complained most bitterly about the inadequacy of annexation laws. For example,

> . . . on annexation . . . the statute is about ten times longer than necessary, filled with special legislation, and is much too cumbersome . . . compared with incorporation it is still easier to incorporate than annex in California. . . . That is not the way it should be . . . too much power is given to property owners and voters. I would be inclined to give agencies such as LAFCO substantially more powers to initiate.
>
> Annexation procedures are time consuming . . . intricate . . . elaborate as hell. . . .
>
> There are many areas that should be in the city, but the statutes are too cumbersome . . . they are extremely time consuming for one small annexation . . . the vote requirements are unreasonable and represent a major problem.
>
> Present law discourages balanced annexation . . . it forces a city to gerrymander in order to exclude those who will vote against. . . .
>
> Annexation is a major problem . . . both the lack of ability on the part of the city to initiate island annexations, and the practical inability to annex large inhabited areas.
>
> No progress has been made with respect to annexing inhabited areas.[2]

Although not as critical in some of the Bay Area urbanized counties, annexation in relatively undeveloped areas can be important to open space preservation programs. It can also be important in developed areas in assuring that unincorporated pockets or islands of land are developed consistent with the open space goals of adjacent corporated areas. Cities, in other words, find little assurance that balanced development will occur, including the orderly preservation of open space, without regulatory land control over their entire planning area. Facilitating annexation can improve the ability of cities to provide open space buffers by controlling growth and development on its fringe, and it can also help to minimize serious coordination problems between cities and counties. The right to initiate annexation of areas adjacent to the city, still dependent on a vote of the residents, would at least place the issue before LAFCO.

Business interests, private electric utilities, and homeowners in unincorporated areas argue against the liberalization of annexation laws. Businesses, principally concerned with the possibility of increased tax potentially resulting from annexation, point to city property taxes and municipal business license taxes—revenue sources that are presently unavailable to counties. Although only 15 California cities provide electric service, private electric utilities fear that cities may use annexation to increase their own electric service area. Homeowners in unincorporated areas apprehend higher taxes and the possible loss of local control of their area's character.

Some argue that cities have permitted development without regard for open space, contending that the ease with which cities annex adjacent unincorporated land areas merely speeds development and compounds existing open space preservation problems. Thus, while increased ability to annex unincorporated areas could be an advantage to progressive cities with strong open space planning programs, it could also serve to affect adversely open space in less committed cities. Opponents assert, moreover, this alternative would perpetuate the narrower interests of some cities, rather than provide for more comprehensive approaches to land use control.

Expanding LAFCOs

Local Agency Formation Commissions exist in every California county and have the responsibility to approve, deny, or conditionally approve proposals for annexation, incorporation, or the creation of special districts. Each LAFCO governing board comprises two city representatives, two county representatives, and one public member, but may also include two special district representatives under authority granted in recent legislation. Although represented on the governing board, local officials apparently have not been pleased with LAFCO's performance. They have criticized LAFCO because they believe decisions tend to be weighted in favor of cities or counties. Others consider LAFCO too political, citing its difficulty in reaching decisions. On the other hand, some local officials believe that LAFCO has been helpful, acting constructively. This viewpoint generally upholds a 1970 evaluation of the statewide operation of LAFCOs conducted by the Institute of Governmental Studies (IGS) at the University of California at Berkeley.

LAFCOs have brought little change in the annual rate of annexation, incorporations, and special district formation ... [but] the significant feature of LAFCO activity appears to be their rejection of unacceptable proposals and the imposing of conditions on others to eliminate undesirable provisions.[3]

Because LAFCOs offer an opportunity under existing law for a review of proposals broader than those received from city and county, and because the involvement of both city and county officials in LAFCO deliberations could strike a balance between city-county considerations, the local planning process might be improved by providing LAFCO with additional responsibility, particularly in the absence of a broader regional or state agency with similar authority. The IGS evaluation found that "the bulk of LAFCO problems occur in dealing with the fringe areas around existing cities,"[4] where they confront critical open space considerations.

If studies indicate that annexation should proceed more rapidly in certain areas, but that individual cities should not receive additional authority, LAFCO might be given the responsibility to initiate or require annexation. Such authority would facilitate the improved management of government services in urban areas and would presumably better enable cities to plan and control development. Counties facing the potential loss of county tax base, however, might well oppose proposals facilitating or requiring the annexation of land to cities. Business, private utilities, and homeowners would also tend to oppose extensions of LAFCO authority.

If annexation is not practical, cities and counties could alternatively be required jointly to zone land within the city "sphere of influence," referring unresolved questions to LAFCO for binding action. Although cities and counties presently engage in cooperative planning activities, the legislative body of either the city or the county need not respect a joint planning decision. Cities and counties might be encouraged to make more permanent, meaningful agreements if LAFCO were mandated to resolve disputes. Of course, more effective cooperation between cities and counties in the planning area would help to assure similar open space goals. This, in turn, should promote consideration of open space before development occurs.

It might also be desirable to provide LAFCO with direct authority in reconciling annexation and incorporation proposals and sphere-of-influence boundaries with city and county plans. The law obliges LAFCO to consider proposals in "conformity with appropriate city or county general or specified plans." It does not include open space plans, however, in determining the sphere of influence, nor does it provide that LAFCO decisions be consistent with the open space plans of local agencies, a requirement ensuring that the future expansion of cities and special district occurs in a manner found by LAFCO to be consistent with the open space objectives of local plans.

Those opposed to these measures argue that they go beyond the primary purposes of LAFCO to promote more efficient government services. Enabling legislation, they say, implies such authority and, in any event, should not be bound inflexibly into state law. Moreover, municipal government might possibly view any increase in LAFCO's authority as an unwarranted, undesirable loss of city control.

Training Programs

Locally elected officials bear the primary responsibility for developing open space plans and meshing supporting future actions. They receive assistance in all counties and most cities from appointed representatives on the planning commission, who are responsible for reviewing planning proposals and recommending specific action to the local legislative body. Effective service on these bodies essentially requires a basic understanding of local planning responsibility and authority. Cities and counties are increasingly obliged to comply with legislative mandates in the planning area and respond to court decisions that continually change regulatory procedures. Yet, drafting and implementing a comprehensive land use plan presupposes an understanding of planning interrelationships, the functions of zoning, and development regulations and prohibitions.

Perhaps local agencies could accomplish more in preserving open space by the vigorous use of regulatory controls. But planning commissioners and local legislators appear to be only generally aware of their real authority. For example, according to a 1972 study of local planning in California conducted by the State Council on Intergovernmental Relations (CIR),

> less than one-quarter of all the cities and counties have an established program designed to train or educate planning commissioners. A majority of the jurisdictions without such a program also lack the services of a professional city planner and, in them, the commissioner is forced to play the role of both layman and technician.[5]

The CIR survey indicates that only 21 percent of those cities and counties had developed an educational program for planning commissioners and, of that number, 37 percent limited it to study sessions related to current planning activities.[6] Accredited training for local officials and the establishment of attendance requirements or incentive programs would help to assure that those serving in local decision-making capacities have some practical insight into the technical and legal framework of planning.

Some communities, not having experienced a need for concentrated planning, might regard training as a waste of time and money. Others might object because some citizens would be unable or unwilling to serve on planning commissions. On the other hand, good planning requires fundamental understanding of the overall area, and a brief training session represents an economical method in achieving improved land use, thus an improved ability to preserve open space.

ADDITIONAL LAND USE CONTROLS

The impossibility of acquiring in fee the land area necessary for open space purposes has now become obvious. Government ability and responsibility to preserve open space by zoning and subdivision regulations has accordingly received more emphasis. Indeed, virtually every major study of open space preservation in California, including the major Urban Metropolitan Open Space Study prepared for the state in 1965, reaches this conclusion. Reliance on land control as a technique to preserve open space has generated discussion regarding its use for this purpose. Recent court decisions and legislation tending to liberalize the authority of public agencies have not clarified existing authority.

It follows that the authority of local agencies to condemn land for open space purposes, to establish a land banking system, compensable regulations, or development rights transfer mechanisms could alternatively supplement land use control.

Authority of Local Agencies to Condemn Land for Open Space

Present law required local agencies to prepare an open space plan and implementation program no later than June 30, 1973. To achieve this, some local agencies may have found it necessary to acquire certain land. Traditionally, public agencies have been able to condemn land for a public purpose, paying the fair market value at the time of acquisition, in order to extend or widen a road, to construct a building, or develop a park. However, whether public purpose includes the right to acquire full or partial interest in land through condemnation simply for broad open space or aesthetic purposes remains unclear. The Government Code provides that

> it is the intent of the Legislature in enacting this chapter to provide a means whereby any county or city may acquire by purchase, gift, grant, bequest, device, lease or otherwise . . . the fee or any lesser interest or right in real property in order to preserve, through limitation of their future use, open spaces and areas for public use and enjoyment.[7]

The "or otherwise" may not provide sufficient authority for local agencies to use condemnation as an open space preservation technique and some experts suggest that the authority of local agencies should be clarified. The California Joint Legislative Committee on Open Space Lands in its 1972 report entitled "State Open Space and Resource Conservation Program for California" has recognized this problem.

> . . . it is recommended that the legislature provide cities and counties the power to administer, manage, acquire, lease, sell and trade open space lands in accordance with adopted open space elements and plans and extend to them the right of eminent domain for condemnation of fee and less than fee interest for open space acquisition.
>
> Cities and counties do not presently have all of these powers and authority to implement their open space programs. Of particular concern is the lack of eminent domain powers for fee and less than fee acquisition for many important categories of open space.[8]

Some public and private agencies support this alternative.

Landowners, concerned with this type of authority because of its potential broad application, have asserted that the unlimited right to condemn land is too nebulous, that its implementation would unfairly restrict individual action. They also believe such authority could result in great loss to landowners because of the difficulty in determining fair market value at the time of condemnation. Others, noting the major departure from traditional condemnation authority, question the constitutional validity of condemnation of less-than-fee property interests.

Land Banking

Bay Area citizens have manifested an interest in restricting and, in some cases, prohibiting growth. While generally not endorsing the "no-growth" concept, some local agencies have rigorously controlled growth. Low density zoning, limitations on the number of building permits issued annually, and more specific development policies have become increasingly apparent throughout the area.

Specialists have suggested a system of land banking (the public acquisition of land for subsequent public or private development) to control growth and development comprehensively, at the same time preserving and more effectively planning for open space areas. It has already been applied to a limited extent by local agencies in California—particularly in the development of tideland areas and by the state in conjunction with acquisition for future highway purposes. Numerous studies, including the recent National Commission on Urban Problems report, *Building the American City*, recommend

> that state governments enact legislation enabling state and/or local development authorities or agencies of general purpose governments to acquire land in advance of development for the following purposes: (a) assuring the continuing availability of sites needed for development; (b) controlling the timing, location, type and scale of development; (c) preventing urban sprawl; and (d) reserving to the public gains in land values resulting from the action of government in promoting and servicing development. At a minimum, such legislation should authorize the acquisition of land surrounding highway interchanges. At such times as development of such land is deemed to be appropriate and in the interests of the region, it could be sold or leased at no less than its fair market value for private development in accordance with approved plans . . . long-term leases should be the preferred method of disposing of any public land, and lease terms should be set so as to permit reassembly of properties for future replanning and development. Legislation should specify a maximum period that such land may be held by the public before lease or sale.[9]

Advocates of land banking, citing government responsibility for comprehensive land use planning, assert that government should be able to control development. Others contend that it can control prices, thus making land available at a minimum cost for low-income housing, public facilities, and other purposes. It also gives government the incremental increase in land values resulting from population growth and public services.

Proposals for land banking generally based on the experience of other countries, notably Sweden, do not lack opponents. A recent Urban Institute report, *Land Banking: Public Policy Alternatives and Dilemmas*, indicates the Swedish example would "mitigate against any simple transferability" to the United States. It points to Sweden's tradition of public land ownership, the relative local governmental fiscal autonomy, the comparative secrecy of Swedish planning with a minimum of citizen participation, and that cities have always played a dominant role in suburban development.[10]

Broadly based land banking would require a state or regional agency. Moreover, the ability of local communities to implement their respective land use plans without the representation of local government officials would be restricted, with little assurance of local accountability. Land banking on a large scale might be impractical because of the large investment required and the impact on the property tax of large land purchases by public agencies. Conceivably, the entire fiscal structure of local government would need revision. Acquiring land for open space and permitting development under state and local regulation might cost less. Public acquisition of large areas might also encourage inflation of private land prices in adjacent areas. Critics of broad governmental intervention in the development process also see the possibility of abuse or mismanagement by authorities in the lease or sale of banked lands. Finally, they claim public ownership of land often means that no one owns it: farmers and tenants not owning their land would have no natural motivation toward conservation.

Compensable Regulation

Legal and political zoning limitations have generally constrained the open space preservation actions of local agencies in the area. Actual or threatened reduction of land values has been the principal limitation on individual property rights resulting from development prohibitions. The National Commission on Urban Problems points out that "it is becoming apparent ... that many public land use objectives will not be achieved by complete reliance on police power techniques.[11] A system of compensable regulation that moves beyond the limitations of pure zoning does not exist in the United States. The recent People for Open Space report, "Economic Analysis of a Regional Open Space Program," describes the concept:

> The term "compensable regulation" means that a landowner would be compensated for any loss in value occasioned by the regulation of his land ... lands to be retained in privately owned open space would be designated, mapped, and zoned for specific uses, such as intensive agriculture, dairy farming, or areas to guide development. Property owners would be guaranteed that whenever they chose to sell their lands in the open market, they would receive at least the price of the lands before regulation, adjusted to changes in the value of the dollar. . . .
>
> Property owners would be taxed only on the open space use of their lands; owners who wish to retain their lands would not be affected by the compensable regulation.

Individual appraisals would be made of each parcel of land . . . and this would become the guaranteed price. Provision would be made for an appeal of these appraisals by property owners. If the owner sells his land for his guaranteed price or more, no compensation is necessary. If an owner is unable to sell for a price equal to his guarantee, a board of review would authorize him to sell at a public auction. After the auction, the owner would file proof with the board of review of the net price received by him and of the costs of the sale. The board would then adjust the owner's guarantee for the land to reflect changes in the value of the dollar since establishment of the guarantee.[12]

Those advocating compensable regulation believe this open space preservation technique, combining full fee acquisition and zoning, may fill an important void, with the advantage of balancing the interest of the landowner and the public agency. Because the designated open space remains privately owned, public agencies need not accumulate the funds for full-fee acquisition, nor must the landowner sell because of competitive land uses or higher taxes. Moreover, traditional concepts of property rights would not be violated, because compensation for prohibitive restrictions would be provided, thus removing a major constraint to effective, lasting regulation of open space.

On the other hand, opponents see several disadvantages. Landowners would lose future increases in their property value. A program involving detailed appraisal of property and unknown actions of private landowners could be impractical because of the dubious permanency of the regulations that assumes the government has condemnation power for open space purposes. Its application to urban fringe, or other areas with high land value, would require, of course, a high guaranteed value and would result in substantial compensation costs, particularly if the regulated land has little or no economic utility. If the administrators consider deregulation of an area desirable but have already compensated the original landowner, the public investment in open space preservation would be lost.

Development Rights Transfer

In recent years this innovative concept, which proposes a different mechanism to accomplish the same objective, has emerged. Development rights transfer was originally designed to preserve historical landmarks. New York City adopted a resolution permitting the transfer of development rights from designated historic landmarks to adjacent lots as early as 1968.[13] A plan similar to the New York ordinance, but incorporating a number of improvements, has also been proposed to protect landmarks in the Chicago Loop area.[14] Legislation enabling development of rights transfer has been introduced in New Jersey and Maryland,[15] and the city of Lafayette in the Bay Area has proposed a transfer ordinance to preserve its hillsides.[16] Based on the Anglo-Saxon "development rights" concept, these propositions legally acknowledged that an owner may build on his land. Rights can be bought and sold separately from the land and from other rights connected with it, subject to reasonable regulation under the police power and power of eminent domain.

One model for applying development rights transfer to open space incorporates features of both the Lafayette proposal and the "Chicago Plan."[17] It involves the initial establishment by a city, county, or regional agency of an open space zone with appropriate controls to protect land recommended for preservation by the general plan. Concomitantly, the jurisdiction designates "development rights transfer districts," undeveloped or partially developed areas where increased residential densities might be accommodated without unduly overcrowding services. "Development rights certificates" would be issued to each land owner whose land is preserved as open space, based on the property's development potential. Previous zoning classifications on the open space land would be used as a base density with factors such as slope density formulae and hillside grading ordinances applied to reach a "modified density." The acres multipled by the modified density would determine the number of certificates assigned to each parcel. Each certificate would have a value of one dwelling unit, or a similar measure of development potential. The number of rights divided into the difference between the market value of the property and its residual value as open space would determine the case value of each development right certificate. A property owner could transfer development potential from one area of his property to another, if plans and regulations permitted, or sell his rights to a developer of another parcel within a "development rights" transfer district. Establishment of planned unit provisions for all undeveloped parcels of five acres or more would allow greater flexibility in accommodating transferred densities. As a safeguard against overdevelopment, a transferee could not increase his authorized density by more than 15 percent. Appropriate deed covenants and restrictions would prevent the reacquisition and application of development rights, once relinquished, to an open space parcel. Taxation would reflect only the open space value of the land. Thus, while the overall number of units would not increase, the distribution and density of development within the city would vary from existing residential zoning classifications.

Development rights transfer would enable the preservation of open space land while compensating the owner for the reduced value of his land. Because the private sector would make compensation and the land would remain in private ownership, excessive government costs, increased tax burdens, liability, and management problems are avoided. The land stays on the tax rolls albeit at a lower assessed value. The increased density of subsequent development results in more efficient land use while existing zoning becomes less rigid, allowing greater innovation in planning.

However, development rights transfer could create problems. One centers on the fluctuation in value of development rights stemming from future market conditions. The success of development rights transfer clearly depends on the creation of development rights, the initial value reflecting an approximation of their intrinsic value on the open market—an unknown factor. Yet, the base density of prior zoning classifications and the land's development value will constrain the initial value. If the value of development rights stays at a high level, developers will not invest the additional capital to increase the authorized density of their projects. Theoretically, the value of an owner's development rights would then decrease, indicating the developer's willingness to pay. The owners of unsold development rights would then be unable to obtain payment for their land. Moreover, as the capability of transfer districts to absorb additional density decreased, the value of development rights would also decrease. Developers might also concentrate their efforts in other jurisdictions, thereby depressing the local real estate market. The elimination of locational factors influencing the open space landowner's potential gain on the sale of his property creates an additional economic disadvantage, because the marketability of development rights certificates would depend on their cash value and supply and demand. Consequently, owners of high-value land would find their investment less marketable than that of property owners with land valued lower.

The creation of a municipal development rights bank, analogous to the Federal Reserve Board, represents a possible means of circumventing these economic uncertainties. The bank would be authorized to sell development rights. To avoid political manipulation, a development rights bank, of course, would be an independent municipal corporation. A problem concerns the congestion and strain on municipal services resulting from increased densities. One New York commentator concludes that

> unused rights will always flow to those areas where the commercial advantages of concentration make transfer economically attractive. If this existing concentration is attended by its usual effects—if the subways and buses are overloaded; the streets, clogged; the air, polluted; and the few remaining open spaces, in the perpetual shadow of surrounding office or apartment towers—then development rights transfer can only make life more miserable.[18]

Similarly, overcrowded schools, inadequate suburban services, and congestion may well increase in the absence of close cooperation between local departments and agencies, careful regulation of new development, and the consideration of service capability in the development rights transfer districts. Moreover, political opposition to increased density, always a factor in local land use decisions, could place local officials in an untenable position, facing development proposals involving transferred development rights.

Opponents of development rights transfer proposals note their dubious impact on increased housing costs, bureaucratic confusion and unwieldiness, and other incentive zoning programs, notably density bonuses for low-cost housing and project design open space. In addition, when no reference point for the establishment of development rights units exists, the problem of arriving at a suitable measure of the land's development potential arises. Finally, transfer proposals engender legal problems, for example, equal protection, although in most cases there appears to be sufficient precedent for legal challenges.

Another comprehensive approach to development rights transfer has the unit value of development rights determined by the community's ability to absorb new development, rather than the individual parcel's development potential. The local planning agency would arbitrarily assign a cash value to one development right, with certificates issued to the owners of undeveloped and underdeveloped land based on the appraised value of their property. The agency would then prescribe the number of development rights for each housing unit and each square foot of commercial and industrial space to be developed, based on the general plan's projected densities. The Professional Engineers Tahoe Committee has suggested that the unit value should reflect the environmental impacts of various land uses.[19]

An owner lacking sufficient rights to fully develop his land would need to purchase additional rights in the open market. For example, an owner of 100 acres of developable land valued at $500,000 might be issued 100 development rights certificates valued at $5,000 each. Planning considerations might determine that each development right enjoys a value of three housing units, thus permitting a 300-home subdivision. However, the developer may wish to develop to the zoned land capacity: four units per acre; thus he would purchase 33 additional certificates at a cost of $165,000 from an owner of restricted property. Closely correlating with general plan objectives, this approach avoids problems of increased density, and other incentive zoning programs remain unaffected.

Unpredictable market conditions, increased housing costs, and administrative complications could create potential problems, with effects on the real estate market for undeveloped land. Developers, faced with a potentially substantial additional capital outlay to develop land to previously allowable densities, might be unwilling or unable to purchase additional development rights. Initially this could result in a depressed real estate market and a drop in land value. Thus owners of developable land would be disadvantaged by the regulations, although future buyers would be relatively unaffected, because open space preservation costs would be transferred from one group of landowners to another. The courts might view the taking of development potential from owners of developable land as arbitrary and unreasonable, therefore unconstitutional. The legal problem involving the imposition of density limitations in conflict with existing zoning classifications also stands out, but it might be avoided by replacing traditional zoning with ordinances linking land use to general plan policy and performance standards.[20]

Any system of development rights transfer is clearly feasible only under certain conditions. The amount of open space land to be preserved, anticipated future growth, existing land values, and environmental tolerance to increased densities will determine the number and value of development rights available for transfer.

IMPROVEMENT OF TAX BENEFIT PROGRAMS

Adjacent land use changes and resultant increases in assessed value often influence a landowner's decision regarding the disposition of his property and discourage the preservation of open space, particularly in urban areas. In some cases, the economic situation allows no choice: it is clearly an advantage to sell or develop. However, available programs permitting him to contract voluntarily with a public agency, thus obtaining benefits in retaining his land, may influence the landowner's decision. Tax benefit programs theoretically hold that private landowners can be encouraged to agree to leave their land in open space for a specified period if its assessed value during that period is reduced. These programs remain basic to the implementation of any overall open space plan because they face the crux of the problem—namely, the economic considerations initially encouraging the landowner to sell or develop his property.

California law presently allows tax benefit programs for lands subject to scenic restrictions, open space easements, and land conservation contracts. The most well known and widely used, the Williamson Act, has been applied to over 11 million acres of California open space. Some critics have contended, nonetheless, that the act should be replaced with a more permanent and selective open space preservation program: "All we're buying for $40 million is some short term holding device . . . for $40 million we could buy the lands and lease them back to farmers."[2][1] However, in the absence of sufficient funds for open space acquisition, abandonment of the act would create a serious gap in open space preservation programs. Measures to improve the Williamson Act and programs to encourage greater reliance on it represent two alternatives, short of abandonment, which address its inherent problems. Tax deferral could also be instituted as a supplemental program.

Measures to Improve the Williamson Act

Legislation restricting agricultural preserves to land designated in local open space plans, limiting agricultural preserves to within three miles of planned urban areas, increasing tax penalties for cancellation and nonrenewal of contracts, and extending the minimum contractual term from 10 to 20 years might improve the Williamson Act.[2][2] These proposals stem from the notion that widespread reliance on the act is undesirable, and that it is more effective in conjunction with other open space preservation programs. More permanent contracts would provide better protection of open space areas and eliminate the act's potential use by speculators to obtain interim tax advantages prior to development, some believe. Prohibition of agricultural preserves beyond three miles from planned urban areas would minimize the fiscal hardships imposed on rural local agencies and reflect limited development potential in outlying areas.

Agricultural interests argue that the exclusion of rural areas fails to recognize increasing economic hardships facing ranching and other farming enterprises, adding that it contradicts a major objective of the act, namely to preserve agricultural lands. Opponents also assert that measures to encourage permanency are premature since the act has only been in existence since 1965, further noting that the restriction of applicability to urban areas together with stronger contractual obligations represents a contradiction that would render the act inoperative.

The Williamson Act in Urban Areas

The view that the act is adequate but that its greater utilization would advance open space objectives underlies proposals to encourage more urban landowners to participate in the program. Increased state subventions to local agencies, tax rebates to contracting landowners, enhanced programs to promote awareness and encourage acceptance of the act among urban landowners, and plans to improve the economic stability of agricultural enterprises might help. Some specialists believe the institution of these proposals would remedy the act's failure to guarantee open space in areas of greatest need. Increased financial support, at least to school districts and other agencies having no open space responsibility, is a justifiable government policy and would augment waning receptivity of some local officials to the act. A tax rebate, based on a fraction of taxes previously paid for open space land's development potential, would perhaps ameliorate the landowner's hesitancy to use the act. New commitments to open space in local plans underscore the need for public officials to institute public information programs concerning property owners entering into land conservation contracts.

Finally, concomitant efforts to ease the difficulties of agricultural production appear essential if farmers and ranchers near urban areas are to maintain economically viable operations. The Santa Clara County Planning Department, commenting on the future of agriculture in the southern Santa Clara Valley, observes that in addition to the development of new crops and improved production practices,

> new methods of marketing some of the existing crops may be a better solution for some of the local farmers close to urban areas . . . production of organically grown fruit and produce, roadside stands, pick-your-own type of marketing, and perhaps, the development of "rent-a-tree" or "rent-a-row" units in which the farmer would supply the land, perform some of the major cultural operations but would leave the crop and its harvesting and disposal to the renter.
>
> . . . recreation immediately stands out as a desirable alternative. . . . Obvious possibilities are hiking, bicycling, horseback riding, camping, hunting, as well as fishing, boating and swimming. . . . The setting aside of designated areas for off-road vehicles and motorcycles may be environmentally more acceptable than permitting wide proliferation of these pursuits where they cannot be readily controlled. Well-planned equestrian centers and possibly some large riding preserves where people could ride over well developed trails with some possible campsites and watering facilities could take advantage of the "horse boom."
>
> . . . Public financed policies to assist such undertakings could include license waiver, improved transportation facilities, and promotional programs. Such policies would need to contain sufficient controls as to maintain acceptable open space and environmental standards.[23]

Increased financial aid and tax rebates raise the question: Would the benefits derived be worth the additional costs? Annual subventions eventually represent a substantial commitment of funds that might be better spent, for example, to purchase development rights. Similarly, whether incentive programs, better comprehension of the Williamson Act, or other measures to promote its implementation will overcome the tendency of landowners to opt for a potentially large profit from the sale of their land, remain problematical.

Voluntary Tax Deferral

The Williamson Act permits owners to restrict the use of their land for a specified time in exchange for permanent tax relief during this period. As an inducement to maintain their land in its present state, landowners would be permitted to defer temporarily all or a portion of current property taxes for a maximum of 20 years. This alternative foresees a significant reduction in current tax liability, decreasing the pressure for immediate land development.

Proposals permitting individuals to defer taxes, criticized as poor public policy on the grounds that such authority will encourage personal fiscal irresponsibility rather than the preservation of open space, may establish a precedent in other disputed areas of taxation. It might also result in excessive costs for government because of more expensive assessment practices and litigation to recover back taxes. At some point, deferred taxes could equal or exceed the value of land in question, placing government in the unhappy position of incurring a loss or forcing an individual to sell his land. A government loss might be passed on to other taxpayers, thus actually encouraging speculation by minimizing current tax liability on an interest-free basis. A tax rebate limit, imposed to prevent forced sale, would constitute an outright grant at the expense of other taxpayers.

FACILITATING OPEN SPACE ACQUISITION

Any open space program needs adequate revenues to acquire land. In this regard, outright acquisition of land by state and local government is the most effective method. However, the "Urban Metropolitan Open Space Study," sponsored by California in 1965, indicated that purchasing all land recommended as open space throughout the state would cost approximately $4 billion. "If only the highest encroachment areas were to be acquired," it reports, "they would cost almost $3 billion."[24] The People for Open Space organization estimated that acquiring approximately 1.4 million acres of Bay Area open space land would need $1.9 billion.[25]

Obviously, state and local agencies lack the revenue sources for an acquisition program of these dimensions. Government agencies have largely deferred many needed capital outlay items, including open space. The League of California Cities reported that "two-thirds of all cities forecast a substantial deficit in revenue for fiscal year 1972-73 just to continue providing existing services at present levels."[26] Despite revenue sharing and the 1972 State Tax Reform Program, counties, schools, and state government confront similar problems.

Thus, present revenues cannot finance an acquisition program. If, as many suggest, acquisition forms a basic part of open space preservation, additional funds must be forthcoming. The 1970 Annual Report of the Joint Committee on Open Space Lands concludes, "It seems certain that the commitment of a substantial amount of money on a regular annual basis is vital if any long range program of preserving open space land is to be realized."[27] Alternatives facilitating state and local acquisition of open space land include permission for local agencies to levy new taxes, provisions for new state and local tax sources, and the sponsorship of a state bond act for open space purposes.

New Taxes by Local Agencies

California's cities and counties now include open space elements in their general plans that incorporate "action plans." Their implementation will conceivably require the planned acquisition of certain open space lands, but local agencies enjoy few revenue sources for this purpose. Before 1972, the property tax represented the major revenue source controlled to some degree by cities and counties. The 1972 State Tax Reform Program, however, limiting local agencies in raising additional revenue from this source, established the property tax rate levied by individual cities and counties in 1972-73 as the tax rate ceiling for those agencies. Adjustments for changes in population and the cost of living by the amount necessary for debt servicing and approved pension plans and by any additional amount approved by the voters subsequent to 1972-73 may nonetheless exceed this ceiling.[28]

Counties had no property tax rate limit, and cities had a $1.00 per $100 of assessed valuation limit before 1972, although cities could exceed the $1.00 limit for various purposes, including parks and recreation. Therefore, enabling local agencies to acquire open space lands may necessitate the reinstatement of city and county authority to exceed their present tax rate limits.

Proponents argue that a reliable source must be available to local agencies for the successful implementation of their open space plans. The permissive authority represented by this alternative would require local communities to assume the political responsibility for imposing additional property taxes. Of course, it would help to make local governing bodies more fiscally responsible, and the basic authority would also provide local agencies with a stable, reliable revenue source for open space acquisition. Because the alternative provides an exception to the overall tax rate limit, sacrificing other important local programs to implement the open space plan would be unnecessary. It recognizes, moreover, an arbitrary property tax rate limit varying from community to community. Periodic exceptions to the limit may be necessary in order to resolve major public problems. In this regard, proponents note that an election cost can be high, and the practical chances of its success minimal—even with an issue as popular as open space preservation.

Opponents note that high property taxes, forcing landowners to develop their property, makes open space preservation difficult. They believe that a greater reliance on the property tax and the relaxation of statutory limitations for one purpose will increase pressures for further exceptions, leading to a gradual erosion of the law. They argue, furthermore, that present law has a flexible quality that permits a community to depend more heavily on the property tax if the issue is sufficiently important to receive a majority vote of approval.

New State and Local Tax Sources for Open Space

Property tax rate limitations and the commitment of existing revenue have led some specialists to propose new sources to finance open space land acquisition. These include property transfer tax, unearned increment tax, and additional sales tax on recreational items.

Property Transfer Tax

A real property transfer tax, long imposed by the federal government, was never used as a major revenue source. In 1967, Congress accordingly repealed the tax, making it available as a new source of state and local revenue. Shortly thereafter, California cities and counties received authority to impose local property transfer taxes, presently levied at a rate of $.55 per $500 of value, applying to the equity in real property being transferred. With application to the purchase price of all real property transfers and with a slightly increased rate, this tax could potentially raise substantial revenue.

The California Assembly Select Committee on Open Space Lands in 1972 estimated that a 1 percent tax, without exemptions, could produce $175 million per annum.[29] Tied to property value, with a stable annual yield, it would tend to increase with economy growth. Because cities and counties presently levy the tax, administrative costs would be negligible. By exempting a minimum transfer, that is, the first $20,000 on all single-family residential property, equity would pose no problem. Because it tends to tax the increase in value from development and provision of public services, in turn creating a need for additional open space, some view this revenue source as particularly appropriate. On a "benefits-received" basis, the tax appears justifiable because the value increase relates to government services. Also, from an open space standpoint, the tax tends to make speculation less profitable, which, to some extent, should contribute to more orderly land development.

The property transfer tax for the acquisition of open space lands becomes a problem because of its present use as a source of revenue for California's cities and counties. Although now a minimal source, local agencies will probably take the position that the state legislature, in providing the initial authorization to impose a 1967 uniform local tax, theoretically reserved the tax for them. Basic opposition will probably come from those viewing it as another property tax, who will argue that it mitigates against providing property tax relief. Developers will contend, moreover, that they already must comply with many costly requirements of public agencies when subdividing land, including the dedication of park land. They will also emphasize the unfairness of the tax, which applies to the total purchase price, rather than the increase in value since acquisition.

Increment Tax

Unlike the property transfer tax, the increment tax, applying only to land, would be levied against that land value representing an increase between acquisition and transfer dates. Variations of the basic proposal could measure the incremental increase between the date of acquisition and a change in zoning, or the development of the property.

Theoretically, an increment tax resembles a property transfer tax, namely, that development and government services enhance land value. Government recaptures a portion of that unearned value through the increment tax, and it thus relates to a need for additional open space, just as the gasoline tax creates a need for additional transit facilities. To the extent that it might curb speculation, it would also impact the overall open space problem. Because the tax would apply to an increase in assessed value, it presumably would measure ability to pay. It should not, however, create an undue burden on landowners because it applies only to an increase in value, remaining unpaid until the actual property transfer.

Although other countries have successfully used an increment tax, critics here contend that it would create administrative problems far outweighing any advantages. In any event, it would clearly impose new requirements on tax administrators. In computing the incremental value, they would perforce distinguish between the inflationary increase and the real growth attributable to development and the provision of public services. They would be additionally responsible for calculating the value of improvements made by the landowner and property taxes paid during the incremental periods, because these would be deducted from any taxable growth and value. They would need to ascertain the accuracy of property assessments on the purchase date and to determine actual value in the absence of a cash transfer. Finally, the increment tax confronts the complex problem of allocating gains between state and local agencies in an equitable manner.

Sales Tax on Recreational Items

The California sales tax applies to tangible personal property, but not to the sale of food, drugs, or personal services. The current rate is 5 percent,* with 3.75 percent earmarked for the state, 1.25 percent for cities and counties. Of the amount for cities and counties, .25 percent emanated from the recent extension of the tax base to gasoline that must be used, in most cases, for public transit facilities. Because of the general concern about placing an increased tax burden on property, some have suggested that the sales tax represents a more likely revenue source to acquire open space land. Perhaps an

---

*Sales tax in San Francisco, Alameda, and Contra Costa counties is 5.5 percent—.50 percent to pay for BART.

additional sales tax on recreational items would be appropriate, they submit, justifiable on the same grounds as the recent extension of the sales tax to gasoline. In other words, just as gasoline is used to provide funds for highways, so should recreational items be used to provide funds for open space acquisition. According to this reasoning, those persons purchasing recreational items are more likely to use and appreciate open space land and, therefore, they should bear a major part of the responsibility for financing its acquisition.

Proponents also note California's long experience with the administration of a state and local sales tax assuring minimum administrative cost increases and the promptly effective resolution of ensuing technical problems. They also contend that economic growth increases and that more leisure time will produce more future revenue. The California Assembly Committee on Revenue and Taxation recently estimated that a 5 percent additional sales tax on the sale of recreational vehicles alone would yield $20 million annually.[30]

On the other hand, critics insist that an additional tax on recreational items will only create undue administrative problems for the state and the businessman. Each "recreational" sale would require a separate determination for the additional sales tax. Quasi-recreational items would add to the general confusion. Retailers would find it difficult to report taxable transactions accurately, thus complicating state auditing. Some experts thus suggest that a surcharge on the overall sales tax would be more appropriate.

A State Bond Act for Open Space

In 1964, California approved a bond to acquire and develop park and recreational facilities, but the funds from this have been expended. A similar State Beach, Park and Recreation and Historical Facilities Bond Act in the amount of $250 million was on the ballot in June 1974, and was approved. It provides $135 million and $90 million to state and local agencies respectively, for the acquisition and development of real property. The balance, $25 million, will be available for the preservation of wildlife and historical resources. The revenues from the bond act, although helpful, remain inadequate to meet the cost estimates for open space projected in the San Francisco Bay Area and in the state.

Those favoring this approach point out that a bond act has traditionally raised a large amount of money for a single purpose without severely affecting the state and local government tax structure or revenue base. Individuals will enjoy future open space preserved today. Thus, a bond act, paid for by future as well as present beneficiaries, becomes particularly appropriate, they asserted. Tax increases, not necessarily producing large annual amounts of revenue, cannot be compared with a bond act and its one-time generation of much revenue. It also permits acquisition of large amounts of land at current costs, thus avoiding future inflationary price increases. Bond act opponents argue that the long-term interest cost will equal, or exceed, any saving accruing from early purchase. They prefer to finance an open space preservation program by a new tax source, more stable and longer lasting than bonds, arguing that the need to act is immediate, and that a bond issue can result in unfortunate delays, failing to provide funds.

EXISTING TAX POLICY CHANGES

Tax revisions seem to many observers the sine qua non of preserving open space land. Although numerous factors undoubtedly prompt a landowner's decision regarding the ultimate use of his property, the tax structure obviously exerts a major influence. The extent to which government agencies rely on the property tax as a source of revenue, for example, or the policies and practices of the local assessor, can directly impact the possibility or feasibility of holding land as open space. The capital gains treatment under income tax laws may also help to encourage or discourage speculation. The allocation of available revenue also bears directly on a government agency's ability to acquire open space land.

Proposals for changes in tax policy to preserve open space include the révision of the local tax base by less reliance on property taxes and more on income taxes, the transfer of responsibility for financing education and welfare services to the state or federal government, the equalization of local revenue sources, and the placement of a heavier tax burden on land, rather than improvements to land.

Revision of Local Tax Base

Cities, counties, school districts, and special districts currently rely on the property tax as their principal revenue source. Experience tells us, however, that the expenditures of public agencies grow faster than the inflationary growth in revenue, generally creating a permanent gap between revenues and expenditures and minimizing the ability of public agencies to plan and implement open space acquisition programs. At the same time, property tax critics contend that it underpins incorrect land use decisions and the premature development of open space land. A recent League of California Cities study of planning indicated:

> Dependence on the local property tax remains the greatest impediment to efficient development and adequate local services. It distorts . . . public and private development decisions, leads to . . . inequitable service levels . . . and is regressive. We strongly need an alternative basic revenue source.[31]

Examining the impact of the property tax on land use decisions, the 1970 report of the California Assembly Committee on Revenue and Taxation indicated in "The Fiscal Implications of Environmental Control" that

> the preliminary investigation by the Committee in this area did not demonstrate that the property tax itself is responsible for the

improper land use decisions under discussion currently, but rather *over dependence* on the tax by local governments is the primary factor.[32]

Broadening the tax base of cities and counties by including income tax revenue might reduce the dependence of local agencies on the property tax, advocates point out, adding, that only the income tax and the sales tax—other than the property tax—can produce sufficient revenues for local agencies. The income tax, of course, provides deductions, personal exemptions, and a progressive rate structure, difficult to achieve in a sales tax. Furthermore, income tax considers all income, while the sales tax only pertains to an individual's income used to purchase tangible personal property items, the proportion of which demonstrably declines as his income increases. The sales tax grows approximately 6.1 percent per year, although the personal income tax averages a 12 percent per year growth.[33] Advocates of greater reliance on the income tax by local agencies emphasize, therefore, that the income tax represents the only revenue source permitting a significantly reduced local agency reliance on the property tax. They also contend that less reliance on the property tax will encourage more rigorous local planning by removing a barrier that has made annexation, and other elements of effective comprehensive planning, difficult to achieve.

Objections to local income taxation focus on specific legislative questions, with one basic issue concerning the relative merits of mandatory or permissive state legislation. Selective adoption of local income tax provisions under enabling legislation raises frequent objection that they will discourage prospective residents from settling in a community, although this is evidence substantiated by states where local income taxation exists. Opponents also object to broad intervention by the state into municipal finances, citing the disparate fiscal requirements and political make-up among California communities.

Another issue concerns the merits of incorporating equivalent property tax roll-back features into state legislation. In the absence of such a requirement, local agencies may allocate income tax revenues for new or expanded government programs rather than reducing reliance on the property tax. Opponents claim that a new local revenue source without concurrent reductions in the property tax ignores widespread public dissatisfaction with excessively high taxes.

The scope of applicability to local agencies also pertains. Legislation directed solely to cities and counties would engender strenuous opposition from those intent on eliminating the present reliance by school districts on property taxation, which has been declared unconstitutional by the state Supreme Court in *Serrano* v. *Priest*. Legislation permitting a variety of local agencies to tax resident income also would create administrative problems and confusion, regardless of authorization for local, state surtax, or state "piggyback" methods of collection.

Finally, fiscal conservatives generally oppose local income taxation, stressing that it fails to address the increasing cost of government and that programs should focus on measures to reduce governmental budgets rather than provide additional revenue sources. Others, discounting the property tax influence on land use decisions, argue that more direct solutions to open space problems are of greater concern. They prefer another method because the income tax already represents a major source of state revenue.

Transfer of Education and Welfare to State or Federal Government

More than 50 percent of the property taxes raised annually by California local agencies finance education and welfare services. To transfer the financial responsibility to state or federal government would significantly impact both education and welfare. For example, if the local cost of welfare and education in California had been transferred to the state in 1973, approximately $4 billion would have been removed from local property tax rolls, representing a significant reduction in local property taxes and a decreased reliance on this revenue. Disadvantages of substantially increased state or federal funding of welfare and education include bureaucratic problems in distributing revenues, redistribution of the relative wealth of school districts, and fewer spending constraints.

Equalizing Local Revenue Sources

Local agency ability to plan and implement open space preservation programs depends to a great extent on their revenue base: the ability of a city or county to raise property taxes specifically depends on the amount of taxable assessed value in a jurisdiction. Sales tax revenue is returned to individual jurisdictions on the basis of its locus, and thus, if a jurisdiction does not have a significant volume of retained transactions, it will not receive adequate sales tax revenue.

Variations in the financing ability of communities lacking resources because of low assessed value or no sales tax base have inhibited efforts to preserve open space. Not only are funds for open space acquisition limited, but also potential open space uses of land tend to be subverted in favor of land uses that improve the local agency's tax base. San Francisco Bay Area open space may thus be the only remaining land available for development. Under the present tax system, some communities lose important revenue, while others may well have enough undeveloped land to proceed with open space preservation and land developmen. programs. One alternative to improve the overall financing ability of communities, to adjust for revenue inequities resulting from an open space preservation program, and to reduce the influence of fiscal considerations on land use decisions involves equalizing local revenue sources.

Advocates of this approach suggest replacing the present local property and sales taxes with a countrywide, regionwide, or statewide tax returned to individual jurisdictions according to a formula reflecting need and taxing ability. A variation involves only the allocation within the county or region of property tax revenue derived from future growth in assessed value. Already adopted in the Twin Cities area of Minnesota, this option requires state authorization to restructure the local property tax so that future revenue derived from growth in taxable assessed value is reallocated over the entire county or region.

The Advisory Commission on Intergovernmental Relations has described the Twin Cities approach, based on a reallocation of 40 percent of the growth in the taxable assessed value of commercial and industrial property:

> The new law works entirely within the present framework of local government ... without changing ... the autonomy of some 300 independent taxing units in the metropolitan area. No metropolitan taxing area is created; all localities continue to make their own policy decisions on levying property taxes. ...
>
> Each community will continue to have a tax base ... the only difference being that beginning with the 1972 valuations a community's valuation will be made up of two parts: That which remains local (not shared), plus its assigned share of the region's growth over 1971. None of the existing tax base of a community will be shared; the shared portion will be 40 per cent of the net growth of commercial industrial valuation after 1971. All other valuation which includes all residential properties, will continue to be used exclusively by the governmental units where the buildings are physically located.
>
> All communities will receive an assigned share of the commercial-industrial growth, determined by its population and adjusted so that a community will receive a large share of its property valuation below the metropolitan average per capita, and a smaller share of its valuation is above average. ...
>
> The law maintains fiscal responsibility, since no jurisdiction can levy against its share of the region's growth anything it is not willing to levy against its own residents/voters. A unique feature of the law is that it introduces base sharing as a separate and distinct concept from revenue sharing.[34]

Critics cite the virtual impossibility of achieving a consensus of the jurisdictions involved, since tax-base sharing will necessarily disadvantage some communities. They also point to the difficulty in defining need and taxing ability, and that equalizing revenues will reduce or remove from local communities the required control of revenues to implement local plans and programs. Moreover, since the elimination of increased tax revenues reduces the attractiveness of certain commercial and industrial facilities to the community, business interests may find government approval increasingly difficult for commercial and industrial expansion.

Change of the Capital Gains Tax

State and federal income tax laws influence the activities of the private sector, including land investment. One feature of the income tax pertains to investors in land and other capital assets when they dispose of their property. Federal law provides that, for a long-term capital gain, that is, investments exceeding six months, 50 percent of the gross gain may be applied toward ordinary income, or the entire gain may be taxed at a fixed rate varying with its amount.[35] Similarly, California law provides that an investor, holding land for less than one year, is taxed on 100 percent of the gain, but only 65 percent if he holds the property from one to five years, and only 50 percent if held for more than five years.[36] Those advocating changes in capital gains suggest that state and federal tax policy should not encourage land speculation and development. Rather, they contend that all income should be similarly treated, with investors discouraged from acquiring land for a preferential tax treatment. Others point to government's responsibility by way of planning and regulating adequate open space, arguing that income averaging does not minimize unusual income increases, and that capital gains remain helpful in protecting large profits in a given year.

Greater Tax Burden on Land

Present property assessment policies generally generate more taxes on improved property than on unimproved property. Reduced taxes on land make it economically feasible to withhold it from the market, causing speculation and higher prices. A heavier tax on improved property tends to discourage the renovation and upgrading of blighted, undeveloped areas. A special supplement to the March 1965 issue of *Nation's Cities* magazine remarks:

> In the suburbs, under-used land is taxed so lightly that prices have multiplied five, ten and twenty fold. The National Association of Home builders, voted 4-1 that high price of land is the builder's most urgent problem. It threatens to price good new single family homes out of the market. It is the primary cause of premature subdivision as builders leap frog far out into the countryside to find land on which they can afford to build—often on land that should be left open . . . cities consume three or four times as much land as they use and . . . many workers must now spend up to 30% of their take home pay on transportation and . . . twenty hours a week getting to and from their jobs.[37]

A heavier tax on land itself, rather than on improvements, could encourage better land use in and around urban centers and discourage the rapid development of suburban and rural land speculation. Theoretically, land taxation based on its locational value reduces its overall cost, particularly in areas away from urban development. This discourages land speculation, helping protect existing open space areas from premature development. Netzer, in his *Economics of the Property Tax*, asserts:

> It is generally agreed that taxes on the value of bare land, . . . rest on the owners of the sites at the time the tax is initially levied or

increased. The tax cannot be shifted, because shifting is possible, under reasonably competitive conditions, only if the supply of sites is reduced. But the supply of land is ... inelastic. Individual land owners will not respond to an increase in land taxes by withdrawing their sites from the market. ... Indeed, their only chance of reducing the burdensomeness of the tax is to seek to raise the latter by encouraging more intensive use of the site they own. Collectively, land owners cannot reduce the stock of land: if individual land owners wish to liquidate ... they must sell the sites to other owners.

Thus, increased taxes on bare land values will reduce the attractiveness of investing in land vis-a-vis other assets, but will not destroy the land itself. Therefore, land prices will fall: the taxes will be capitalized. Land rents before taxes are unchanged, but because of higher taxes, after tax returns are lower, and investors offer less for land. ...[38]

Opponents of site value taxation, contending that theory will never work in practice, point out the possibility of a partial shift to site value taxation because of its differential impact on individual properties. They also believe that the free market truly regulates land value and that tax policy does little to encourage development or control urban land speculation. They contend, moreover, that a heavier land tax could actually encourage the premature development of land, particularly in transitional areas. Finally, they suggest that site value taxation could complicate assessing practices by requiring a separate land valuation and improvements rather than one value to the overall parcel.

NOTES

1. William Holliman, "Invisible Boundaries and Political Responsibility: A Proposal for Revision of California Annexation Laws," *Pacific Law Journal* 3 (1972): 534.

2. League of California Cities, "Planning and Management in California Cities: An Assessment of Legal Impediments and Technical Assistance" (Sacramento, 1971), p. 15.

3. LeGates, op. cit.

4. Ibid., p. 94.

5. California Council on Intergovernmental Relations, "Local Government Planning in California" (1972), p. 8.

6. Ibid., p. 52.

7. California Government Code, Section 6950.

8. Eckbo, Dean, Austin, & Williams, "State Open Space and Resource Conservation Program for California," for California Legislature Joint Committee on Open Space Lands, April 1972, p. 20.

9. National Commission on Urban Problems, *Building the American City* (U.S. Government Publication, 1968),

10. Sylvan Kamm, "Land Banking: Public Policy Alternatives and Dilemmas" (Washington, D.C.: The Urban Institute, December 1970), p. 16.

11. Ibid, p. 250.

12. Development Research Associates, "Economic Analysis of a Regional Open Space Program" (San Francisco: People for Open Space, 1970), pp. 20-21.

13. New York City Zoning Resolution, 1968, Section 74-79.

14. John J. Costonis, "The Chicago Plan: Incentive Zoning and the Preservation of Urban Landmarks," *Harvard Law Review* 85, no. 3 (1972): 574-632.

15. "New Land Development Legislation Will Affect Real Estate Investment," *The Mortgage and Real Estate Executive's Report* (March 7, 1973), p. 2.

16. Lafayette City Planning Department, "Open Space, Conservation Element of the General Plan" (proposed, 1973).

17. Costonis, op. cit., p. 590.

18. "Development Rights Transfer in New York City," *Yale Law Journal*, December 1972, p. 371.

19. J. N. Littlefield, Memorandum to Members of the Professional Engineers Tahoe Regional Committee (September 29, 1971), p. 3.

20. F. Bair, "Is Zoning a Mistake?" *Zoning Digest*, 1962, p. 249; and Luther L. McDougal, III, "Performance Standards: A Viable Alternative to Euclidean Zoning?" *Tulane Law Review*, 47, no. 2, February 1973, pp. 256-83.

21. Arthur Lubow, "Farmers' Tax Break Goes into Pockets of Land Corporations," Sacramento *Bee*, September 5, 1972, p. B1.

22. AB 2138, introduced by Assemblyman Dunlap in the 1971 California legislative session.

23. Peter J. Lert and W. W. Wood, Jr., *Agriculture—A Look at its Future*, prepared for Santa Clara County Planning Policy Committee, Urban Development/Open Space Subcommittee (June 28, 1972), pp. 9, 10, and 12.

24. Eckbo, Dean, Austin, & Williams, *Open Space: The Choices Before California* (San Francisco: Diablo Press, 1965), p. 25.

25. Development Research Associates, op. cit., p. 33.

26. League of California Cities, *The Municipal Fiscal Crisis* (1972).

27. California Legislature, Joint Committee on Open Space Land, *Final Report* (February 1970), p. 32.

28. Chapter 1406, Statutes of 1972.

29. Wilma Mayers Krebs, "Real Estate Transfer Tax," in *Funding for Acquisition of Open Space Lands: Three Approaches* (California Legislature Assembly Select Committee on Open Space Lands, October 1972), p. 10.

30. Assembly Committee on Revenue and Taxation, *The Fiscal Implications of Environmental Control* (December 1970), p. 104.

31. League of California Cities, "Planning and Management of California Cities," op. cit., p. 29.

32. Ibid, p. 93.

33. Annual Reports of the State Board of Equalization, Franchise Tax Board, and Office of Legislative Analyst of the State of California.

34. Advisory Commission on Intergovernmental Relations, *Tax Base Sharing For Twin Cities*, Special Bulletin (1972).

35. Internal Revenue Service, Federal Statutes Relative to Personal Income Taxation.

36. Franchise Tax Board, State of California Statutes Relative to Personal Income Taxation.

37. "Are Property Taxes Obsolete?" *Nation's Cities*, March 1965, p. 26.

38. Dick Netzer, *Economics of the Property Tax* (Washington, D.C.: The Brookings Institution, 1966), pp. 33, 34, and 36.

9

REGIONAL AND STATE COORDINATION: THE REAL ISSUE

California has, in recent years, displayed considerable interest in open space preservation. The legislature created the Joint Committee on Bay Area Regional Organization, the Joint Committee on Open Space Lands, and the Office of Planning and Research, the latter required to "give immediate and high priority to the development of land use policy. . . ." The state constitution was amended to provide: "it is in the best interest of the state to maintain, preserve, conserve, and otherwise continue in existence open space lands. . . ." The Williamson Act has also facilitated the preservation of open space. Other legislation obliged local agencies to prepare open space elements for their general plan and to develop specific implementation programs and environmental impact statements in conjunction with new development projects.

Regional and some local agencies have made laudatory efforts to preserve open space by improving land use planning, making more effective use of regulatory powers, and acquiring open space land. Despite these accomplishments—or perhaps because of them—the real issue confronting the San Francisco Bay Area centers on the need to coordinate the open space-related activities of cities, counties, and other local government agencies on a regional and statewide basis. Numerous studies and discussions concerning open space preservation, coupled with past and present attempts at coordination, indicate a regional or state open space plan should be prepared to assure that individual agencies achieve common open space goals. Further, an open space plan should include an open space lands classification system, distinguishing statewide, regional, and local land and establishing priorities for acquiring open space. An estimate of the cost of open space land to be acquired should be combined with a description of other open space preservation techniques and implementation programs. Effective implementation of a coordinated open space program obviously cannot be voluntary and a mechanism is needed to assure that local open space actions are consistent with regional and state open space goals. Finally, an effective program of open space preservation must rely on land acquisition.

POWERS

An agency responsible for coordinating a regional or statewide open space preservation program needs to be empowered to assure meaningful actions. Depending upon the full extent of its planning responsibilities, we believe the agency must have the ability to acquire open space land by purchase or eminent domain, to develop parks, and to raise and allocate revenue for open space. Activities of Bay Area regional agencies and their studies of open space preservation show the state or regional open space agency should assure that development within the state or region is consistent with its overall open space plan.

Those advocating enforcement powers look to economic sanctions, such as withholding state-shared revenues, for compliance with state or regional plans. Some local agencies contend these arbitrary procedures disrupt the economy, thus creating hardships. Authority to impose building moratoria in noncomplying communities could be given to the open space agency. Similar authority of regional water quality control boards suggest this as an effective last resort to achieve compliance. However, neither sanctions nor moratoria address the problem of subsequent local land use decisions inconsistent with regional open space objectives. The open space agency might exercise authority over proposed development of land within areas designated as "significant," but only on the appeal of a local land use decision. This would provide leverage to state or regional agencies over actual land use in areas with important open space value, but not usurp present community authority to plan and regulate land use.

Perhaps some state or regional agency should regulate land use within areas designated as open space in the state or regional plan, in order to minimize confusion, eliminate duplicating reviews, assure uniform application of development criteria, and guarantee preservation of open space lands with state or regional significance. However, those believing in local land use decisions oppose the transfer of responsibility for all land use decision in open space areas to a state or regional agency.

THE STRUCTURE OF AN OPEN SPACE AGENCY

In addition to the range of powers accorded to an open space agency, an unresolved issue rests on the government organization for coordinating state, regional, and local goals pertaining to open space preservation. The creation of a single-purpose regional open space agency, a multipurpose regional agency with responsibility for planning and enforcing an open space preservation program, a regional study commission with specific temporary powers relating to the use of open space, and a state open space agency easily come to mind.

Retain the Status Quo

In the San Francisco Bay Area we find many cities, counties, special districts, regional agencies, and state regulatory bodies informally interacting to undertake joint planning on a more formalized basis through the Association of Bay Area Governments (ABAG), active in land use planning and open space preservation. ABAG has prepared plans for regional land use, open space, the coastal zone, and a regional growth policy, at the same time cooperating with other land use and open space related agencies, including the Bay Conservation and Development Commission (BCDC), the two newly created coastal commissions, the Metropolitan Transportation Commission (MTC), and the East Bay Regional Park District (EBRPD). Although ABAG's ability to implement regional plans depends on voluntary cooperation, it has developed into a regional agency.

Of course, we can achieve a coordinated regional open space program with the status quo. Those favoring this approach argue that achieving effective coordination becomes an evolutionary process, unable to balance competing interests through mandated coordination attempts. They point out that ABAG, assuming an increasingly important role in matters of regional significance, has identified regional problems, collected related data, and prepared practical and realistic plans. ABAG's record reveals its success in educating cities and counties about the importance of open space preservation problems. Retention of the status quo supports ABAG's long-standing efforts to place the regional problem in perspective and continue meaningful involvement in regional planning activities under a system not eroding cities' and counties' current authority for land use planning. Finally, creation of an additional open space agency could undermine ABAG's planning and coordinating accomplishments, adding to the confusing responsibility among regional agencies. Conversely, ABAG may have reached its functional limit. An additional organization in this case may be needed to ensure regional open space plans. Status quo critics cite the need for an agency with the ability to act on a regional basis, although they recognize ABAG's admirable preparation of a regional open space plan. They believe, however, that a minimal ability to veto public and private agency development decisions has now become essential, to make sure open space areas are not put to an alternative use.

Establish a Single-Purpose Regional Agency

Government organization in the area pertaining to regional problems has largely centered on single-purpose regional or state agencies. Existing single-purpose agencies have only a planning responsibility or the provision of service in specific functional areas, but regional agencies with a planning responsibility can also implement plans. For example, MTC can allocate revenue to local agencies and BCDC reviews development proposals affecting its jurisdictional land and water areas.

Following this precedent, a new single-purpose regional open space agency might be desirable. Indeed, establishing single-purpose regional agencies causes minimal disturbance for existing local agencies, yet they can exercise all powers in one area of responsibility that might otherwise be conferred upon a multi-purpose agency. Although the creation of a multipurpose regional agency may eventually be necessary for planning and operating purposes, it would be premature until the assembly of all data and the preparation of an integrated regional plan. A single-purpose regional agency would not necessarily frustrate the eventual establishment of a multipurpose agency. However, single-purpose agency legislation could require its consolidation with a multipurpose planning agency whenever such an agency arose. A single-purpose agency aimed solely at the preservation of open space would be more politically acceptable, thus easier to establish.

Opponents of the single-purpose regional agency argue that effective coordination of the decisions and actions of all Bay Area agencies requires the establishment of a multipurpose regional agency. They suggest that open space preservation depends on the ability to integrate the plans of those regional agencies impacting land use and open space. Although a single-purpose agency could be given a veto power over development proposals of other agencies, this authority would not ensure balanced land use and adequate open space throughout the nine counties. Creating a single-purpose agency would make more difficult the eventual establishment of a multipurpose agency because existing agencies traditionally resist attempts to consolidate their functions or erode their authority. Another single-purpose agency would also contribute to the low public visibility and accountability that similar agencies in the area presently experience. Finally, creating a regionwide open space agency could result in fiscal inequities for some area residents, particularly if the functions of existing regional park districts, that is, East Bay Regional Park District, Mid-Peninsula Regional Park District, and Marin County Regional Park District, were assigned to a new regional agency.

Establish a Multipurpose Regional Agency
with Enforcement Powers

A number of single-purpose regional agencies have been created in response to crises, and generally speaking, to deal with a singular, technical problem. Since the real issue with respect to open space concerns the overall question of land use and development, its preservation transcends the land use decisions of most of the single-purpose regional agencies already existing.

Thus, when considering regional growth and development and the effective implementation of land use plans, the coordination of activities of various single-purpose regional agencies, as well as existing local agencies, becomes important. The establishment of a multipurpose regional agency with the specific responsibility of preparing and implementing an open space plan should not be overlooked. Establishment of a multipurpose regional agency is based largely on the idea that balanced urban development, including the preservation of appropriate open space areas, necessitates consistency between local land use decisions and regional development goals. Balanced urban development requires a comprehensive master plan for the regional aspects of transportation, air quality, water quality, liquid waste, solid waste, and similar regional problems, as well as open space. Although the responsibility for broad regional planning implies enforcement capabilities, the multipurpose agency need not assume the operating responsibility for existing single-purpose regional agencies. From an open space standpoint, it would be undesirable that the new multipurpose agency have operating responsibility.

Proponents of the multipurpose approach argue that it will result in improved political accountability for land use planning and development decisions. Planning activities of existing agencies would be subject to centralized review for consistency with regional goals, and it would be unnecessary to create new single-purpose regional agencies for open space planning or similar activities. They also contend that tax inequities would be reduced to the extent of achievement of broader financing of open space planning or acquisition.

Opponents of the multipurpose regional agency cite unresolved questions regarding the desirability of this appraoch. No consensus exists, they say, regarding the optimum size for such an agency, and conflicting reports on economies of scale, as well as the experience of other areas, indicates that an overall cost increase could be the only result. Rather than prematurely creating such an agency, critics of the multipurpose approach suggest that it would be more desirable to wait until all necessary data regarding regional problems are available and the scope and nature of necessary regional planning and control are known.

Establish a Regional Study Commission
with Specific Temporary Powers

Many unresolved questions regarding the nature of a new open space planning agency become apparent. What is the specific nature of its responsibility? What authority should it have? How should the governing board be constituted and selected, and what is its relationship to existing regional and local agencies?

A regional study commission might develop a rational proposal. Following the BCDC precedent, the study commission would also have temporary control, that is, veto power, or major land use decisions affecting the preservation of open space with regional or statewide significance. Proponents point out that open space can be essentially stabilized during the planning period, because the planning process and the temporary regulatory controls will occur simultaneously. This approach should also maximize cooperation between the study commission and local agencies. Proponents argue this approach not only permits the immediate implementation of regulatory controls while an orderly planning process is underway, but also provides additional time to mobilize public support for the ultimate program recommended by the study commission.

Opponents point to the apparent sufficiency of extant open space preservation studies, contending that another study will not assure the adoption of an effective program for coordinating open space preservation. They note the availability of necessary information to develop an action program and that assigning responsibility for preparing and enforcing a regional open space preservation program remains to be accomplished. Unreasonable and undesirable delays might prove costly. Landowners might claim they were damaged because of a "freeze" on land use during the temporary planning period.

Establish a State Open Space Agency

Perhaps the state should play an important role in land use and open space preservation. The federal government has seriously considered a National Land Use Policy to encourage states planning for the conservation and development of their land resources. The recent report of the League of California Cities on planning impediments is relevant:

> Local planning should relate to national goals. . . . There is no coordinated body of state policies, and there is no state organization. . . . This, by all odds, is the most serious single deficiency in California. One of the biggest impediments to city planning is that California has failed to establish priority of land use or take strong action in designating areas that should remain unused.
>
> Planning procedures in cities must be subject to overall requirements . . . otherwise [it] will always be one-sided. . . . our council doesn't want to annex problem areas, even though they are within our sphere of influence . . . it only wants to annex land that will produce revenue. . . .
>
> A regional planning agency meeting . . . state standards should be required . . . law. Each city and county should be required to incorporate that part of the regional plan which affects areas in the city into the city's general plan. The city should be required to comply with the regional plan in the construction of public facilities and in zoning and rezoning property within the city.[1]

The California State Development Plan also expresses the basic need for a state land use policy:

> The development of a statewide land use policy is essential to the satisfactory future management of California's resources. Mechanisms must be established for resolving . . . demands for land; for priorities for state programs; and for examining land use issues within the broad context of a consciously developed, desirable general pattern of development. . . .
>
> Assumptions about land use are implicit in almost every evaluation of issues and policies affecting the major functional areas of resource management. Decisions are made in the development of highway and water programs; in planning to meet recreational needs; in the . . . Federal and local government; in numerous independent approaches to watershed management; in the management and disposal of state owned land; and . . . the use of land for agricultural purposes.

State government affects land use by its taxation policies, enabling legislation, grants-in-aid and by its programs of research, technical assistance and education. The vacuum in land use policy has resulted in practices which lack ... understanding of the interrelated aspects of land management and development and economic growth.

If California is to determine its own destiny and shape its own growth patterns, it must do so consciously. The lack of deliberate, comprehensive policy commits [it] to reacting to growth patterns it does not conscientiously control, and in effect, becoming a party to urban and economic development patterns which have emerged out of a policy vacuum.[2]

Recent activities in other states suggest that California must do more than establish broad policies. The 1972 Joint Legislative Committee on Open Space Lands Report summarizes states' activity pertaining to land use and open space preservation:

Hawaii, Maine, Vermont and Colorado have all adopted state administered land use laws ... they all involve use of the state's power to zone or district areas of critical state concern [and] spell out the division of responsibilities between state and local governments.

States which have adopted significant state level controls over limited land and water areas are: ... California, with the San Francisco Bay Conservation Development Commission; then Maine (shoreland zoning); Michigan (scenic rivers and Great Lakes shorelands); Delaware (coastal zone act); Oregon (water areas of the state); Maryland (wetlands); North Carolina (beach erosion and coastal wetlands); New York (Hudson River Valley and St. Laurence-Eastern Ontario Commissions, Agricultural District Law, Adirondack Park Agency); New Jersey (wetlands); Alaska (zoning power in unorganized areas); Rhode Island (coastal resources management, protection of intertidal salt marshes, coastal wetlands, fresh water wetlands); Massachusetts (coastal and inland wetlands); Wisconsin (shoreland zoning); Minnesota (shoreland development); Washington (coastline protection); Connecticut (tidal wetlands); Georgia (coastal marshlands).

Flood plain control is exercised ... at the state level by Michigan, Nebraska, Massachusetts, Wisconsin, Minnesota and Montana.[3]

A state agency might help achieve a coordinated program of open space preservation. Proponents argue the state has already shown a willingness to regulate land use by creating agencies, for example, BCDC, Lake Tahoe Regional Planning Authority, and the State and Regional Water Quality Control Boards, proving a state interest in comprehensive land use planning and open space preservation. However, proponents believe the establishment of comprehensive goals and policies remain insufficient because they are meaningless without enforcement. Advocating an active program of enforcement, they emphasize it does not exclude regional participation in land use planning and open space preservation. In fact, they argue, the needs, problems, and methods of implementaton vary, making regional activity desirable. They suggest that development decisions relate to state and regional goals for open space preservation. The state program, of course, can be much broader in terms of incorporating elements designed to provide financial and technical assistance for open space preservation, but at a minimum; proponents submit that a strong state program of land use planning, including enforcement ability, has become necessary to achieve open space preservation coordination.

Virtually no one opposes the concept that the state should assume a more active role in land use planning and open space preservation, although its actual role is unclear. At one end of the spectrum we see the establishment of policies and suggested guidelines for local and regional agencies, at the other end, substantial control over land use. The private sector generally supports a stronger state and regional role, but it is concerned about administrative and other problems that may arise. Local and regional agencies express a preference for guidelines, but any erosion of local planning and land use control troubles them. The role of state government pertaining to land use planning and open space preservation must evolve and become an essential element of any program to achieve comprehensive land use planning and effective open space preservation.

NOTES

1. League of California Cities, "Planning and Management in California Cities: An Assessment of Legal Impediments and Technical Assistance" (Sacramento, 1971), p. 24.

2. California State Office of Planning, *California State Development Plan Program, Phase II Report* (Sacramento: State Printing Office, 1968), p. 195.

3. California Legislature Joint Committee on Open Space Lands, *State Open Space and Resource Conservation Program for California* (April 1972), p. 16.

POPULATION OF BAY AREA CITIES
IN 1950, 1960, AND 1970

County & City	1950	Census 1960	1970	Percent Change 1960-70
Alameda				
Alameda	64,430	63,855	70,968	11.1
Albany	17,590	14,804	14,674	-0.9
Berkeley	113,805	111,268	116,716	4.9
Emeryville	2,889	2,686	2,681	-0.2
Fremont		43,790	100,869	130.3
Hayward	14,272	72,790	93,058	28.0
Livermore	4,364	16,058	37,703	134.8
Newark		9,884	27,153	174.7
Oakland	384,575	367,548	361,561	-1.6
Piedmont	10,132	11,117	10,917	-1.8
Pleasanton	2,244	4,203	18,328	336.1
San Leandro	27,542	65,962	68,698	4.1
Union City		6,618	14,724	122.5
Contra Costa				
Antioch	11,051	17,305	28,060	62.1
Brentwood	1,729	2,186	2,649	21.2
Clayton			1,385	
Concord	6,953	36,000	85,164	136.6
El Cerrito	18,011	25,437	25,190	-1.0
Hercules	343	310	252	-18.7
Lafayette			20,484	
Martinez	8,268	9,604	16,506	71.9
Pinole	1,147	6,064	15,850	161.4
Pittsburg	12,763	19,062	20,651	8.3
Pleasant Hill		21,376	24,610	15.1
Richmond	99,545	71,854	79,043	10.0
San Pablo	14,476	19,687	21,461	9.0
Walnut Creek	2,420	9,903	39,844	302.3
Marin				
Belvedere	800	2,148	2,599	21.0
Corte Madera	1,933	5,962	8,464	42.0

County & City	1950	Census 1960	1970	Percent Change 1960-70
Marin (continued)				
Fairfax	4,078	5,813	7,661	31.8
Larkspur	2,905	5,710	10,487	83.7
Mill Valley	7,331	10,411	12,942	24.3
Novato		17,881	31,006	73.4
Ross	2,179	2,551	2,742	7.5
San Anselmo	9,188	11,584	13,031	12.5
San Rafael	13,848	20,460	38,977	90.5
Sausalito	4,828	5,331	6,158	15.5
Tiburon				
Napa				
Calistoga	1,418	1,514	1,882	24.3
Napa	13,579	22,170	35,978	62.3
St. Helena	2,297	2,722	3,173	16.6
Yountville			2,332	
San Francisco				
San Francisco	775,357	740,316	715,674	-3.3
San Mateo				
Atherton	3,630	7,717	8,085	4.8
Belmont	5,567	15,996	23,667	48.0
Brisbane			3,003	
Burlingame	19,886	24,036	27,320	13.7
Colma	297	500	537	7.4
Daly City	15,191	44,791	66,922	49.4
Half Moon Bay		1,957	4,023	05.6
Hillsborough	3,552	7,554	8,753	15.9
Menlo Park	13,587	26,957	26,734	-0.8
Millbrae	8,972	15,873	20,781	30.9
Pacifica		20,995	36,020	71.6
Portola Valley			4,999	
Redwood City	25,544	46,290	55,686	20.3
San Bruno	12,478	29,063	36,254	24.7
San Carlos	14,371	21,370	25,924	21.3
San Mateo	41,782	69,870	78,991	13.1
South San Francisco	19,351	39,418	46,646	18.3
Woodside		3,592	4,731	31.7
Santa Clara				
Campbell		11,863	24,770	08.8
Cupertino		3,664	18,216	97.2
Gilroy	4,951	7,348	12,655	72.4
Los Altos		19,696	24,956	26.7

| | | Census | | Percent Change |
County & City	1950	1960	1970	1960-70
Santa Clara (continued)				
Los Altos Hills		3,412	6,865	01.2
Los Gatos	4,907	9,036	23,735	62.7
Milpitas		6,572	27,149	13.1
Monte Sereno		1,506	3,089	05.1
Morgan Hill	1,627	3,151	6,485	05.8
Mountain View	6,563	30,889	51,092	65.4
Palo Alto	25,475	52,287	55,966	7.0
San Jose	95,280	204,196	445,779	118.3
Santa Clara	11,702	58,880	87,717	49.0
Saratoga		14,861	27,110	82.4
Sunnyvale	9,829	52,898	95,408	80.4
Solano				
Benicia	7,284	6,070	8,783	44.7
Dixon	1,714	2,970	4,432	49.2
Fairfield	3,118	14,968	44,146	194.9
Rio Vista	1,831	2,616	3,135	19.8
Suisun City	946	2,470	2,917	18.1
Vacaville	3,169	10,898	21,690	99.0
Vallejo	26,038	60,877	66,733	9.6
Sonoma				
Cloverdale	1,292	2,848	3,251	14.2
Cotati			1,368	
Healdsburg	3,258	4,816	5,438	12.9
Petaluma	10,315	14,035	24,870	77.2
Rohnert Park			6,133	
Santa Rosa	17,902	31,027	50,006	61.2
Sebastopol	2,601	2,694	3,993	48.2
Sonoma	2,015	3,023	4,112	36.0

Source: California Chamber of Commerce, Economic Development and Research Department.

BOOKS

Babcock, Richard, 1969. *The Zoning Game*. Madison: University of Wisconsin Press.

Civacy-Wantrup, S. V., 1952. *Resource Conservation Economics and Policies*. Berkeley: University of California Press.

Dana, R. H., Jr., 1957. *Two Years Before the Mast*. New York: Collier and Son.

Eckbo, Dean, Austin & Williams, 1965. *Open Space: The Choices Before California*. San Francisco: Diablo Press.

Friedmann, John and William Alonso, 1964. *Regional Development and Planning*. Cambridge: M.I.T. Press.

Herring, Francis W., ed., 1965. *Open Space and the Law*. Berkeley: University of California, Institute of Governmental Studies.

Hutchinson, W. H., 1969. *California: Two Centuries of Man, Land, and Growth in the Golden State*. Palo Alto: American West Publishing Company.

Johnson, Harry L., ed., 1969. *State and Local Tax Problems*. Memphis: University of Tennessee Press.

Little, Charles E., 1960. *Challenge of the Land*. Open Space Action Institute.

McHarg, Ian L., 1969. *Design with Nature*. Garden City, N.Y.: Natural History Press.

Ratcliff, Richard U., 1949. *Urban Land Economics*. New York: McGraw-Hill.

Reilly, William K., ed., 1973. *The Use of Land: A Citizen's Policy Guide to Urban Growth*. New York: Thomas Y. Crowell.

Rhea, Gordon C., Carl R. Schenker, Jr., and Stephen L. Urbanczyk, 1972. *California Land Use Primer: A Legal Handbook for Environmentalists*. Stanford Environmental Law Society.

Schmertz, Milfred F., 1970. *Acquisition, Conservation, Creation and Design of Open Space for People*. Washington, D.C.: American Institute of Architects.

Scientific American, ed., 1969. *Cities.* New York: Knopf.

Wallace, David A., 1970. *Metropolitan Open Space and Natural Process.* Philadelphia: University of Pennsylvania.

Whyte, William H., 1970. *The Last Landscape.* Garden City, N.Y.: Doubleday.

REPORTS AND MONOGRAPHS

American Enterprise Institute, 1973. "Land Use Policy and Planning Bills." *Legislative Analysis* No. 11, 93rd Cong., Washington, D.C.

American Society of Planning Officials, 1968. "Problems of Zoning and Land Use Regulation." Research Report No. 2, prepared for the National Commission on Urban Problems, Washington, D.C.

Associated Home Builders of the Greater East Bay, Inc., 1972. "Growth Cost—Revenue Studies."

Association of Bay Area Governments 1971. "Physical Resources of the San Francisco Bay Area." Technical Report P-2494. 0.

————, 1972. "Urban Growth Policy for the San Francisco Bay Region." Issue Paper No. 1.

————, 1972. "Formulation of Regional Growth Policy for the San Francisco Bay Region." Issue Paper No. 2.

————, 1973. "Zoning and Growth in the San Francisco Bay Area." Issue Paper No. 3.

————, 1973. "Financing Open Space for the San Francisco Bay Region."

————, 1973. "How to Implement Open Space Plans for the San Francisco Bay Area." 3 Vols.

Bank of America National Trust and Savings Association, 1967. "Economic Growth and Development in the San Francisco-Oakland Metropolitan Area."

Bosselman, Fred P., 1968. "Alternatives to Urban Sprawl: Legal Guidelines for Governmental Action." Research Report No. 15. Washington, D.C.: U.S. Government Printing Office.

California Council on Intergovernmental Relations, 1971. "Local Agency Formation Commissions."

_____, 1972. "Local Government Planning in California."

California Legislature Assembly Select Committee on Open Space Lands, 1972. *Funding for Acquisition of Open Space Lands: Three Approaches.*

_____, 1973. "Open Space Zoning Handbook."

California Legislature Joint Committee on Open Space Land, 1969. "Preliminary Report."

_____, 1970. "Final Report."

_____, 1971. "Techniques and General Legal Aspects of Preserving Open Space."

_____, 1972. "State Open Space and Resource Conservation Program for California."

California Public Outdoor Recreation Plan Committee, 1970. "The Scenic, Scientific and Educational Values of the Natural Landscape of California." Department of Parks and Recreation.

California Wildlife Conservation Board, 1963. "A Report on the Achievements and Objectives of the California Wildlife Conservation Board, 1947-63."

Carman, Hoy F. and Jim G. Polson, 1971. "The California Land Conservation Act of 1965: Land Owner Participation and Estimated Tax Shifts." University of California, Agricultural Extension Service. No. 71-4.

Citizen's Advisory Committee on Open Space, 1970. "Final Report." California Legislature, Joint Committee on Open Space Lands.

Coke, James G. and John J. Gargan, 1969. "Fragmentation in Land Use Planning and Control." Research Report No. 18, prepared for the National Commission on Urban Problems, Washington, D.C.

Committee for Economic Development, 1970. "Reshaping Government in Metropolitan Areas."

Commonwealth Club of California, 1963. "Preserve Open Space in California?." Transaction No. 1, Vol. 58, no. 1.

_____, 1964. "What Should Be Our Wilderness Policy?." Transaction No. 3, Vol. 58, no. 3.

_____, 1968. "How to Solve Regional vs. Local Need in Development of San Francisco Bay?." Transaction H, Vol. 62.

Development Research Associates, 1970. "Economic Analysis of a Regional Open Space Program." San Francisco: People for Open Space.

Doerr, David R. and Raymond R. Sullivan, 1964. "Property Taxation and Land Use." Part IV of *Taxation of Property in California*, Assembly Interim Committee on Revenue and Taxation.

Environmental Quality Study Council, 1972. "Draft Report on Land Use." California State Environmental Quality Study Council.

Fellmeth, Robert C., ed., 1971. The Ralph Nader Task Force Report on "Land Use in the State of California." Washington, D.C.: Center for the Study of Responsive Law.

Foin, T. C. et al., 1972. "The California Land Conservation Act in Sacramento County: Implementation and Effectiveness." California Legislature, Assembly Select Committee on Open Space Lands.

Fujimoto, Isao and Phillip J. Symonds, 1971. "Regional Organization in California." Davis: University of California.

Golany, Gideon, 1973. "New Towns Planning and Development: A Worldwide Bibliography." Research Report 20, Washington, D.C.: Urban Land Institute.

Heyman, Ira Michael, 1968. "Powers, Volume I: Regulation-Legal Questions." San Francisco Bay Conservation and Development Commission.

Kamm, Sylvan, 1970. "Land Banking: Public Policy Alternatives and Dilemmas." Washington, D.C.: The Urban Institute.

Kent, T. J., 1970. "Open Space for the San Francisco Bay Area: Organizing to Guide Metropolitan Growth." Berkeley University of California, Institute of Governmental Studies.

Land Use Subcommittee of the Advisory Committee, U.S. Department of Housing and Urban Development, 1972. "Urban Growth and Land Development: The Land Conversion Process." Washington, D.C.: National Academy of Sciences.

League of California Cities, 1970. "Changing Roles for Cities."

————, 1971. "Planning and Management in California Cities: An Assessment of Legal Impediments and Technical Assistance."

League of Women Voters, 1973. "Land use at the state level—the growing edge." *Current Focus*, Washington, D.C.: League of Women Voters Education Fund.

LeGates, Richard T., 1970. "California Local Agency Formation Commissions." Berkeley: University of California, Institute of Governmental Studies.

Livingston and Blayney, 1971. "Open Space Development vs. Palo Alto Foothills Environmental Design Study." Palo Alto: Central Services.

Lobe, Natalie, William Gosnell, and Elaine Gerber, 1972. "Paying for Open Space: A Method and Analysis." Baltimore: Regional Planning Council.

Lovelace, Eldridge and William Weismantal, 1961. "Density Zoning: Organic Zoning for Planned Residential Development." Technical Bulletin No. 42, Urban Land Institute.

Lum, David T. E., Samuel G. Camp, and Karl Gertel, "Hawaii's Experience in Zoning." Research Report 172, University of Hawaii, Agricultural Experiment Station.

Marcov, O'Leary and Associates. "Open Space for Human Needs." The National Urban Coalition.

Metropolitan Council of the Twin Cities Area, 1971. "The Impact of Fiscal Disparity on Metropolitan Municipalities and School Districts."

Milpitas Planning Department, 1971. "Milpitas Community Comprehensive Land Use Economic Study 1969-1970." (in cooperation with Milpitas Unified School District and Milpitas Sanitary District).

Murphy, Francis C., 1958. "Regulating Flood Plain Development." Research Paper No. 51. University of Chicago, Department of Geography.

Nature Conservancy, 1970. "Legal Aspects of Land Acquisition under the Nature Conservancy." Washington, D.C.: Nature Conservancy.

Netzer, Dick, 1968. "Impact of the Property Tax: Effect on Housing, Urban Land Use and Local Government Finance." Research Paper No. 1 (prepared for the National Commission on Urban Problems).

Odell, Rice, ed., August 1971. "Conservation Foundation Letter: A Report on Environmental Issues." Washington, D.C.: Conservation Foundation.

_____, October 1971. "Conservation Foundation Letter: A Report on Environmental Issues." Washington, D.C.: Conservation Foundation.

Palo Alto Planning and Development Commission, 1972. Staff Report, "Regulation to Preserve Foothills Open Space."

Patri, Tito, David C. Streatfield, and Thomas J. Ingmire, 1970. *The Santa Cruz Mountains Regional Pilot Study: Early Warning System*. Berkeley: University of California.

People for Open Space, 1969. "The Case for Open Space in the San Francisco Bay Area." San Francisco.

Pietzsch, Mike, 1972. "Legal Guidelines for Implementation of the Open-Space Element of the General Plan of the City of Mountain View." Mountain View, Calif.: City Attorney's Office.

Plimpton, Oakes A., 1972. "Legal Analysis of Conservation Easements as a Method of Privately Conserving and Preserving Land." Washington, D.C.: Nature Conservancy.

Post, Alan, 1971. "Report on Open Space and Taxation." California State Legislature.

Real Estate Research Corporation, 1972. "Economic Analysis, Foothills Environmental Design Study." Palo Alto, Calif.

Recht, Richard J., 1970. "Open Space and the Urban Growth Process." Research Report No. 31. Berkeley: University of California, Center for Real Estate and Urban Economics.

Regional Planning Council, 1967. "A Land Bank for the Baltimore Region—a Suggested Approach for Implementing the Regional Plan." Baltimore.

San Francisco Bay Conservation and Development Commission, 1967. "Government: Part of a Detailed Study of San Francisco Bay."

Santa Clara County Planning Department, 1969. "A National Wildlife Refuge for South San Francisco Bay."

————, 1970. "An Inventory of Parks and Recreation." Santa Clara County.

Scott, Stanley and John C. Bollers, 1968. "Governing a Metropolitan Region: The San Francisco Bay Area." Berkeley: University of California, Institute of Governmental Studies.

Security Pacific National Bank, 1971. "San Francisco Bay Area Report: A Study of Growth and Economic Stature of the Nine Bay Area Counties." Economic Research Division.

Siegel, Shirley Anderson, 1960. "The Law of Open Space." Park, Recreation and Urban Studies Project of the Tristate N.Y. Metropolitan Region.

Smith, Fred, 1973. *Man and His Urban Environment*. New York: Rockefeller Brothers Fund.

Stanford Environmental Law Society, 1971. "San Jose: Sprawling City." Stanford University Law School.

_____, 1971. "The Environment and California's Highways." Stanford University Law School.

Stedman, Karhnyn, 1966. "Skyline Landscape of the San Francisco Peninsula Cities." Council for Foothills Planning and Research.

Strong, Ann Louise, 1963. "Preserving Urban Open Space." Washington, D.C.: U.S. Government Printing Office.

_____, 1965. "Open Space for Urban America." Washington, D.C.: U.S. Government Printing Office.

Sussna, Stephen, 1967. "Land Use Control: More Effective Approaches." Research Monograph No. 17. Washington, D.C.: Urban Land Institute.

U.S. Advisory Commission on Intergovernmental Relations, 1963. "The Role of the States in Strengthening the Property Tax." Vol. 1.

_____, 1968. "Urban and Rural America: Policies for Future Growth."

U.S. Department of Agriculture Economic Research Service, 1968. "Open Space: Its Use and Preservation." Miscellaneous Publication No. 1121, Washington, D.C.: U.S. Government Printing Office.

U.S. Environmental Protection Agency, 1972. "The Relationship Between Environmental Quality and Land Use." Washington, D.C.

U.S. Senate Committee on Interior and Insular Affairs, 1972. "National Land Use Policy Background." Washington, D.C.: U.S. Government Printing Office.

University of California, Western Center for Community Education and Development. "Open Space in California: Issues and Options."

Urban Land Institute, 1961. "New Approaches to Residential Land Development." Technical Bulletin No. 40.

_____, 1965. "Taxation and Land Use in Metropolitan and Urban America." Research Monograph No. 12.

_____, 1970. "Land: Recreation and Leisure." Abstract from Land Use Symposium 1970.

_____, 1973. "San Francisco Bay Area . . . Today." Project Brochure, ULI 1973 Fall Meeting.

Vance, James E. Jr., 1964. "Geography and Urban Evolution in the San Francisco Bay Area." Berkeley: University of California, Institute of Governmental Studies.

Whyte, William H., 1968. "Securing Open Space, for Urban America: Conservation Easement." Technical Bulletin No. 36, Urban Land Institute.

PLAN AND POLICY DOCUMENTS

Association of Bay Area Governments, 1966. *Preliminary Regional Plan for the San Francisco Bay Region.*

———, 1969. *Regional Open Space Element: Supplement Report RP-3.*

———, 1970. *Regional Plan 1970:1990 San Francisco Bay Region.*

———, 1971. "Project Review Policies and Procedures."

———, 1972. *Regional Open Space Plan, Phase II, San Francisco Bay Region* (Summary).

———, 1973. *Regional Ocean Coastline Plan for the San Francisco Bay Area.*

California Department of Navigation and Ocean Development, 1972. "Comprehensive Ocean Area Plan."

California Department of Parks and Recreation, 1972. *California Outdoor Recreation Resources Plan.*

California State Office of Planning, 1968. *California State Development Plan Program.* Sacramento: State Printing Office.

California State Office of Planning and Research, 1972. *Environmental Goals and Policies.*

California Tomorrow, 1971. "The California Tomorrow Plan—a First Sketch." San Francisco.

Contra Costa County Planning Commission, 1970. "Recreation Element of the General Plan for Contra Costa County."

Duncan & Jones and Ribera & Sue, Inc., 1971. *Interim Report—Parks, Recreation and Open Space Program: Phase I.* Santa Cruz Planning Department.

Mountain View Planning Department, 1972. "The Proposed Open Space and Conservation Element Chapter 7-A, City of Mountain View General Plan."

Palo Alto Department of Planning and Community Development, 1972. "The Open Space Element of the Palo Alto General Plan."

San Francisco Bay Conservation and Development Commission, 1969. *San Francisco Bay Plan*.

San Francisco Department of City Planning, 1971. *The Urban Design Plan for the Comprehensive Plan of San Francisco*.

————, 1972. "Improvement Plan for Recreation and Open Space: A Proposal for Citizen Review."

————, 1972. "Programs Recommended for Carrying Out the Improvement Plan for Recreation and Open Space."

San Jose Planning Department, 1972. "Urban Development Policies."

U.S. Office of Management and Budget, 1971. "Evaluation, Review and Co-ordination of Federal and Federally Assisted Programs and Projects." Circular No. A-95 (revised).

ARTICLES

Architectural Record, 1970. "Land as a Public Resource vs. Speculative Commodity." (June) pp. 138-42.

Barrow, James C. and J. Dean Jansma, 1970. "Impact of Public Land Programs on Local Government Finances." *American Journal of Agricultural Economics* 52: 363-71.

Belser, Karl, 1967. "The Planning Fiasco in California." *Cry California* (Summer), pp. 10-13.

————, 1970. "The Making of Slurban America." *Cry California* 5, no. 4: 1-22.

Blayney, John, 1971. "A Clinching Case for Open Space." *Cry California* (Winter), pp. 3-9.

Business Week, 1970. "Correcting San Jose's Boomtime Mistakes," (September 19), pp. 74-76.

————, 1972. "The Land Use Battle That Business Faces," (August 26), pp. 40-50.

Cahn, Robert. "Where Do We Grow from Here?" *Christian Science Monitor*, May 21-June 5, 1973.

California's Environment, 1972. "An Environmental Controversy: The Williamson Act and State Land-use Policy." 7.

Cameron, Juan, 1973. "Growth is a Fighting Word in Colorado's Mountain Wonderland." *Fortune* (October), p. 148.

Cantor, Arnold, 1968. "State and Local Taxes: The Case for Reform." *AFL-CIO American Federationist* 75: 9-15.

Costonis, John J., 1972. "The Chicago Plan: Incentive Zoning and the Preservation of Urban Landmarks." *Harvard Law Review* 85, no. 3.

Demaree, Allan T., 1970. "Cars and Cities on a Collision Course." *Fortune*, vol. 81, February, pp. 124-28.

Fattermeyer, Edmund, 1973. "We're Building a New Kind of Togetherness." *Fortune* (October), p. 130.

Forbes, 1970. "Revolution in Suburbia," (April 1), pp. 24-32.

Frazer, Jack B., 1970. "In Santa Clara Valley: The Debris of Development." *City* 4: 21-9.

Gaffney, Mason, 1969. "Land Planning and the Property Tax," *AIP Journal*, pp. 178-83.

Gotherman, John E., 1971. "Municipal Income Taxes." *Municipal Finance* 43, no. 3: 127-32.

Gurko, Stephen, 1972. "Federal Income Taxes and Urban Sprawl." *Denver Law Journal* 48, no. 3: 329-51.

Hady, Thomas F., 1970. "Differential Assessment of Farmland on the Rural-urban Fringe." *American Journal Of Agricultural Economics* 52: 25-32.

Hagman, Donald G., 1964. "Open Space Planning and Property Taxation—Some Suggestions." *Wisconsin Law Review* 4: 629-57.

Harris, Michael, 1969. "Our 19th-century State Lands Commission." *Cry California*, 4, no. 4, pp. 18-40.

Harvard Law Review, 1962. "Techniques for Preserving Open Space" 75: 1622-44.

Harvith, Bernard E., 1969. "Subdivision Dedication Requirements—Some Observations and an Alternative: A Special Tax on Gain from Realty." *Albany Law Review* 33: 474-90.

Heyman, Ira Michael, 1968. "The Great Property Rights Fallacy." *Cry California* (Summer) pp. 29-32.

Isard, Walter, and Coughlin, Robert E., 1956. "Municipal Costs and Revenues Resulting from Community Growth." *AIP Journal*, 22, no. 3, 122-41.

Issel, William E., 1972. "A-95 Used to Address Housing Imbalance." *AIP Newsletter*, pp. 11-12.

Knetsch, Jack L., 1963. "Land Values and Parks in Urban Fringe Areas." *Journal of Farm Economics* 44: 1718-26.

Kolderie, Ted, 1969. "Strategies: Having Started with Sewers, the Twin Cities Council Goes After Tougher Regional Problems." *City*, 3, no. 4, pp. 34-37.

Krivetsky, Henry C., 1970. "How Should We Select a Regional Governing Body?" *Commonwealth Club Transactions*, Part 2, 64, no. 31: 1-24.

McGivern, William C., 1972. "Putting a Speed Limit on Growth." *ASPO Planning* 38, no. 10: 258-85.

Marcus, Norman, 1971. "Air Rights Transfer in New York City." *Law and Contemporary Problems*, 36, no. 3.

Mikesell, John L., 1971. "Local Sales Taxes in North America." *Municipal Finance* 43, no. 3: 133-40.

Morgan, Neil, 1973. "Running Out of Space." *Harper's Magazine* (September) p. 59.

Osmundson, Theodore, 1970. "How to Control the Flood Controllers." *Cry California* (Summer), pp. 31-38.

Passow, Shirley S., 1970. "Land Reserves and Teamwork in Planning Stockholm." *AIP Journal* (May), pp. 179-88.

Prentice, P. I., 1969. "The Case for Taxing Location Values: A Memorandum for a Metropolis Considering Property Tax Reform." *American Journal of Economics and Sociology* 28, no. 2: 147-58.

Prestbo, John A., 1971. "Sprawl of Cities Stirs Fears that Agriculture Will Run Out of Space." *Wall Street Journal* (July 10).

Pryde, Phillip R., 1972. "New Strategies for Open Space." *Sierra Club Bulletin* (February), pp. 9-11, 18-19.

Schoop, E. Jack, 1971. "The San Francisco Bay Plan: Combining Policy with Police Power." *AIP Journal* (January).

Sesser, Stanford N., 1971. "The Nation Debates an Issue: The Economy vs. the Environment." *Wall Street Journal* (November 4), p. 1.

Sikorsky, Igor I., Jr., 1972. "A-95: Deterrent to Discriminatory Zoning." *Civil Rights Digest* (August), pp. 17-19.

Snyder, J. Herbert, 1966. "A New Program for Agricultural Land Use Stabilization: The California Land Conservation Act of 1965." *Land Economics* 42, no. 1: 29-41.

Sparks, Bertel M., 1971. "Changing Concepts of Private Property." *Freeman* 21: 583-98.

Stocker, Frederick D., 1971. "Effects of Taxation on Urban Land Use." *The Appraisal Journal* (January), pp. 57-69.

Stollman, Israel, 1972. "Ramapo." *Planning* 38, no. 6: 108-09.

Stuart, Darwin G. and Robert B. Teska, 1971. "Who Pays for What: A Cost Revenue Analysis of Suburban Land Use Alternatives." *Urban Land* 30, no. 3.

Thorwaldson, Jay, 1973. "The Palo Alto Experience." *Cry California* (Spring), pp. 4-17.

Time Magazine, 1973. "The Land Boom," October 1.

Volpert, Richard S., 1970. "Creation and Maintenance of Open Space in Subdivisions: Another Approach." *California Homeowner* (March) (condensed from UCLA *Law Review* 12, no. 3, March 1965).

Wagner, Walter F., Jr., 1970. "Alternatives to Urban Sprawl: New Processes, New Involvement." *Architectural Record* (November).

Walker, Mabel, 1971. "Major Impacts on the Property Tax." *Municipal Finance* 43, no. 3: 117-21.

Watkins, T. H. and William Bronson, 1971. "The California Earthquake Hazard: A Future Built on Sand." *Cry California* (Fall), pp. 5-17.

White, Bertram C., 1971. "Coastline Crisis." *Pacific Law Journal* 2, no. 1: 226-44.

Worsnop, Richard L., 1971. "Property Tax Reform." *Editorial Research Reports* 1, no. 6: 102-20.

Yale Law Journal, 1972. "Development Rights Transfer in New York City," 82, no. 2: 338-73.

Yearwood, Richard M., 1970. "Land Subdivision and Its Control." *American Journal of Economics and Sociology* 29, no. 2: 113-26.

Zimmerman, Joseph, 1970. "Metropolitan Reform in the U.S.: An Overview." *Public Administration Review* (September/October), p. 531.

CONFERENCES AND HEARINGS

Association of Engineering Geologists, 1971. *Environmental Planning and Geology*. Proceedings of National Meeting, October 1969. Washington, D.C.: U.S. Government Printing Office.

California Legislature, 1969. Hearing of Joint Committee on Open Space Lands, San Diego, California, September 15-16.

_____, 1969. Hearing of Joint Committee on Open Space Lands, Fresno, California, October 13.

_____, 1969. Hearing of Joint Committee on Open Space Lands, San Francisco, California, November 3-4.

Forrest, Clyde W., 1968. "The Private Property and Public-Interest Conflict Proceedings." Urbana: University of Illinois, Institute on Law and Planning.

Joint Committee on Internal Revenue Taxation, 1969. Summary of Testimony on Capital Gains, Washington, D.C.: U.S. Government Printing Office.

Smith, Ned C., ed., 1967. Summary and Proceedings of the First Professional Level Conference on Open Space Preservation Methods, Lake Minnewaska, N.Y., Open Space Action Committee, New York.

MISCELLANEOUS

Kent, T. J., Jr., 1968. "Home Rule and Limited Metropolitan Government" (statement presented at National Conference of the American Society of Planning Officials, May 1968).

McCracken, Michael, 1971. "The Local Agency Formation Commission: An Open Space Trustee?" Stanford Law School.

Sedway, Paul H., 1971. "The New Open Space and Conservation Elements: Implications for Planning, Zoning and Future Legislation" (paper presented to the San Francisco Bay Area Planning Director's Association).

Syracuse, Lee A., ed. *Building our Community* (a series of periodical papers on subdivision design), Nos. 1-5.

Taber, Stephen L., 1972. "Open Space in California Subdivisions" (essay for the University of the Pacific, McGeorge School of Law, in cooperation with U.S. Department of Agriculture).

ABOUT THE EDITORS

EDWARD ELLIS SMITH, a member of the board of governors of the Commonwealth Club of California, is a vice president of the International Division of Crocker Bank, San Francisco. A writer and lecturer, he is the author of *The Young Stalin, The Russian Department of Police, The People's Republic of China*, and other works. As a regular officer in the United States Army, the Central Intelligence Agency, and the Department of State, he served at a number of posts in the United States and abroad. Mr. Smith graduated Phi Beta Kappa from West Virginia University. He did graduate work in political science and economics there, and later, at Stanford University.

DURWARD S. RIGGS, executive director of the Commonwealth Club of California, graduated from the University of California, Santa Barbara, later attending graduate school at San Francisco State University and Southern Oregon College in political science and international relations. Mr. Riggs has edited numerous Commonwealth Club publications including *Local, State and Federal Roles in California's Water Development* and *How Much Government is Good for Business?* He has travelled widely and studied at first hand the problems of open space in urban areas.

COMMUNITY DEVELOPMENT STRATEGIES: Case Studies
of Major Model Cities

George T. Washnis

EXCLUSIONARY ZONING: Land Use Regulation and
Housing in the 1970s

Richard F. Babcock and
Fred P. Bosselman

IMPACT OF FEDERAL LEGISLATION AND PROGRAMS
ON PRIVATE LAND IN URBAN AND METROPOLITAN
DEVELOPMENT

Joseph L. Stevens

LAND BANKING IN THE CONTROL OF URBAN
DEVELOPMENT

Harvey L. Flechner

NONGROWTH PLANNING STRATEGIES: The Developing
Power of Towns, Cities, and Regions

Earl Finkler and David L. Peterson
Introduction by William J. Toner

THE POLITICAL REALITIES OF URBAN PLANNING

Don T. Allensworth

THE POLITICS OF LAND USE: Planning, Zoning, and the
Private Developer

Robert R. Linowes and
Don T. Allensworth